SECOND EDITION

Investigative Reporting

Investigative

SECOND EDITION

Reporting

By **PETER BENJAMINSON**
and **DAVID ANDERSON**

IOWA STATE UNIVERSITY PRESS / AMES

PN4781
.A59
1990

First Edition © 1976 David Anderson
and Peter Benjaminson

Second Edition © 1990 Iowa State
University Press, Ames, Iowa 50010.
All rights reserved. Manufactured in
the United States of America. ∞ This
book is printed on acid-free paper.

Peter Benjaminson, a former investigative reporter for the *Atlanta Journal*
and the *Detroit Free Press,* is the
author of *Death in the Afternoon:
America's Newspaper Giants Struggle
for Survival* (Andrews, McMeel, &
Parker, 1984) and *The Story of Mo-
town* (Grove, 1979).

David Anderson, a former reporter
and editor for newspapers and wire
services in Chicago, Detroit, and Minneapolis, works for a political and
fund-raising consulting firm.

Library of Congress Cataloging-in-Publication Data

Benjaminson, Peter
    Investigative reporting / by Peter Benjaminson and David Anderson. — 2nd ed.
    Rev. ed. of: Investigative reporting / David Anderson and Peter Benjaminson. c1976.
    ISBN 0-8138-0197-4. — ISBN 0-8138-0193-1 (pbk.)
    1. Investigative reporting. I. Anderson, David. II. Anderson, David. Investigative report-
ing. III. Title.
PN4781.A59 1990
070.4'3 — dc20   90-4361
                                                                                    CIP

CONTENTS

PART III: Techniques

APPENDIX: Investigative Examples

PREFACE

This book has been written with two goals in mind—to help the beginning or student journalist understand some of the techniques basic to investigative reporting, and to inspire working journalists, whether novices or veterans, to undertake more investigations.

We have sought to illustrate the realities of investigative reporting: the evasiveness of subjects, the anxiety of editors and news directors, and the numbing frustration of repeatedly running down bad tips and unworthy hunches. We also have tried to show that such problems are routine and should not be cause for disappointment. Finally, we have sought to convey some of the satisfaction felt by a journalist who has done a difficult job well. We want to encourage more of the careful, thorough, dogged journalism that has come to be known as investigative reporting, wherever it might appear.

Although our print backgrounds have undoubtedly influenced our perspectives, this book is meant for all reporters: newspaper, magazine, radio, and television. Chapter 19 deals exclusively with investigative reporting for television, but the principles of investigative reporting and many of its techniques remain the same for all media.

We began writing the first edition of this book in 1972, during and shortly after the Watergate experience. We wrote this edition, the second, during 1988 and 1989. Much has changed during the intervening years, and although the basics of investigative reporting as we set them out have not changed since we first wrote about them, we have added to and amended this edition to reflect the relevant changes in technique that have occurred. Besides the new chapter about television, we have added chapter 13, on investigating with a computer. We have also added a discussion of the Freedom of Information Act to chapter 5. Finally, we've replaced all but one of the investigative stories in the first edition's appendix with more recent and relevant examples, including investigative stories from radio and television.

Although computers and the Freedom of Information Act were barely mentioned in the first edition of this book, and all of the examples reprinted in the appendix were from newspapers, reviewers hailed it as "a valuable book for working journalists as well as students and teachers" (*Writer's Digest*), "glutted with useful advice, sprinkled adequately with informative anecdotes and written in a lively, readable style" (*Investigative Reporters and Editors Journal*), "ages ahead of the latest star stories" (*Hartford Advocate*), and "refreshingly irreverent" (*News Leads*). We hope the second edition continues in this tradition.

One of the reasons we added a chapter on investigative reporting for television is that local television stations are much more involved in investigative reporting than ever before. In fact, investigative reporting seems to have become institutionalized at both local newspapers and local broadcast stations. Ninety-eight percent of editors and news directors responding to a 1986 survey sponsored by Investigative Reporters and Editors (IRE) said investigative reporting had become a regular or occasional activity in their newsrooms.

Although investigative activity may have decreased somewhat in the late 1970s and early 1980s, it is on the rise again at the local level, as the 1986 survey indicated. Fifty-one percent of the editors and 56 percent of the news directors responding to the IRE survey said their reporters did more investigative reporting in 1985 than five years earlier. Fifty-eight percent of newspaper editors responding said their papers printed one to five investigative stories in 1985, and 40 percent of the television respondents said they aired one to five investigative stories that same year.

It has been pointed out that because most newspapers publish 365 issues a year and most news programs broadcast daily, these figures are not encouraging. Such an argument, although true as far as it goes, fails to take into account the gargantuan size of many investigative projects. It also fails to acknowledge the greater care taken by today's reporters and editors to insure accuracy in their investigations, an effort less evident during investigative reporting's immediate post-Watergate flush. Finally, the argument fails to take into account what we consider a significant historical question: How many investigative stories did the average newspaper or broadcast station publish each year before the toppling of President Nixon?

On the national level, however, the picture is a dark one. As *New York Times* columnist Anthony Lewis pointed out in 1988, the cozy press-government relationship that died during the adversarial reporting of Vietnam and Watergate has reestablished itself. Although some national reporting remains aggressive and unafraid, most of it has become gingerly and protective. American politicians, reacting to Watergate and its aftermath, have roused the people against aggressive reporting and have turned many reporters back into mere stenographers. The Washington press corps, on the whole, no longer deals with the situation in the real world. It deals only with what politicians say about that situation. The press was in this condition when the first of the Watergate events occurred, shaking it out of its lethargy for a few years before it was bullied back into docility.

But investigative reporting is alive and well in thousands of cities, towns, and rural areas across America and retains a foothold, tenuous though it may be, in some of the great cities of this land, including Washington, D.C. To the hope that investigative reporting will regain its place in the national as well as the local consciousness, this book is dedicated.

And to **Jim Neubacher,** 1949–1990, who demonstrated throughout his professional life that the duty of the reporter is "to comfort the afflicted and afflict the comfortable."

ACKNOWLEDGMENTS

In writing this book, we have received much encouragement and many helpful suggestions from professionals and laypeople alike. We also have been inspired by the work of many investigative reporters across the country, some of whose stories appear in the appendix. We are particularly indebted to Duane Lindstrom, who gave much time to the original outline; to Jay Brant, who wrote the section "The Law Itself" in chapter 8; to Don Shelby, who wrote the chapter on investigative reporting for television; and to David Walonick, who wrote the chapter on investigating with computers.

We would also like to thank Elizabeth Abrams, Thomas Adcock, Ted Anderson, Miriam Balmuth, Karlyn Barker, Anne Benjaminson, Roslyn Bernstein, Arthur Block, Jennie Buckner, James W. Carey, Dan Chusid, Susan Cook, Richard Cunningham, Kathy Daley, Dennis DeNitto, Patty Dingus, Elisabeth Donovan, Ron Dorfman, Pat Doyle, Joel Dreyfuss, Oz Elliott, Gordon Felton, Roger Flaherty, Dan Galinson, Ken Goldstein, Terrence Gorman, Susan Harrigan, Gary Hayes, John Head, Louis Heldman, Lucia Herndon, Nancy Heusted, Michael Hoyt, Joy Huang, Walter Jacobson, Fred Jerome, Fred Jordan, Jon Katz, Felix Kessler, Joe Kirby, Jack Krauskopf, Bill Kunerth, Menina Lucas, Donna Martin, Richard McLeer, Sandra McJimsey, Melvin Mencher, Claudia Menza, Ruth Miller, Josh Mills, Robert Miraldi, Susan Mistler, Jim Neubacher, Judy Neuman, Ladd Neuman, Mary Nichols, Paul Noglows, John Oppedahl, Richard Petrow, Sam Pizzigati, John Polich, David Pollak, John Rhodes, Susan Rossen, Barney Rosset, Jerry Sass, Jim Savage, Mark Schulman, Robert Schultz, Rosemary Sheffield, Neal Shine, Scott and Barbara Siegel, Bill Silag, Bill Smith, John Smyntek, Mitch Stephens, Carol Sternhell, Dan Sullivan, Kim Sykes, Hiley Ward, Steve Weinberg, Linda Whitman, and the editors and reporters at the various newspapers at which we've worked over the years.

In addition, there are a number of investigators whose work we sought to emulate years ago and who, although they do not know it, are largely responsible for the book. Among them are Donald Barlett, Robert Caro, William Clements, Henry DeZutter, Jim Dwyer, Seymour Hersh, Morton Kondracke, Morton Mintz, Jack Nelson, Art Petacque, Mike Royko, James Steele, Pete Waldmeir, Lois Wille, and Pamela Zekman. We would suggest that the beginning journalist could do nothing so profitable as to spend some time watching these men and women work, reading their stories, and watching and listening to their broadcasts.

PART I

Basics

CHAPTER 1

The investigative reporter

Everybody knows what an investigative reporter is. He's the guy with the dangling cigarette, the grim visage, the belted trench coat, and the snap-brim fedora. He slinks in and out of phone booths, talks out of the side of his mouth, and ignores other, lesser reporters.

He never had to learn his trade. He was born to it. He sprung from his mother's womb clutching a dog-eared address book and his real father's birth certificate. He has an interminable list of contacts. His job consists largely of calling the contacts and saying "Gimme the dope." The contacts, of course, always have the dope at their fingertips and are only too glad to part with it. He has all the time in the world to pursue sleazy characters through seamy intrigues. He appears in the city room only every two or three months to drop his copy on the desks of his astonished editors, mumble a few words, and disappear again into the night.

This book is written in the belief that there is no such person. For one thing, he may be a she. For another, many general-assignment reporters, political reporters, and feature writers — in print and broadcast journalism — wind up doing investigative reporting from time to time. In fact, any reporter who does the job well is already part investigator. Those who merely record the public words of people powerful enough or clever enough to attract the media's attention are publicists or stenographers; they are not journalists.

The only workable definition of an investigative reporter is a reporter who spends a lot of time doing investigations. But uncovering information, particularly information that has been deliberately concealed, requires a certain type of personality. According to conventional wisdom, that personality consists mainly of extraordinary patience or, put another way, an extremely high threshold of boredom. We think, however, that in addition investigative reporters share a certain abiding faith in human nature: a faith that someone, somehow, is working against the public interest.

While this may seem the epitome of cynicism, it is a useful attitude for an investigator. Suppose an investigative report reveals that a governmental agency is hiring civil servants because, and only because, they worked in a political campaign. In most cases when this sort of abuse is reported, it is discovered to have been going on for years. It is quite probable that during those years many persons in that city or state believed that the government officials involved were perfectly honest. If the investigator had shared that attitude, the story would never have been written.

We sincerely doubt that there is a city or county in the country where right now some public officeholder, private businessperson, or foundation official is not engaging in a practice that will result in an investigative story in the months or years to come. It's basic human nature. The opportunities for personal profit in public and corporate life are so great that some officials will always succumb to temptation. For example, they may know for days or weeks in advance when important decisions about buying and selling land will be made and may capitalize on their advance knowledge.

But even reporters cynical enough to see plots where others see only plans do not always take the time to do the necessary digging. A third trait common to most good investigators, therefore, is the belief that many illicit acts cannot be covered up forever—or even for very long. Powerful officials and institutions are often corrupt and frequently are careless with evidence. They brag to their friends, file incriminating documents in public offices, and trust people they have no reason to trust. The investigator knows that these people can be led to blurt out their misdeeds in a moment's befuddlement.

Just as there is no such thing as the perfect crime, there is no such thing as the airtight conspiracy. The clues are always there. If a reporter digs hard enough, long enough, and with enough intelligence, the clues will be found. Often what separates the investigator from other reporters is a willingness to dig. The challenge of unraveling, say, a complicated land scheme will drive an investigator to spend weeks on end closeted with dusty real estate records. In fact, the more difficult the investigation, the more involved the scheme, and the more clever the people or organizations behind it, the longer the investigator will want to spend researching the story.

The work ultimately involved in investigative reporting is not unlike the work involved in many other professions. It's painstaking, careful, logical, and complete. Good lawyers do it when preparing for trial, archaeologists do it when examining the ruins of ancient civilizations, and historians do it when analyzing the past. Unlike most historians, however, investigative reporters do their work while the subjects of their research are still around to see the results. Although historians face problems of incomplete and lost records, investigators must face outright hostility and obstruction. Generally, the corrupt do not fear the judgment of history as much as they fear exposure, prosecution, conviction, and disgrace. That is why they conceal their activities and why reporters often must go to unusual lengths to uncover those activities.

Investigative reporting, then, is simply the reporting of concealed information. Some investigations concern activities of public officials, such as corrupt politicians; others concern activities of corporations, political organizations, charities, and even foreign governments. Often investigations uncover some sort of financial fraud.

In subsequent chapters, we will show the novice investigator how to uncover concealed information using a variety of methods, none of which involve any magic and none of which require any special abilities. Obviously, some reporters have personalities more suited to dealing with certain kinds of people than do others. Charm, however, is not half as important as a willingness to work hard and think carefully.

CHAPTER 2

Ethics of investigative reporting

Many fundamental techniques of investigative reporting involve actions some would label as dishonest, fraudulent, immoral, and perhaps even illegal. Because investigative reporting aims at bringing corruption, hypocrisy, and lawbreaking to public attention, it is reasonable to expect the members of the news-gathering profession to act as ethically as possible. And if all the information a reporter ever needed for investigations was on file, in legally available public records, there would be no problem: Reporters could be completely candid in dealing with people under investigation. But the major fact of investigative reporting is that people frequently go to great lengths to conceal damaging evidence.

Public officials, for example, tend to conceal ownership or interest in any company doing business with their agency. It is unlikely that a reporter suspecting such an arrangement would be able to prove it by knocking on an official's door and saying, "Hi. I'm here to uncover malfeasance. Any canceled checks you'd like to show me?" Generally, before confronting the subject of an investigation, the reporter would seek confirmation of the official's financial links to the company, perhaps by posing as a businessperson. That, of course, is dishonest. Reporters are often caught in the classic ethical dilemma: They're damned if they do and damned if they don't. By lying to the double-dealing official, the reporter will offend the ethical sensibilities of many people. But if the story doesn't appear, that corrupt official will continue to profit at public expense.

Most reporters use deceptive methods to gather information—on the theory that in a democracy the public's right to information out-weighs a public official's right to expect complete candor from journalists. Deceptive methods are justified, however, only when greater harm will be done to the public if the information remains concealed than the harm done to individuals by its publication. A reporter should never resort to questionable methods if the information can be obtained in another way.

In those cases that are difficult to judge, most reporters tend to err on the side of dishonesty to obtain the information. The underlying assumption is that society has more to gain from an accurate, thorough reportage of events than it has to lose from the discomfort of the corrupt. Most professional journalists would prefer not to find themselves in a position of withholding important information from their readers simply to avoid worrying about their own personal ethics. Their overriding goal is to inform the public. Nevertheless, at some point, every investigative reporter who is in the least bit sensitive questions the ethics of the profession.

Most investigative reporters take tremendous criticism from the friends and families of people they expose. They are accused of sensationalism, bias, and irresponsibility. Sometimes the subjects of investigations have nervous breakdowns, are jailed, or commit suicide. After a few such experiences, even the most jaded reporters begin to question their motives, their methods, and their fitness to sit in judgment on others. What accolades most investigators receive — whether pats on the back or lucrative prizes — come primarily from other journalists or from partisans who see their own cause being advanced by the reportage.

Even more disturbing than purely ethical considerations are the illegalities involved in many investigations. Reporters have been indicted, convicted, and jailed for stories they wrote, for acts they committed in gathering their information, or for refusing to answer a judge's questions. In at least one case an investigative reporter had to find work in another state to avoid prosecution. In all probability, a much greater percentage of investigative reporters would find themselves afoul of the law were it not that many prosecutors fear the consequences of hostile media on election day.

Many reporters, most frequently columnist Jack Anderson, have obtained classified information. Yet consider for a moment Section 793 of Title 18 of the *United States Code*. Commonly known as the Espionage Act, this law provides a wide and sometimes fatal range of penalties for anyone who, "having unauthorized possession of, access to, or control over any . . . information relating to the national defense, which information the possessor has reason to believe could be used to the injury of the United States or to the advantage of any foreign nation, willfully communicates . . . the same to any person not entitled to receive. . . ." Clearly, a lot of newspapers have violated this and other laws, particularly in covering defense and foreign affairs. Yet the stories made possible by these and similar criminal acts have been good journal-

ism. To say that the *New York Times,* the *Washington Post,* and other
newspapers, magazines, and broadcast stations should not have printed
stories about, for instance, major flaws in expensive new weapon systems being used by the U.S. armed forces is to say that employees of
those media organizations have the right to decide what the public
should know and what it should not know.

Many journalists and their attorneys have argued that because of
the First Amendment, laws such as the Espionage Act do not apply to
newspapers. But many prosecutors have argued otherwise. The final
authority on whether a law has or has not been broken is the judge
hearing a particular case. If the judge rules that a reporter has broken a
law, then the reporter has broken the law. Other journalists have argued
that when they break the law, they are justified because laws that result
in censorship of the news are bad laws and journalists have a moral
obligation to break them. Enough has been said about the morality or
immorality of breaking "bad" laws that we feel no need to add to the
debate. We would only say that some laws, particularly those written by
politicians to protect politicians—what we would term antidisclosure
laws—fairly beg to be broken.

A few years ago in Michigan, for example, the state senate went so
far as to begin construction of a wood-and-glass cage for the news corps
in which the volume of the floor debate might have been subject to
control by the senate leadership. Would reporters be acting properly in
attaching a suction microphone to the partition without the senate's
permission? We think they would be. Or consider an Illinois law that
permits land to be owned in secret trust. Under this system public officials can buy, sell, or rezone land without public disclosure. Consequently many Illinois public officials have made fortunes in real estate,
often at the taxpayers' expense. Would a reporter be acting properly in
using deception to uncover and report on the ownership of such trusts?
We think so.

Regardless of the questionable ethics of such antidisclosure laws,
reporters are left in the position of attacking public officials for breaking
some laws (those outlawing conflict of interest, for example) while the
reporters themselves have broken other laws (those forbidding the theft
of documents, perhaps) to prove the conflict of interest. The argument
that hypocrisy is excused for reporters, or that the ends justify the means
only in journalism, is a hard one to uphold. The longer one is in journalism—or in any position to observe social processes close up—the more
apparent it becomes that there are no such things as ends. Nothing is
ever ended; there are no final solutions. If the means, the methods by
which people try to reach the ends, are immoral, then there is only

immorality. It has been argued that despite good intentions, the dishonest journalist is only adding to the general immorality. But the argument that means never justify ends presupposes ethical absolutes in which all acts are either good or bad, and there are no greater and lesser evils.

Suppose, for example, a city seems unable to enforce the building code in a particular tenement, and a reporter is informed that the building is secretly owned by a building inspector. The owner listed in the tract index says the building was sold to someone else and says that the purchaser's identity is none of the reporter's business. To what lengths should a reporter go to find out who currently owns the building? Should he or she lie? Should it make a difference if the building is dangerous? Should it make more of a difference if someone, perhaps a child, was killed falling through a rotted porch railing?

In their book *All the President's Men, Washington Post* reporters Bob Woodward and Carl Bernstein wrote that they lied to employees of the Committee to Re-Elect the President (CREEP). (Their interviews with the CREEP employees took place during the investigation of a complex scandal, which mostly involved illicit campaigning and fundraising practices on behalf of President Richard Nixon's 1968 reelection campaign and came to be known as Watergate.) The two reporters told various CREEP campaign workers, generally in late-night visits to their homes, that other, unnamed workers said they might be willing to talk. It wasn't true. But it was, according to the two, an effective door opener.

The facts of Watergate, like so many other investigations, could not be dug out of publicly available records. In many such cases, the only recourse to ignoring the story is to trick those involved into revealing the facts. These tactics often create great animosity between public officials and journalists: Only a small minority of public officials either welcome or appreciate aggressive reporting. Most would prefer that reporters "let public officials carry out the mandate they were given by the voters"—which is another way of saying "Look, they elected me, so who are you to question what I do?"

As a result, most state and local governments still go out of their way on occasion to sidestep the relevant open-meetings and open-records laws. Public policy is still occasionally hammered out behind closed doors, and records that could be used to spotlight corruption or mismanagement are kept from reporters and from the public (see chapter 5). In our opinion, reporters who do not do everything possible to halt such practices or find out what happens in such meetings concede too much of the public's right to know—a right that is not theirs to give away.

In cases in which enterprising reporters unearth genuinely harmful information—perhaps plans that compromise the national defense—one could argue that if a reporter found the information, it's probably nothing new to the enemy.

The problems of method are not the only ethical questions that confront investigative reporters. Questions range from matters of personal integrity to the choice of appropriate language when it comes time to write. Unfortunately, reporters sometimes make errors, sometimes exaggerate or fabricate, and sometimes engage in conflicts of interest themselves.

Some publish or broadcast quotes from anonymous but always articulate "observers" whose views happen to coincide with their own, although many editors refuse to allow reporters to use unattributed quotes without a compelling reason to do so. Most reporters clean up the quotes they put in their stories, particularly when they're quoting less educated people. (Phrases tend to become complete sentences, for instance, whereas people rarely speak in complete sentences.) But too often the cleanup results in a quote that is more akin to what the reporter wants to hear than what was originally intended.

All reporters at one time or another come across published or broadcast stories they suspect are untrue. Unfortunately, it's often a custom among journalists to look the other way, a kind of I-won't-embarrass-you-if-you-won't-embarrass-me ethic. Local and national press councils, bodies aimed at giving individuals a forum in which to air specific grievances against the media, have not caught on, except in Minnesota. The National News Council closed down in 1984 after eleven years of operation. And the number of ombudsmen, specially appointed columnists who criticize their own newspaper in the columns of that newspaper, has grown only slowly. The first was appointed in 1967; twenty-two years later only thirty-eight ombudsmen were at work on America's 1,645 daily newspapers. The country's two major journalism reviews, *Columbia Journalism Review* and *Washington Journalism Review,* both concern themselves primarily with the East Coast. This means that in newspapers outside New York or Washington, only a serious mistake is likely to come to the public's attention. Newspapers do not often cover themselves or each other, possibly because they fear destroying each other's credibility. The excuse most commonly advanced, however, is that the public is not interested in the media's problems. By ignoring one of the country's major institutions, however, investigative reporters are in another hypocritical position. They'll take on almost anybody, it seems, but another reporter. (For exceptions, see examples 4 and 7 in the appendix.) If a major newspaper or TV station reports something falsely, that is just as newsworthy as if the government tells a lie, and as such it should be investigated and reported. Catching an errant reporter or newspaper is no more difficult than any other investigation and generally is much easier. An investigator can almost always find someone on the inside who is willing to cooperate.

The most common, if not the most dangerous, form of media corruption is what is euphemistically termed a freebie. Freebies are little bribes. They include everything from free meals to liquor at Christmastime to all-expense-paid junkets. Although many newspapers, magazines, and broadcast stations have adopted guidelines regulating the acceptance of freebies by their staffers, the guidelines are sometimes violated or are too liberal to begin with. Many such codes still allow reporters to accept gifts worth $25 or less; with the average reporter's annual salary still at approximately $20,000, however, $25 may mean more to a reporter than it does to those more highly paid.

Reporters, particularly investigators and political reporters, should be somewhat cautious about how they handle their private affairs, to avoid even potential conflicts of interest. That doesn't mean journalists can't go out carousing and tearing the tags from pillows on occasion. But it does mean that a reporter about to inherit a half-interest in Sony shouldn't write stories complaining about the high tariffs on foreign television sets.

Obviously, reporters live in the same world as everybody else. They are susceptible to charges of being prohomeowner if they own homes or of being antihomeowner if they rent apartments. Labor writers are occasionally damned by one faction or another, depending on whether or not they are members of the Newspaper Guild. One businessman speaking before a group of publishers told them that because they paid their employees so little, reporters were invariably biased in favor of the poor.

A reporter who gets too close to sources by taking handouts is not only unethical but also stupid. Even if he or she doesn't get caught, the reporter may wind up so compromised that blackmail is risked. Even the most harmless freebie can hurt. One of the authors lost the grab for the bill at a restaurant while seeking to bluff his luncheon guest into admitting taking a bribe. The author had eaten a tuna-salad sandwich. The bluff hadn't worked (the official had been an investigative reporter himself), and a story never appeared. For the next two years, though, whenever an investigation was dropped or fell behind schedule, his editors wanted to know how much tuna salad was involved. But most important, it is only human nature to be affected by a public official who gave you a gift at Christmas or by a businessperson who sold you a new car at cost. A reporter may go a little easier on such benefactors than the evidence warrants or may even go a little too hard in attempting to compensate. It is better not to get into such a position in the first place.

The most difficult problems that arise in investigative reporting are the everyday decisions about what is or is not newsworthy, what facts should be included in a story, whether certain actions really are unethical or illegal, and in what perspective the facts should be reported. In most instances on important stories, these problems are discussed at length by the reporters and editors involved. The debate generally centers around whether the paper has a molehill or a mountain on its hands. Reporters seem most often to overplay their own discoveries, and editors to downplay them. Reporters are defending their egos, seeking better placement of the story in the paper, and perhaps feeling overimpressed by the difficulties they surmounted in obtaining the information.

Editors tend to attach little weight to attempts to cover up a story and must worry about how articulately they could defend the story to an irate publisher. Obviously, it is good for a reporter's career to win major prizes, and at many newspapers it is better for an editor's career to remove as much controversy from a story as possible. Serious charges against powerful people can bring all kinds of trouble for a newspaper: charges and countercharges, lawsuits or threats of a suit, and even arousal of the advertisers. Believing that reporters are not infallible, most newspaper editors take a decidedly devil's-advocate role to test a story before publishing it. A reporter who has done careful research and is certain of the information is not bothered by hard questions.

The problem becomes most difficult, however, when the two sides disagree on whether certain actions of a person or institution warrant exposé treatment. Sometimes editors will ask questions like, Why are we singling out this guy when everybody does it? The reporter is likely to answer, Because he's the one we caught, and that's his tough luck. Obviously, if the person in question has done something wrong and it's important that the public know, the story should be printed. If the paper has information that the practice is common, that should be printed also.

Sometimes there is a difference of opinion among professionals as to whether certain kinds of behavior are wrong and whether they are worthy of coverage. Perhaps an editor will ask a reporter to investigate a presidential candidate's extramarital sex life. The reporter may think such conduct does not warrant a story. Should the story be given to another reporter who believes that fooling around is an abomination? Should the story idea be dropped? What about that percentage of readers who think a presidential candidate's morals and character are important? Should they be ignored? Don't they have as much right to information as anyone else?

Reporters must also exercise great care not to draw conclusions, or even make inferences, that can't be directly supported by the facts at hand. That sounds fairly simple, but a lot of otherwise good stories have been wrecked or almost wrecked by a reporter who tried to stretch the evidence just a little bit too far. If a reporter charges, on good evidence, that a person has committed terrible act A and also hints that he may have done horrible thing B, the culprit is in an excellent position to deny B, denounce the investigator as an overzealous moron, and walk away more or less unscathed. On the other hand, if a reporter is certain a person committed both A and B but neglects to mention B, then he has given that person a privilege that is not his to give. People in a democracy have a right to learn everything they can about actions that affect their interests.

Many good investigations are killed or watered-down for one of the following reasons:

"So what if she's a partner in a business with people who are breaking the law? That's guilt by association."

"How can we say he's guilty of conflict of interest (or anything else) when he hasn't been convicted? After all, a person is innocent until proven guilty."

The guilt-by-association dogma holds that a newspaper shouldn't say a man is a thief just because he hangs around with thieves. In a strictly logical sense, that is true. Were it not, one could accuse all prison guards, probation officers, and judges of murder because they hang around with murderers. But when it comes down to cases, the guilt-by-association homily prevents a lot of newspaper readers from learning that the county prosecutor spends time at the racetrack with syndicate types or that a county judge is a partner in a real estate business with city commissioners who are rezoning their own land. Obviously, these are facts to which readers are entitled.

That judge may be conspiring with the commissioners if she knows they are voting on their own land. Depending on the relevant conspiracy statute, however, the judge may not have committed any crime. But her strange sense of ethics ought to become a matter of public record anyhow. The same is true of a state legislator, for example, who campaigns on a platform of Victorian morality, votes for long jail sentences for drunks, and yet drinks heavily once out of the sight of constituents.

A lot of reporters are slowed by the dictum that a person is innocent until proven guilty. Many take that to mean a newspaper can't say a person did something unless a court has concurred. However, because a good investigation leads to direct knowledge of the events, a journalist should feel free to report them whether or not a judge has agreed. The only caution here is language. The word "murder," for example, is a legal term. It cannot accurately be said that a man murdered someone unless he has been convicted of that crime, and even then it should be said he was "convicted of murder." But a reporter who clearly sees a person shoot can accurately report what was seen—a shooting. By the same token, if it is established that a city councilperson owned a parcel of land on January 28, 1988, and voted to rezone that land that same day, it can be said he had conflicting interests when he voted. If, however, one wishes to go a step further and bring in the conflict-of-interest law, it should be said only that the councilperson was "in apparent violation of the state conflict-of-interest statute."

Any editor who really believed that a person could not be said to have committed a reportable, scandalous act until proven guilty of it in court would have investigative reporters do little more than gather their evidence, present it to the local prosecutor, and sit back awaiting a verdict. "Innocent until proven guilty" simply expresses the common law's intent to afford defendants due process. What it says is that a person cannot be punished by a police officer or a prosecutor. It does not say a newspaper cannot report events without the prior approval of the courts, even if some of those events may involve a person's breaking the law.

A final word on newspaper ethics. We think almost all of the mistakes, dishonesties, and indiscretions of journalists can be traced to a single cause—their desire to further their own careers. That is what has fostered the "scoop mentality": reporters' competing not to better inform the public but to beat the competition to a story that is about to break anyhow. That is why a widow may be informed of her husband's untimely death by reporters masquerading as cops. That is why a lot of advertisers are still able to edit newspapers.

The profession would be a lot better off if those who are in it for their own advancement would find some other career. A reporter who starts worrying too much about becoming executive editor should do the readers a favor and quit. So should those editors who always find an excuse either not to do the story or to do it in such a way that it puts the readers to sleep and leaves untouched the problems at which the story was aimed.

What to investigate

There is no institution of any standing, anywhere, that wouldn't be improved by a bit of investigation. After all, Boy Scout officials in North Carolina were found to be padding troop rolls in 1983 in hopes of getting larger United Way allocations, and the Los Angeles area United Way organization was revealed in 1986 to have loaned hundreds of thousands of dollars in interest-free, unsecured, and unrepaid loans to five of its executives. Other malfeasances have been unearthed at Boys Town in Nebraska, among the Shriners of North America, and in the fund-raising techniques of organizations set up to aid widows of policemen and to care for dying children. Presidents, presidential candidates, senators, representatives, governors, federal judges, cops, and even investigative reporters have all been caught violating their public trusts.

American citizens are oppressed, in some small and in some not so small ways, by clogged and archaic criminal justice systems, by outmoded and degrading bail-bond systems, by school systems that graduate illiterates, by health-care systems that care miserably for millions of people while ignoring millions more, by inadequate and unfair taxation systems, and by acts of corrupt officials. This is not to say that everyone in America is miserable. Far from it. But it does mean that opportunities for investigation are often staring the reporter in the face.

In fact, there aren't nearly enough investigative reporters to go around. As a result, choosing subjects to investigate is one of the most crucial aspects of investigative reporting. The correct choice of an investigative target could mean not only professional satisfaction for a reporter but also a more healthy community at large. And no matter how good a job of investigation a reporter does, if the topic is boring or trivial, the story will be boring or trivial.

Too often, reporters choose their investigations not because of the scope or significance of the story they hope to produce but because the information on the topic is easily obtainable and the need to expend great labor on the story is minimal. That causes too many reporters to wait by their telephones for the right tip or for an insider to come along and hand them an all-but-well-written story. True enough, a reporter is hired to write stories, and if a story presents itself, there's no reason why it shouldn't be written. But the most useful stories are usually those originated by a reporter. A tipster turned away by the press will often take the inside information on criminality in high places to a prosecutor or police agency, and the story will come out eventually.

In our opinion, it's the stories about those institutions everyone takes for granted—the state medical board and how it regulates crooked and incompetent physicians, the local probation department and how it supervises parolees—that are the most rewarding. They would never appear without original research by the reporters. For example, in Chicago it had long been understood that control of the Cook County assessor's office was a political necessity for the Democratic machine—not only for the large number of patronage jobs in the office but also because a hardworking and sufficiently dishonest assessor was a very effective campaign fund-raiser. For decades the matter lay untouched by the press, save for the usual gossip by reporters in bars. There would be a great story if only a link could be shown between the machine's fund-raising and the campaign contributors' property tax assessments. But it seemed that too many contributors and too many buildings were involved, the contributions were too well hidden, and the assessment process was just too complicated.

At least it seemed that way until two reporters for the *Chicago Daily News,* William Clements and Charles Nicodemus, sent out form letters to the Cook County sheriff, clerk, assessor, and other county officers saying that as part of their newspaper's preparation for covering the upcoming election, they wanted an appointment and an in-depth explanation of how each office worked. Naturally, the assessor, P. J. "Parky" Cullerton, didn't try to impede or sidetrack the reporters until it was too late. He released one of his top assistants to give the reporters a three-day course in assessing. After that, Clements and Nicodemus did their own assessments of more than two dozen of the biggest buildings in downtown Chicago.

While that was going on, WMAQ-TV commentator Walter Jacobson managed to talk his way into a fund-raising party for Cullerton, where the camera recorded the presence of many of the biggest property owners in the city. Why, Jacobson asked his six-o'clock-news audience, were all those people there, and what did they want? Although Jacobson could not say for certain that the big realtors were benefiting from the assessor's magnanimity, the implication was clear. When the facts came out several months later in the *Daily News,* they were appalling. Clements and Nicodemus had spent three months in the assessor's office. They found a two-year-old skyscraper that was being assessed as if it had depreciated for nearly a hundred years. The assessors maintained they were given information by the building's owner that justified the low taxes, but they refused to let reporters see it, saying the information was confidential. When all the stalls were over, the reporters were able to conclude that no such information existed, that no information would have warranted such a tax break, and that the average Chicago taxpayer was carrying the burden of taxes not levied against influential owners.

Clements estimated that the city's taxpayers were making up for somewhere between $5 million and $20 million annually—just on the buildings he and Nicodemus investigated. Because those buildings represented only about 10 percent of the new high rises in the city, the loss to the city coffers was considerable. Furthermore, a number of the underassessed buildings were owned or operated by men serving on Cullerton's campaign committee, and other major building owners regularly attended a wide range of Democratic fund-raising functions. Following the *Daily News* story, other papers ran some excellent recovery investigations detailing even more abuses. For example, a suburban community newspaper found that a number of posh country clubs were assessed at only 6 cents a square foot while land around them sold for as much as $10 dollars a square foot.

Several other investigative stories in Chicago stemmed from a decision by a public-interest law firm to examine all recent major land transactions in or near downtown Chicago. A city official involved in a large urban renewal project on the near West Side was found to have received about $15 million in suspicious payments, although he had invested no money in the renewal project himself. Then there was the railroad, tax-exempt by state law. It was selling off surplus land to developers who continued not paying taxes on the land, even though they were not exempt. Large parking lots existed on land slated for other uses by government contracts, and city-owned land was being sold to aldermen's friends in return for bank stock. In fact, in all but a few cases of private land sales, the law firm found either conflicts of interest or violations of law. Perhaps the most shocking case was uncovered by Ralph Whitehead and Duane Lindstrom, former investigators for the law firm who were then working for Lerner Newspapers in Chicago. They found that a large hotel on land near the downtown area had negotiated a ninety-nine-year lease on the land from the city's continually bankrupt school board in return for 3 percent of the hotel's drink revenue. A realtor friendly to those who negotiated the lease was president of the school board.

Some people say that Chicago is exceptionally corrupt. We would point out that it's possible that Chicago has a reputation for corruption not necessarily because it is more corrupt than other big cities but because until recently it supported several fairly independent newspapers and television stations with large numbers of competing investigative reporters.

A fertile field for investigation is land purchase, real estate speculation, and other business dealings by public officials. Since the dawn of this republic, when, according to some historians, delegates to the constitutional convention used inside information to deal profitably in bond markets, public officials have been in a peculiar position. On the one hand, they are charged with doing what they think is best for the public in formulating public policy. On the other hand, like most red-blooded Americans, they do not shun financial gain. In many cases, not only would they like money above and beyond their salaries for their personal satisfaction, but they desperately need those funds to finance the ever-growing expense of public campaigning. Again and again their financial needs, coupled with their privileged position at the helm of society, lead them into a conflict of interest: the illegitimate meshing of their own needs with their concept of what is for the public good.

The best place to begin searching for such conflicts is in the various campaign contributor lists now kept by most states and counties. In some presidential and other elections, people who are not self-interested often become excited enough to give generously to campaigns of their choice. But when a low-level official receives large contributions, it's time to be suspicious and try to find out if the official gave or will give something in return. Some gifts to politicians come in forms other than campaign contributions, such as stock deals, limited partnerships, cut-rate houses and cars, consulting fees, real estate commissions, insurance purchases, finder's fees, and even legal fees. Public officials who run businesses on the side, including real estate brokerages, law firms, and insurance agencies, can easily disguise such payments. They can also list them on their income tax forms and pay taxes on them, thus avoiding prosecution by the Internal Revenue Service or the embarrassment of writing "Bribe—$100,000" in the income section of their Form 1040 for all to see. Such quids pro quos are so common in politics that some cynical investigative reporters think of government mainly as a vending machine for the corrupt: A relatively small amount of money goes in, and a large amount of money comes out. The public, of course, pays the difference.

Persistent rumors that a person is a crook of some sort also bear looking into. The rumors may have been started by political enemies, but they may be true. Journalists should watch too for signs of government employees living beyond their means. One reporter spent so much time riding in a Chicago squad car that the cops, accustomed to his presence, spoke openly in front of him. The reporter learned that one of the cops, a patrolman, owned a second home in Florida, a camper, four automobiles, including a Ferrari and an Alfa Romeo, and a jewelry collection of undetermined size. A revelation of this kind, of course, does not make a story—at least not yet. Perhaps the government employee married well or inherited a fortune. (The acquisition of money through marriage or inheritance can be verified in probate court, by marriage licenses, and with business records; see chapter 6.) Or perhaps the money came from gambling. Lobbyists have been known to lose large sums to favored politicians regularly, at the poker table.

But, we repeat, the most fruitful investigations will often be of those institutions that function so unobtrusively and with so little fuss that the public assumes they are doing their job as well as it can be done. A careful look at any long-established institution will often reveal a dense bureaucracy, grown up by custom and accretion, that is no longer doing the job that most people, if they thought about it, would want performed. The concerned reporter who is interested in her long-run as well as her short-run journalistic reputation will attempt to dig into the operations of such agencies and let the public know how they can be reformed or improved.

One of the most popular ways to do this is for a reporter to get on the receiving end of one of these institutions and write about what it's like. Several reporters who could pass for eighteen-year-olds have enrolled themselves in high schools and written stories that had school administrators and bureaucrats explaining themselves for months afterward. Others have had themselves committed to mental institutions and have written revealing series about conditions inside. Reporters have taken jobs in automobile factories, as ambulance drivers, in garment-district sweatshops, and as helpers to drug dealers preparing dope for distribution, to name but a few. But such participatory journalism is not always necessary or desirable. In most cases the nonparticipatory techniques of investigative reporting, which this book describes, can be employed to investigate both institutions and individuals. After all, institutions are merely groups of people, and no reporter has ever been able to investigate an institution without investigating the official or unofficial activities of the people involved.

Those reporters too lazy to look for something new to investigate should remember that many people stop reading newspapers or paying much attention to TV news programs because they've "heard it all before," heard the same topics being investigated again and again. According to a 1988 study by Jack Doppelt of Northwest University's Medill School of Journalism, the investigative stories with the most impact are those concerned with a new topic. People like learning something they don't already know.

A final note: The responsible investigator should avoid trivial sensationalism or should at least follow it up with some thoughtful investigation in the same field. For example, although the work habits of a single garbage-truck crew might make an interesting story and photo layout, a reporter could spend time researching and writing a more valuable story comparing sanitation costs and contracts in various cities and drawing the relevant conclusions for local public policy.

Sources
and
Records

CHAPTER 4

Attracting and evaluating sources

Although a reporter may spend day after day searching out a clue important enough to justify beginning a full-scale investigation, it's possible to chance upon a prizewinner by picking up a city-room phone to order a pizza and having a heavy breather at the other end of the line announce that the price of anchovies was fixed by an international cabal of fish-farm executives meeting in the back of his shop. The reporter wasn't exactly straining any investigative skills by picking up the telephone, but with any ambition at all he or she is off on the next investigation.

This is the easiest way to receive tips—unexpectedly. Attracting and encouraging tips, however, as well as developing and cultivating sources and evaluating and using the information they provide, all require forethought and preparation. Once the source is whispering sweet somethings in the reporter's ear, the reporter has, by definition, already attracted him. Unless the reporter's name came in a dream or the phone number was dialed at random, it is likely that the source had a specific reason for calling that particular newspaper or that particular reporter.

Many newspapers and broadcast stations, especially those in small towns, are overprotective of the institutions in their communities and see themselves as town boosters, not community critics. These papers and stations rarely print or broadcast investigations aimed at major figures or institutions in their towns, and when they do, they weaken the stories by casting them as denials by spokesmen for those institutions. If a source has some information that would tend to discredit an institution in such a community, it is unlikely she will provide her information to a reporter for a paper that covers its community in such a way.

Sources appear to differentiate among reporters as well as among newspapers. Real estate writers who are virtual public relations agents for the home-building industry are not going to receive tips about massive scandals in that industry. Even unsophisticated readers may realize intuitively that tips given to such writers would not result in news stories.

Once a reporter becomes well known, there is no problem encouraging sources to call. Even if a reporter has a big name, though, it has to be the right kind of big name. It's possible that columnist William Buckley, at least until a few years ago, was almost as well known as columnist Jack Anderson, but Anderson probably received a hundred or more solid tips for every dollop of information phoned to Buckley. That's because Anderson is seen by many as a champion of the little man, a friend of the griper, and an avenger of evils perpetrated by officialdom. Buckley—although he may not deserve his public image—is seen by many as a representative of and spokesman for that officialdom.

Doing investigative stories is one way to attract sources. But there are other ways to indicate to potential sources that a reporter is in the market for information. If a journalist is interested in tips relating to a particular person who is suspected of wrongdoing, it may be possible to persuade an editor to okay profiles, features, or hard news stories about that person. It doesn't matter—as long as the reporter's byline appears on all of them. The bylined stories invariably attract sources who have information about the person. (That is why it is so common to read newspaper stories charging someone with committing illegal acts A, B, and C, then to pick up the paper two days later and read that he also committed illegal acts D and E. Either sources not contacted by the reporter came forward or sources who had known about D and E but withheld their knowledge from the reporter were cajoled into coming forward by the stories about A, B, and C.) Reporters are rarely concerned about alarming the subject of an investigation with this approach. Most well-known people are egoistic enough to believe that even their routine movements are worthy of public notice, so much so that it would be unlikely they would spend much time wondering about a spate of stories about them. Experienced investigators, however, are careful not to produce paeans of praise about the person they're pursuing, for fear they'll scare off the sources they're trying to attract.

Another effective method of attracting sources is to appear on a television talk show. Viewers who hear a voice and see a face are much more likely to contact the reporter than if he or she remains merely a byline. A reporter who projects an interest in investigative stories often finds that people are so anxious to get in touch that they'll forward information not only about the subject discussed on the air but about a variety of other matters as well.

Landing a beat assignment is another way to attract sources. Bylined stories about a particular institution that appear month after month will readily suggest to the general public that the author is a potential recipient of information about that institution. Tips may come also from the members of the institution the reporter is assigned to cover, as long as the reporter indicates she is open to tips from the lower-downs as well as from the higher-ups. Perhaps the easiest way to attract tips, in fact, is to act like a human being instead of the stereotypical reporter of late-night-movie fame. Experienced reporters attempt to meet as many people as possible in all walks of life and to be as charming as possible when meeting them. They avoid dogmatism if drawn into an argument with a source, and they let the source know they are open to new ideas, especially new story ideas. They don't begin scribbling notes the first time a source mentions a well-known name. They attempt to act as casual as possible while remembering as much as possible. They talk less and listen more. Most important, they treat with special courtesy those people who usually are treated curtly: waitresses, clerks, counter-people, students, and low-level bureaucrats. It pays when the favor is returned in the form of a news tip. Good reporters are not born with a long list of contacts; they make them.

Sources, of course, may have varied motives. Often the source is simply a conscientious public servant who sees a wrong being committed and thinks the public ought to know about it. This person usually turns to the media only after unsuccessful attempts to interest superiors in ending the wrongdoing; the media are often the only effective outlet for civil servants who wish to remain honest and still do their jobs. Other sources may reveal information to revenge themselves on one of their superiors or colleagues who they believe has done them an injury. Although their motives are less pure than those of public servants who wish to right a wrong, the information they provide need be taken no less seriously, just more cautiously.

Some information is provided inadvertently by people in government or private industry who like to gossip. When talking to reporters about their work, these inadvertent sources may not realize that the information they provide may result in a newspaper investigation that their employer will not appreciate. Sometimes sources are just average citizens who stumble across interesting information. Because these people are unused to bearing important secrets, or because they have been disbelieved and are frustrated by the burden of information they carry, their words often spill out in a confused rush to the first reporter polite enough to listen to them.

All these sources are in marked contrast to informants who, after providing a reporter on one or two occasions with leads that result in stories, come to consider themselves as inside dopesters. Having adopted this self-image, they begin to look for more tips to sustain it. In some cases they become volunteer adjuncts to a reporter's investigative effort, all the more valuable from one perspective because they are unpaid, highly motivated, and probably not as well known as the reporter they are voluntarily assisting. They are valuable not only because they are able to provide information from their own store of knowledge but also because in a pinch a reporter can often call on them to dig out a specific piece of information. Their names should be kept on file—with one caution. These people are not necessarily ethical and by definition are not professional. Every one of their tips must be thoroughly checked out, especially if the reporter senses that newly discovered journalistic egos are driving the volunteers to exaggeration. It's the reporter, not the source, who is responsible for reportorial inaccuracies.

Whatever the motives or aspirations of the source, it's the information, not the source, that should most concern the reporter. Tips should be judged on their individual merit rather than on the motives of the person who conveys them. A disgruntled contractor who had lost a bid on a city contract, for example, talked with Vesta L. Kimble, a reporter for the *Baltimore News American,* in 1982. The result was a 1983 series in that newspaper that revealed the establishment of front companies for the purpose of gobbling up the 10 percent of construction contracts reserved for minority businesses. These firms purported to be minority-owned and minority-controlled when in fact they were owned and controlled by whites.

There are numerous other examples of self-interested sources providing useful tips to investigators. Self-interest is almost invariably the motive when, for example, campaign aides to a candidate inform a reporter of alleged misconduct by their opponent. During one primary election race for Cook County (Chicago) state's attorney, an aide to a reform candidate told a reporter that Mayor Richard Daley's chosen candidate had been active in partisan politics while serving on the bench. Such activity was a violation of the ethics rules laid down by the Illinois Supreme Court. The charge was damaging to the machine candidate's campaign; self-interest obviously motivated the tip. But the reporter began to check out the story, despite the source. Interviews with a number of recently fired or disgruntled machine election workers enabled the reporter to establish specific dates when the judge presided over affairs at party headquarters. Interviews with machine functionaries in adjacent wards indicated that the judge had issued formal invitations to neighboring machine politicians to attend party meetings in his ward, a rather blatant sign of partisan activity.

The reporter checked his newspaper's photo file on the judge—a good way to discover surprising things about who someone's associates are, without leaving your office—and found a year-old picture of the judge with his arms extended horizontally, suggesting that two people had been cropped out of the picture. The reporter spent another hour in the photo library and eventually found the missing parts of the same picture in the separate photo files kept on the other two politicians. When contacted by the reporter, the photographer who had taken the picture remembered where he had taken it—at a party fund-raising luncheon.

Confronted, the judge was successfully bluffed (a technique discussed in chapter 12) into revealing other improper partisan activities. Unfortunately, however, the story was killed when the judge successfully persuaded his friend the publisher to do him a favor.

But as often as not, partisan leaks don't hold water. For example, when a black Wayne County (Detroit) circuit court judge launched a mayoral campaign in Detroit, rumormongers insisted he was linked to gangland drug figures and was a crook himself. A month-long investigation of the rumors ensued. The reporter assigned to the story traced each rumor back to its source, and in each case the alleged source denied authorship of the tale. Checks of public records indicated that the judge was living no higher than his salary warranted. Although he had been associated with drug figures before being named to the bench, in each instance he was acting as an attorney for those figures. And although his shady clients had indeed contributed to his successful campaign for a judicial seat, the judge listed their contributions on the required campaign reports.

One of the most persistent rumors about the candidate was that when asked why he wanted to run for mayor even though the mayor's salary was lower than a judge's, the candidate reportedly replied that he would make a lot more money as mayor. This was taken to mean that he planned to accept payoffs as the city's chief executive. Months later, when another black candidate entered the mayor's race, rumormongers began attributing the same story to him. So perhaps both men, both black, had been victimized by racially biased tipsters. In any case, because no evidence was ever found to support the rumors about the judge, no story was ever written.

Whatever its apparent initial worth, however, no tip should be completely ignored. Reporters shouldn't fly off the handle when someone calls and says "I read your story today and see you don't like Senator X" or "It's pretty clear you agree with me that Mayor Y is trying to pull a fast one." The person who volunteers such remarks is probably not just making small talk but more likely is attempting to feel out the reporter's attitudes. If the reporter can possibly agree with whatever the source blurts out (or at least remain silent), the source, feeling comforted by what seems to be ideological fellowship, may tell the reporter something useful. Experienced investigators ignore whatever may annoy them about a tipster's small talk, manner, or appearance. None of these is necessarily relevant. Some people act crazy yet have accurate information. Others look, act, and dress like bankers yet spout thirdhand nonsense.

Perhaps the classic example of this is Sherman Skolnick, a self-styled Chicago "legal researcher." Skolnick saw lots of conspiracies among the powerful to do harm to the powerless and was widely regarded as an endless source of unprovable stories. He will tell you, for example, that one of the authors of this book is a Central Intelligence Agency spook (untrue).

The problem with Skolnick, however, is that every once in a while he is absolutely right. For a long time he insisted on repeating to various reporters that former Illinois governor Otto Kerner, then a federal judge, was a crook. Eventually a jury agreed.

Skolnick also repeatedly charged that two Illinois Supreme Court justices were crooks who had taken shares in a bank that had a case before their court. Much laughter ensued. Skolnick said that none of the Chicago newspapers would print the story because officials of both newspaper chains had been given stock in the same bank. More laughter. A short time later both judges were removed from the bench for conflict of interest, and investigators unearthed public records showing that, indeed, a dozen members of the media — newspaper publishers and editors along with radio and television station owners and news directors — had been given stock in the bank.

Reporters who took Skolnick seriously wasted a lot of time; reporters who ignored him missed many excellent stories. Old-time newsroom hacks would automatically have dismissed Skolnick as a nut. They would also dismiss all the old ladies who walk into newsrooms with bags full of aging records, and all the people who telephone slurred stories to newspaper city desks. Some of these people may indeed be a bit insane, but they often have stories to tell, often surprisingly well-documented and detailed stories, and they shouldn't be rejected out of hand by news hawks too busy rewriting handouts to spare the time to listen to them. After all, prizewinning stories sometimes begin with what seem to be off-the-wall tips.

A Detroit reporter, for example, was once visited by an immigrant from Barbados who took an hour of what the busy reporter considered precious time to tell a patently ridiculous story. The man alleged that one of the Wayne County (Detroit) commissioners, a woman, had picked him up on a Caribbean beach while she was on vacation. They became lovers, he said. She brought him back to the United States, where they were to be married. During the few months their marriage lasted, he told the reporter, the Commissioner had attempted to start a prison riot in Ohio, had tricked him into perjuring himself, and had threatened him and others with a pistol. The immigrant's self-interest in the dissemination of this tale was obvious; the commissioner was suing him for divorce, and federal immigration agents were attempting to deport him. Even worse, from the reporter's point of view, the man could produce no evidence in support of his version of his love affair with the commissioner. Now, what could be more ridiculous than listening to his story? But the amused reporter, fancying himself a humanitarian, waited patiently through the entire tale and walked back to his office with an indulgent smile on his face.

Within a matter of days the Detroit police commissioner accused the county commissioners of refusing to fund an intergovernmental police agency because accusations against one of the commissioners were being investigated. The reporter who had listened condescendingly to what he had thought were insane ramblings suddenly found himself the sole possessor of enough background information to write a good story about the reasons underlying the squabble between the cops and commissioners. Not devastating reporting, but informative nevertheless.

No two tips, of course, are of equal value. A reporter who answers the telephones in any newspaper's city room for half a day will converse with callers who will tell him that giant grasshoppers are eating every house in the neighborhood or that myopic martians are molesting the water heaters. But the reporter who answers these phones often enough will eventually be contacted by some startled businessperson who picked up the wrong briefcase on a visit to city hall and now possesses a copy of an agreement between the mayor and the local Mafia don to split rake-offs from crooked contractors. The problem is to separate the substantive tips from the creations of malicious imaginations.

Columnist Jack Anderson failed miserably in this task at a crucial juncture in the 1972 presidential campaign. Without adequately checking the facts, he reported on national radio an unverified tip that had been telephoned to him — that Democratic vice presidential candidate Tom Eagleton, who had already admitted a history of mental distress, had been ticketed for drunk driving on several occasions. No evidence ever materialized to support this report. Later, Anderson alibied unforgivably: He said he couldn't take the time to check the report because he might have lost the scoop if he did.

What Anderson didn't have — documentation — is what most often separates good tips from bad. Any tip is incalculably stronger if it can be verified or at least corroborated on paper. A document indicates that a third party, and usually an official third party, is involved in the case. In addition, possessing a document will probably help get the story published. It can reassure an editor and the newspaper or station's lawyers that there will be something more solid than a few whispered words to rely on if and when the story must be defended in court. Best of all, though, is an admission by your investigative subject that the deed was his. (Securing such confessions is discussed in chapter 12.)

In the absence of documentation, identical or corroborating accounts of the same facts from different sources—if possible, with different biases—are of roughly equal value. Three reporters from WCVB-TV in Needham, Massachusetts, acting on a tip from a relative of a youngster who had been recruited into a door-to-door sales operation, put together a shocking story from corroborating accounts they elicited from teenagers who had left such operations, from police officers, and from Massachusetts state officials. Their story revealed that the teenagers recruited to sell magazines and household cleaners with promises of high earnings and exotic travel were forced to work fourteen hours a day, six days a week, and were given barely enough money for food. Profits went to those at the top, not the kids. Crowded into cheap motel rooms, the teenagers who failed to sell were often beaten, and the girls were encouraged to engage in prostitution.

Even before seeking out corroborating evidence, however, the reporter should try to put the source in a position that will force documentation or verification of the account. The reporter should take the source over the same ground two or three times to see if the story changes with each telling. Or the reporter could attempt to wring from the source a detail that can be checked with a second, preferably neutral source. For example, if the source is encouraged to mention a specific street corner or address at which some incident took place, or to state firmly what the weather was like at a particular time, then the information can be checked against street maps or old weather reports. If the source's account is verified initially, detail by insignificant detail, the reporter can begin to check out the more significant allegations.

Some sources, especially professional bureaucrats who are accustomed to collecting paper and are protected by civil service statutes, are able to provide reporters with massive documentation. For example, a Detroit reporter was approached by an employee of that city's auditor-general. The auditor's assigned task was to prevent other city officials from misspending public funds or falling into conflicts of interest. The employee, protected by his union and by civil service regulations, felt free to tell the reporter that the auditor had engaged in just the sort of folly he was charged with preventing: He had hired his own son with city funds to teach his employees "report writing." The employee buttressed his account with copies of letters from the auditor to the city civil service commission and to a local university arranging for the course, an invoice from the university for the course cost, a city voucher indicating that payment had been made, and a diploma from the course signed by the auditor's son. The signature would have been especially useful to the reporter had the auditor denied the existence of the arrangement, because another copy of the son's signature could easily have been obtained, and the two compared. But as it happened, the auditor-general admitted all after the reporter confronted him with the information.

After this story was printed, the auditor began to harass his talkative employee. He restricted the employee's vacation time, cut his telephone calls, and so on. The reporter, in part because he did not want it said around city hall that his sources would be mistreated, wrote a story about the mistreatment. The harassment ended, and the auditor took early retirement.

If a reporter finds that documentation is vital to a story, and the source, on initial contact, doesn't provide it or an indication of where it might be found, there is no reason the reporter can't ask the source to get it. The reporter can tell the source that without documentation or verification there won't be any story. Some reporters specialize in pep talks that will persuade their sources to take the risks necessary to obtain the crucial documentation.

For example, suppose an assistant city assessor calls a reporter to say that the chief city assessor is ordering the underassessment of buildings owned by the chief's cousins. (A lower assessment means lower property taxes.) But the assistant won't provide the reporter with copies of the relevant paperwork because the boss would find out and fire him. At this point, the reporter could accept his demurral and begin a laborious check of birth and marriage certificates, telephone books, and city directories in an effort to identify and locate the assessor's cousins and the properties they own. The reporter could prepare an evaluation of the worth of the buildings owned by the cousins and then compare that assessment to the official city assessment. With some effort, a good story could be produced this way. (See chapter 3, for example.) But it would be much easier if the reporter had the work sheets setting out the assistant assessor's appraisal of the worth of the buildings, the chief assessor's veto of that appraisal, and the substitution of a lower figure. It would be a much stronger story as well, because it would show the assessor's role in the tax favoritism.

The reporter's task is to give the timid tipster a course in investigative journalism that will convince him either that any participation in the story can be successfully concealed or that his job is safe in any case. The reporter can appeal to his sense of righteousness and indignation: "You mean you have a Harvard doctorate in assessing gas stations, and some dingbat who doesn't have brains to be a janitor, much less your boss, tells you to forget all you know so that his relatives can cheat on their property taxes?" Thus the reporter gives the source a way to vent his anger and help the reporter at the same time. If the source is afraid that by copying only his own assessment work sheets the boss will know who to blame, the reporter can suggest he copy the work sheets of the other assistant assessors as well, thus involving and protecting them all. If the reporter has a personality and a reputation that are sufficiently forceful and persuasive, it may be possible to convince even the most timid bureaucrat that he need not worry, because publication of the story will put the boss in the spotlight and preclude any revenge or harassment.

Once information from a source has been solicited and evaluated, the reporter must decide if that potential story is worth the time it will take to document and write. Perhaps a reporter is informed that a certain contractor, now dead, bribed a certain city official, also now dead, in cash ten years ago in Madrid. The only witness was a slow-witted, nearsighted towel attendant in a Spanish bordello whose mother is head of the secret police. Chances are the reporter will never prove that story. Of course, if the bribe was substantial, if by giving it the contractor illicitly secured the contract to pave every park in the city, and if, since the paving, skinned knees have become the number one crippler of local schoolchildren, the reporter may wish to start hunting up the official's heirs, friends, enemies, and tour guides to verify the story. But in the time that is likely to take, the reporter may be able to discover, research, and write two other stories of greater importance.

In deciding if a story is worth the time, a reporter should talk to other reporters. Maybe they have already heard, researched, and debunked information similar to what the reporter has received. Maybe they know the source. Maybe they're already writing the story. Nothing is quite as discouraging as working for days on a top-notch investigative piece only to discover that another reporter is typing out a final draft while you're still looking for the phone booth your source called from.

Experienced investigators know that they'll have to produce stories if they're to continue to attract sources. They try to avoid disappointing sources by not using their information. If a reporter's publisher routinely kills investigative stories for reasons unrelated to good journalism, the reporter should either quit investigating or quit the paper, because the flow of tips will soon dry up. Reporters need not worry, however, about disappointing those sources who inadvertently provide them with what we choose to call overhead tips. Reporters are often alerted to potential investigative stories by public officials and ordinary citizens who inadvertently tip off a reporter to the need for an investigation in a specific area while they publicly discuss another, perhaps less newsworthy issue. Alertness is essential in recognizing the importance of such offhand assistance.

A reporter for the *Hoboken* (N.J.) *Reporter,* for example, overheard a brief mention of the city-owned Hoboken Cemetery at a city council meeting in 1986. (None of the other reporters attending the meeting picked up on the remark.) He found out that the graveyard had not been properly cared for in years, although the cemetery trustees had $1 million in the bank and spent more than $50,000 a year. As a result of his story, cemetery conditions improved dramatically, and the city got a handle on what was happening to a fairly sizable chunk of its money.

A few years earlier a *Detroit Free Press* reporter covering the deliberations of the Detroit city council overheard council members talking about the complaints of their constituents that legally parked, relatively new cars were being towed away by a firm under contract to the police department's abandoned-auto section. By talking to the irate citizens and by digging in public records, the reporter was able to determine that the police inspector in charge of abandoned cars and an associate of organized-crime bosses had been owners of the towing firm. The reporter discovered that numerous cars had been falsely designated as abandoned and then towed away, sold, or stripped for profit by the firm. The reporter also learned that the towing firm, managed by a former felon, had been illicitly granted a city license by police detectives who were later indicted in other bribery cases. The published stories resulted in the reorganization of the abandoned-auto section of the police department and an end to city contracts for the towing firm, not to mention fewer official car thefts on the streets of Detroit. And none of those reforms would have been achieved without the reporter's attention to talk among the city council members about complaints from their constituents.

CHAPTER 5

An introduction to records

Them are three kinds of records: those the law entitles the public to see, those the law prohibits the public from seeing, and those not mentioned by the law. Good investigators do not admit the existence of a category of records that they cannot see. As far as they are concerned, the only important distinctions among the three kinds of records involve the methods best suited to getting at them and the relative difficulty in doing so. In any case, some of the official distinctions among records don't make much sense. Income tax records, for example, are hard to get. Property tax records, on the other hand, are easily obtained. For some reason a person's income tax is confidential, but the same person's property taxes are everybody's business.

With a few exceptions, record keeping is fairly consistent from state to state and from city to city. Which kinds of records are public and which are not, however, varies widely.

Congress passed the federal Freedom of Information Act (FOIA) in 1966, but many journalists ignored it until 1974, when Congress amended it — over President Gerald Ford's veto — to make it generally useful. According to the act, all federal records are available to the public on request, unless those records fall under one of the nine categories of exempt information that government agencies are permitted, but not required, to withhold. Many states enacted similar freedom-of-information acts.

Although the Reagan administration attempted to gut the act, the federal FOIA has served as the basis for numerous major investigations in the past few years and will continue to do so unless it is amended out of existence or repealed. For instance, the act has been used to force the government to reveal the names of the more than two hundred workplaces in the United States where the government had identified but not notified 250,000 workers of increased risks of cancer, heart disease, and other illnesses due to working conditions. A *New York Times* reporter discovered through use of the FOIA that tons of nuclear fuel, which terrorists could use to construct atomic weapons of their own, were missing from American nuclear power plants. Two academic researchers revealed that President John F. Kennedy almost died from Addison's disease before he was killed by an assassin's bullet and that President Franklin D. Roosevelt used twenty-nine aliases when being treated at Bethesda Naval Hospital to conceal his health problems from American voters. (See the appendix for more examples of FOIA use.) Reporters, scholars, businesspeople, and private citizens are constantly making use of the federal act and its state equivalents to unearth valuable information and journalistic bombshells.

Unfortunately, use of the act requires tremendous patience, persistence, and maturity because many government bureaucrats, loath to reveal the public information in their keeping, attempt to delay sending out information requested under the act, in the hopes that the requester will eventually lose interest and go away. However, a number of organizations have sprung up to help journalists and other members of the public overcome bureaucratic resistance to successful use of the act. Detailed manuals have been published containing easily understandable instructions for using the act, including sample request letters to copy. Among the most helpful of such manuals is *How to Use the Federal FOI Act* (available for $3 a copy from the FOI Service Center, 800 Eighteenth Street, N.W., Suite 300, Washington, DC 20006). Individual states also publish guides to their own FOIAs, open-government laws, and privacy laws. New York state, for instance, publishes *Your Right to Know: New York State's Open Government Laws* (available from the Committee on Open Government, NYS Department of State, 162 Washington Avenue, Albany, NY 12231, Phone 518-474-2518).

Aside from the formal requirements set out by the laws themselves, experienced FOIA users offer many tips to reporters who seek timely results from FOIA requests. For instance, Jack H. Taylor, Jr., a reporter for the *Dallas Times Herald,* has suggested finding out exactly where the particular record you want is stored, finding out if a state agency has the records you want before you appeal to a federal agency, being as precise as possible in defining the records you're requesting, and stating in advance your willingness to pay fees (you can specify a maximum amount) while at the same time asking for the waiver from such fees that is often granted to journalists.

Bureaucrats, who often seem to believe they own the material the public has paid for and left in their care, often try to prevent public access to it, no matter what the federal or state FOIA says. For some time one big-city police department permitted reporters to view arrest reports but not to photocopy them or even take notes from them. Other agencies insist that reporters fill out a form for each record they wish to see. In many cases a copy of the form is then sent to politicians whose records are viewed, to alert them to a possible investigation. Whether these bureaucratic blocking moves are legal or not depends on the public-records act in the state involved. (State acts usually apply to local governments within that state as well as the state government itself.)

Reporters should not hesitate to use the various FOIAs when confronted with blocking techniques. But try a simple and polite request first. It saves times and aggravation. And who knows? It just might work. Even within the same government office, the accessibility of the records often depends on which clerk is approached first, how he or she is handled by the reporter, and whether the clerk (or the clerk's boss) is mad at the reporter's newspaper or station that day.

The federal FOIA and many state FOIAs allow journalists to appeal to the appropriate courts if they are told they can't see the records the law entitles them to see. And although it may involve time and expense, a lawsuit or two may greatly enhance the situation by softening up bureaucratic resistance. It is certainly better to litigate the matter than to take no for an answer. Once a city's police department has lost a suit to a journalist seeking access to crime statistics reports, for example, it is unlikely that the fire department will bother to prevent reporters from reading fire or arson reports. But filing a suit or asking for a court order prematurely may damage an entire investigation by alerting those under scrutiny. If a reporter needs a court order to get certain records and wants to avoid tipping off those under investigation, the wisest course may be to seek access to a similar but different set of records. For example, if the reporter is looking for a record of all the narcotics arrests by a certain policeman, the newspaper or broadcast station could sue for access to records of all the gambling arrests by another policeman.

Beyond avoiding court appearances, there are a number of other good reasons reporters do everything they can to get the records clerks on their side. The clerks can show reporters the short cuts. They can also help with the digging and, once they have joined in, are not likely to alert the people being investigated. Furthermore, the clerks are in an excellent position to provide needed information in the future. Presidents, governors, mayors, and department heads come and go with the political tides. But bureaucrats, mostly under civil service and union protection, remain. When a newspaper's reporters are good to them, they come to view that newspaper as a shield to protect them from marauding politicians and as an outlet for their own grievances. As such, records clerks can be invaluable to investigators. Besides, working among friends is easier on one's nerves. After publishing a few investigations, a reporter usually has an ample supply of enemies.

Gaining access to public records is only part of the battle. Knowing what kinds of records are kept is even more important. Too often, reporters presume that because they have not previously heard of a certain type of record, it does not exist. Fortunately, ours is a society of paper shufflers: Hardly a deal is made, an action taken, or an official statement uttered that is not committed to paper and filed somewhere. Who knows how many Pulitzer Prize stories are scattered in file cabinets all over the country?

Discovering what kinds of information are recorded and where they are kept is not as difficult as it sounds. Just as society abounds with people who fill out and shuffle forms, it abounds with people whose job it is to know what records are kept and who has them. If the information a reporter seeks is on paper, somebody put it there and knows how to retrieve it. Knowing who these people are and talking to them is a substantial part of most investigations.

People who regularly deal with records of interest to reporters include lawyers, particularly public service lawyers, who tend to specialize in ecology, civil rights, housing, fraud, and corruption. Certain defense lawyers are familiar with a variety of public records, and some of them can be helpful on stories dealing with organized crime. Federal prosecutors (assistant U.S. attorneys), state attorney general's staffers, local prosecutors, and lawyers working for the vast number of federal and local regulatory agencies are also experts on records available in their own and related fields. Often they can be persuaded to obtain information for reporters that reporters could not obtain for themselves. Court clerks, city clerks, county clerks, and legislative clerks are all knowledgeable about what kinds of things are a matter of accessible record, where they are kept, and how to read them. Librarians at public, law, and school libraries can be helpful in explaining indexes and directories, and many are adept at locating government studies quickly.

Legislative aides, city council staff researchers, law clerks, and researchers for various city, state, and federal agencies spend lots of time doing the same sort of research required of investigative reporters. A reporter working on a story about why the river is yellow downstream of the local varnish factory should talk with staffers at the Environmental Protection Agency or the state department of conservation. They may know of reams of information about the varnish company that could dovetail nicely with what the reporter can find elsewhere.

Lobbyists will often help with investigative research, as long as it's not aimed at them. They too are paid to know what's going on.

Federal Bureau of Investigation agents (many of them accountants and lawyers), Internal Revenue Service agents, Federal Strike Force agents, U.S. marshals, and local police investigators are sometimes helpful. They are more likely to disclose what is available and how to get it than to help reporters directly, but sometimes they will be of active assistance if they are certain it will not compromise their job security.

Politicians can be helpful too. In the course of mudslinging campaigns, they come across a lot of mud but also some useful and accurate information. They know where the bodies are buried and the records are kept. Experienced investigators find that it's often fruitful to mention the name of the subject of an investigation to some politicians of the opposing party.

Private detectives rarely hold a person's head underwater to get information these days. They're more likely to be sending record requests to government agencies. And numerous private eyes are willing to cooperate with reporters, especially if those reporters have information to trade.

Researchers for labor unions, consumer groups, community organizations, and special-interest groups also deal regularly with public, and sometimes not-so-public, documents. Because a lot of these people tend to move in and out of government work, they often have excellent contacts in many agencies. Persons active in the many Public Interest Research Groups (PIRGs) across the country can also be helpful. Without the power of the press or the terror of subpoena behind them, they have to rely heavily on public records research and have become quite adept at it.

Academicians, professors, graduate students, and even undergraduates often accumulate vast information, either from records or on their own. Sometimes they get information that a reporter can't get, because their sources aren't worried about it turning up in a newspaper. Every now and then some graduate seminar studying, say, community power sets off to investigate why the construction of a local interstate highway resulted in the condemnation of only certain parcels of land, and it comes up with some interesting findings.

Last, and probably most important, are other reporters and editors. Suppose a reporter has spent a week working on persistent reports that the local circuit judge, who convicts blacks four times as frequently as whites, is a member of the National Socialist White People's party. The reporter spends days in the county clerk's office going through old records but can find nothing linking the judge to any right-wing groups. She mentions it to the reporter at the next desk, who suggests calling the Anti-Defamation League in Washington. She does, and the league offers to send a pamphlet written by the judge entitled *Never Kick a Nigger in the Shin When You Can Hit Him on the Head Instead.* The point is that no single reporter knows as much about where to find things as all reporters put together. An experienced investigator who is stumped on a story starts talking to colleagues. If they can't help, the reporter might seek aid from absent predecessors by thinking through investigations from years past and looking them up in the newspaper's library.

It is unlikely that talking to a dozen or more persons in the categories mentioned above would not turn up something useful, or at least something encouraging. There is not a public record available on the subject of property, for example, that an experienced real estate lawyer does not know about. Too many reporters begin investigations on topics new to them without spending enough time talking to experts in the field.

If the experts don't know, there are organizations that do. Various states (such as Minnesota), journalism schools (such as the one at the University of Missouri), chapters of journalistic organizations (such as the Society of Professional Journalists, formerly Sigma Delta Chi), and societies (such as the Iowa State Historical Society) have published guides to the private and public documents available in their geographic areas or areas of specialization. Investigative Reporters and Editors has published *The Reporter's Handbook,* edited by John Ullmann and Steve Honeyman (New York: St. Martin's Press, 1983), a useful and detailed guide to public records nationwide. Don't give up searching for that elusive record without consulting one of these guides.

Even those documents the law forbids reporters or the public to see can be obtained. We doubt that there is a large newspaper in the country whose reporters at one time or another haven't written stories based on classified military documents, personnel records, interoffice memos, or federal income tax returns. The Pentagon papers, and records obtained in a burglary of the FBI office at Media, Pennsylvania, were passed among newspapers like so many news releases. Yet it is not necessary to work in Washington or for a major media outlet to obtain even the most esoteric documents. For example, the Lerner chain of community newspapers in Chicago obtained U.S. Army intelligence bulletins setting out the policy for army spying on civilians and instructing agents on techniques.

A good investigator never forgoes an investigation because it can be documented only by inaccessible records. It is simply a matter of measuring the importance of the story against an estimate of the time required to obtain the records and then deciding whether to go ahead. Without trying to get the necessary information, the reporter will never know what is available.

One reporter, desperate for the names and addresses of some recent immigrants, went to a regional office of the U.S. Immigration and Naturalization Service. He was told that the records were confidential, by law. Before giving up, the reporter gave half a dozen immigration officials a low-key pep talk on how long he had worked on the story, how much it meant, and how the lists could help clear up a major scandal. For all he knew, either the director or one of the department heads sitting in on the meeting was a part of the scandal. But, he continued, if the list came to him in the proverbial brown-paper wrapper, he would obviously have no idea who sent it. The director leaned back in his chair, laughed, looked out the window, and said, "Listen, son, I'm afraid you've been watching too much television. We don't break the law here. We don't even bend it in this office." A few days later the list arrived at the reporter's newspaper, in a plain pink envelope, not a brown one.

More public records are available in various government offices and private files than most journalists realize. Many reporters tend to ignore these files because mucking around in them can be tedious and because the reporters mistakenly believe that stories flowing from file cabinets are duller than stories flowing from people. On all but the most complicated stories, however, file-cabinet research seldom takes more than a few days. And it's only tedious when a reporter is working a dry hole; relevant documents are rarely dull. More important, documents are used mainly to prepare for interviews. Even if the records prove an iron-clad case, a reporter must still interview the people involved to get their reactions, retractions, and explanations. Properly written building-code stories, for example, are not about building codes or even buildings but about the people who own them, the people who must live in them, and the officials who find it convenient or profitable to look the other way.

CHAPTER 6

Public and private records

P eople are born, go to school, marry, divorce, receive salaries, give to charity, buy and abandon automobiles, travel, buy goods on the installment plan, change their names, open businesses, join professions and armies and governments and churches, contribute to and borrow from museums, acquire guns, buy stocks, and die. It's a rare person who goes through life without signing papers and creating documents that an investigative reporter might look up in some office someday. The paragraphs below contain capsule descriptions of documents that most people produce, what an experienced investigator can do with them, and where they can be found.

Make it easier on yourself when you're trying to find a record by remembering these tips: (1) If attorneys, debt collectors, real estate people, or title searchers need a certain record, it will be easily available to anyone, including you. (2) If the agency that produced the record won't give it to you, try one of the agencies the originating agency may have sent it to. The receiving agency is usually much less interested in maintaining the confidentiality of the records than the originating agency is. Or try agencies that routinely collect information primarily recorded by other agencies, such as the courts at all levels, whose records are easily accessible. Another example: State motor vehicle departments collect a great deal of information on licensed drivers that doesn't have much to do with their driving. Those departments then make the information available to anyone who writes in for it. (3) Never end an interview without asking the person you're interviewing if she knows of any records, documents, or reports that might be helpful to you and where you can obtain them.

In many cases, as soon as you find the records you're looking for, they will suggest a story. Looking up the accident reports for a city and finding that a large percentage of its traffic accidents occur at a certain corner will immediately suggest a story to most reporters. If, however, you find the record of your choice and can't figure out what to do with it, *try comparing reality with the information on the record.* If there's a discrepancy, you may have a story. For instance, try comparing the names of the registered voters on a certain block with the names of the people who actually live there.

Or compare the records you find with other records. For instance, compare lists of contributors to the mayor's election campaign with lists of those who sell goods or services to that city. Computers make such a task relatively easy, even if each set of records contains millions of bits of information. (See chapter 13.)

Or compare the records with what human sources tell you. If there's a discrepancy, either your sources or the records are lying. If all else fails, and you still believe something is amiss, *investigate the record-making agency.*

Airline manifests

Although they often deny it, airlines keep records of the passengers on most flights. A public relations person is more likely than a counter clerk to show such a manifest to a reporter. The clerk will probably suspect that the reporter is an employee of the company who is checking up on him. The public relations person may be an ex-reporter and may understand how crucial it sometimes is to be able to write that two particular persons were on the same flight to, say, Colombia. Reporters sometimes ask others—a government agent with subpoena power, for example—to obtain manifests for them.

If a reporter's ethical standards are low enough, it's often possible to find out where the subject of an investigation is going by calling the airline's reservation office, posing as the subject, and asking for reconfirmation of the subject's reservation.

Records of state-owned aircraft are also available. In Georgia, for instance, a reporter in 1981 requested and received flight reports from the state's Office of Air Transportation on every flight Governor George Busbee had taken on state aircraft. Included in each report was the origin, destination, takeoff and landing time, total flight time, total wait time, number of passengers, miles flown, aircraft ID number, pilot name, copilot name, name of the agency the flight was billed to, and name of each passenger. A reporter who couldn't write at least a passably interesting story with such a treasure trove of information—about a well-known public figure flying around the state and region with other private and public figures in tow on taxpayer-purchased aircraft piloted by taxpayer-paid employees — should resign from journalism and embark upon some less taxing profession.

Audits and consultants' reports

Every now and then some public agency decides to hire an outside consultant to check its efficiency. If the consultant reports back that the agency has been doing a good job, a press release is issued. If the consultant says the agency is wasteful, inefficient, stupid, lax, and criminally negligent, nothing is made public.

The Wayne County (Michigan) Road Commission hired a consultant to study its operations during the 1970s, and when the consultant came back with a report that area roads were getting four to eight times as much salt as snow and ice conditions warranted, the board quietly accepted the report. Had the beat reporter covering the meeting not burned himself with a stray cigar ash and jerked awake at the moment the report was accepted, no one except the board members would have known of its existence. When the reporter asked for a copy of the consultant's report, the board secretary said it was not a public document because it had not been formally accepted. The reporter argued that it was a public-paid study of a public agency and was discussed at a public meeting. After much arm waving and yelling, the reporter got the document. It wasn't a great story, or even an investigative story, but the example illustrates two principles. First, covering a beat and waking up at the right moment often leads to good discoveries. Second, if all else fails, threaten to go berserk.

Bank records

The federal government requires banks to keep copies of relatively large checks written by their customers. Most banks, rather than segregate some checks from others, keep copies of all checks their customers write. A source at the bank, or in a federal agency, might be willing to show such records to a journalistic investigator.

Birth records

For most persons, birth records are usually on file in a public office, such as the health department or the county clerk's office with jurisdiction over the area in which the person was born. One problem with birth certificates is that the reporter usually has to know where a person was born before he can check the birth certificate. Because many people wish to obtain copies of their own birth certificates, most jurisdictions have made the retrieval of the certificates relatively easy. If a reporter is looking for someone else's birth certificate, however, it may be more difficult because some bureaucrats consider birth information private. But a friendly smile or the right contacts can do wonders.

Birth certificates come in handy when a reporter is following the nepotism trail and wishes to find out if a certain official has in-laws on the payroll. By obtaining the official's birth certificate, the reporter may find the maiden name of the official's mother on it and then be able to search for public payrollers with the same last name. Some jurisdictions, however, do not include parents' names on birth records issued to second parties.

Business records

If Terry Smith wants to open Smith's Video Store, several choices are available. All the routes, however, require filing signed forms with public officials. In most states, Smith can go into business under what is called an assumed name. That is, Smith assumes the name "Smith's Video Store" for business purposes. In some jurisdictions, assuming a name for business purposes is called "doing business as," and the forms involved are called "dba" forms.

To assume a business name, Smith must get the approval of the clerk or other county official in the county in which the store will be located. The clerk will check the files to see that no one else is operating a business under that name. If the check shows that the name is free, Smith will pay a small fee and file for the name. Smith's application, as approved by the clerk, will be kept on file so that others—including reporters—will be able to see who operates Smith's Video Store. If Smith wants to run the store under a partnership agreement with someone else, Smith will file a copartnership agreement with the county clerk. That form will contain information about both Smith and the partner and will be signed by both.

Smith could also run the store as a corporation, in which case Smith would go through the process of incorporation and then file papers with a state office, usually the secretary of state. In many states Smith would be required to reveal the names and addresses of all the incorporators and directors of the firm, the amount and type of stock issued by the firm, the number of shares held by each incorporator, a description of the work the firm intended to engage in, and the name and business address of its local representative. Although salary figures for officers and directors are not included in incorporation papers, that information is often found in proxy solicitations sent to stockholders, because adjustments of those figures must be approved at stockholders' meetings. Nonprofit corporations are required to file similar reports.

Both profit and nonprofit corporations in most states are also required to file annual statements. In some states the annual reports are even more detailed than the articles of incorporation. Most of the information originally submitted is repeated and updated, and a complete corporate balance sheet is filed, detailing corporate assets and liabilities. Often parent and subsidiary corporations must also be listed, along with the name and address of the person or firm that helped the corporation prepare its annual report.

The information provided on such forms varies greatly from state to state. In some states annual reports are neither required nor filed, and in others they are called franchise reports and may be filed with the state's franchise tax agency. (A franchise is a government-granted right to do business, and certain business taxes are known as franchise taxes.) In some states in which annual reports are filed as franchise tax reports, the papers are not available for public inspection, allegedly because they contain tax information.

Because attorneys must know who runs what in order to know whom to sue, access to and copying of business records have been routinized in most states where the information is available. (See chapter 7 and Uniform Commercial Code Records in this chapter.) In some states all the forms are on file with each county clerk. In others the files have been centralized at the state capital and are available by mail or phone, usually for a small fee. In some states the same forms are available from both sources.

The problem is that in most states business forms are not cross-indexed by the name or names of the people involved. In other words, a reporter can't find out what firms someone is connected with simply by looking up that person's name. Another problem is that out-of-state companies do not always register in all the states where they do business, so a reporter often must write or call another state's capital to obtain the records. (When in doubt, start with Delaware, the most popular filing state among multistate corporations.) What this country needs is a national cross-referenced corporate index, which would allow an investigator to look up information about a firm, no matter where it did business, as well as look up individuals and discover what companies they were associated with, wherever those firms happened to be located.

Even a reporter not engaged in a particular investigation involving business records finds it wise to make a friend or two in the office where such forms are filed. Occasionally someone will take out an assumed business name that trades on the name of a public agency or better-known corporation. Perhaps a high pressure bookselling firm will register the name "Official New York School Books, Inc." in hopes that its salespeople can confuse potential customers in door-to-door sales pitches.

(See Securities and Exchange Commission Records in this chapter for business records kept by the federal government.)

Cab company records

In most cities cab drivers are required to note the pickup times and destinations of each fare they take. This makes cabbies relatively reliable sources if they can remember which face went with which trip on their manifest.

Campaign contribution and expenditure records

By law, campaign finance records are filed with election officials or county clerks in most jurisdictions. The laws governing the filing of such records vary from state to state. In some jurisdictions, statements must be filed during the campaign; in others, by a certain date after the campaign. On most forms, the candidate must list expenses and specify how much each person contributed toward the primary, the general election, or both. Reporters often find it fruitful to compare lists of campaign contributors with lists of those awarded government contracts and political appointments. (This process has been computerized in recent years. See chapter 13.) Information on firms receiving contracts is usually available from the purchasing unit of the jurisdiction involved. Because the occupations or businesses of campaign contributors are often not listed on the financial records, reporters may be reduced to calling the contributor's home during business hours and obtaining his or her office telephone number from a family member. If no one at the business will give the name of the business, the telephone number can be looked up in numerical order to discover the address, firm, or person to which it belongs. (See Crisscross Telephone Directories in this chapter.)

Unfortunately, many candidates raise a lot of campaign money at fund-raising dinners or parties at which contributions take the form of ticket purchases. Most campaign finance-disclosure laws do not require that ticket purchasers be listed because the price of one ticket is usually and purposefully set below the amount of the minimum campaign contribution that must be reported. This maneuver allows fat cats to give huge amounts to favored candidates without attracting any notice by buying hundreds of tickets to a candidate's fund-raising party. All that may appear in the records filed by the candidate is "fund-raising party, $200,000." A savvy reporter, however, will attend the party or at least interview persons who attended. It is unlikely that any big shots would have bothered to attend if they had not given money or bought some tickets. And fat cats who made large contributions may give out the tickets they have purchased to their friends or employees, who may know where the tickets came from. Also, it will be difficult for everybody who attended to forget who else was there.

Charity records

Many charities and nonprofit organizations are frauds of one form or another, and even some fairly legitimate charities make questionable decisions about raising and spending the public's money. Fortunately, investigations of charities are fairly easy because their books must be filed annually with state agencies and are open to public inspection. Also, charities (as well as colleges, churches, medical clinics, and hospitals) must file detailed forms with the Internal Revenue Service, and those forms are available to the general public, including investigative reporters. Furthermore, in most charities there are likely to be a number of people who are in it solely for the public service involved and whose cooperation is not difficult to obtain.

The main difficulty with investigations of charities, nonprofit organizations, and other good works occurs when it comes time to publish the story. Even the most corrupt charities can easily drape themselves in the flag, motherhood, and apple pie. Most have taken great pains to cultivate widespread public and publisher approval of their activities.

Charity fraud usually consists of one or more of three standard elements: Some of the money raised is not spent for the purposes listed; the funds are raised through deception or coercion; or some of the money collected is not reported. Shady charities often overlook laws requiring them to file their books with the appropriate state agency. A reporter can sometimes pressure the agency to requisition those forms if the charity has not filed them. Nonprofit Blue Cross and Blue Shield organizations in various states are also required to file voluminous information annually with the appropriate state agencies in the respective states. And all charities must file Form 990 with the IRS. This form lists the group's income and outgo in detail, as well as the salaries of its major officers and other pertinent and interesting information. (Private foundations must file the more detailed Form 990-PF, also available to reporters and the public.)

Legitimate, honest charities and nonprofit corporations rarely have qualms about showing reporters their books or answering questions, beyond the nervousness that normally greets journalists' hard questions. Even some of the crooked outfits will make a display of happily showing their books, believing that the average reporter couldn't understand them anyway or knowing they are inaccurate. Don't let all the numbers scare you. Looking at a set of books is not difficult once you understand the basics of accounting. A quick aid is *How to Read a Financial Report,* a booklet published by Merrill Lynch, Pierce, Fenner, and Smith and available without charge at their brokerage offices.

In dealing with a charity, a reporter needs to find out how much money the charity collected over a set time period, how much was spent raising the money, and how much went to the charity's cause. Then he or she must do whatever spot checking is possible to determine if the figures are accurate. The reporter should obtain the names and addresses of some of the larger donors and contact them to find out if their personal records correspond to the entries in the charity's books. The same should be done with some of the named recipients. It is important that the reporter choose the names; the charity's officers may select only a sample they know is bona fide. The reporter is not checking to see if the books balance—that the credits equal the debits. Books always balance. He or she is checking the accuracy of the reported income and outgo and looking at such things as officers' salaries and expense accounts.

Among the most common charity frauds are the myriad police and fire fighters' benefit funds. Generally, the organizations assert that the money raised goes to widows, orphans, retired fire fighters or police officers, and other worthy groups. They sell meaningless advertisements in magazines that either don't exist or are not well distributed. They also sell window decals to shopkeepers. The purpose of the decals is to ward off arsonists, robbers, and burglars, encourage the fire department or cop on the beat to watch the store, and, not incidentally, ward off rival police charities. As such, these so-called police or fire fighter charities are but thinly disguised protection rackets. They may advertise that they give $1,500 to the spouse of each police officer or fire fighter killed in the line of duty. Typically, there may be six such deaths a year, but the charity raises hundreds of thousands, if not millions, of dollars.

Up to 80 or 90 percent of the contributions to many charities goes for administrative overhead. We know of one charity designed to promote the culture of a certain ethnic group that kept 100 percent of what it raised over a five-year period. Stories about such charities are made even more interesting when the reporter takes the trouble to ask the responsible authorities why they have permitted the abuses to continue unchecked. The reporter may find that the authorities take a harder line on consumer and ecology organizations than on more "patriotic" charities.

It is wise to remember that investigating charities may hit close to home. Many newspapers support local United Fund or Red Feather drives, and many publishers have pet charities.

City directories

Not to be confused with telephone directories, city directories list residents alphabetically and are published for most cities. These handy books give the street address, the telephone number, the spouse's first name, the employer's name, and the business address (or a description of the kind of work an individual does) and note if someone is a member of the armed forces. Most large newspapers buy the latest editions of city directories, and they are used constantly. City directories are often published in the same volume as crisscross telephone directories. (See Crisscross Telephone Directories in this chapter.)

City licenses

In many cities, people who engage in a variety of occupations—fruit peddlers, junkyard owners, sidewalk florists, and so on—must pay a city tax and carry a license. They are usually required to file a detailed application for the license, and the application is available on request to the public. The range of occupations covered by license bureaus is vast. In New York City, for example, a person must have a city license to hold a block party, be an able seaman, embalm, exterminate, grade hay and straw, smoke on piers, establish a seaplane base, store rubber cement, make sausages, transplant hard-shell clams, and open a deli. Each license application contains personal and occupational information that could be useful to an investigator.

Congressional records

Congress investigates more subjects than newspapers have the time or space to cover. A call to a local congressman or a college or public library that has been designated as a depository for government documents is the fastest way to obtain a copy of a congressional hearing report. Going through a local congressman is also the quickest way to obtain various studies produced by the executive branch. For both types of reports it is wise to get the names of staffers who did the legwork on the reports, because the final document is often a watered-down abbreviation of the original investigation. The staffer who spent a year investigating the topic is likely to have some strong feelings about the material that was left out and may be quite willing to pass it on.

Congressional hearing records are used by newspapers and broadcast stations when they want to call someone a mafioso but don't want to be sued for libel. The paper or station merely reports that the person was identified as a mafioso in a hearing held by a House or Senate committee that looked into organized crime. The problem with this practice is that not everyone so identified was proved to be actively involved in organized crime, and it is also possible that not everyone who was in the Mafia or associated with mafiosi ten years ago still is.

Crisscross telephone directories

Primarily for the benefit of salespeople, crisscross phone directories have been printed for most major population areas. In these directories, persons are listed not by the alphabetical order of their names but by the alphabetical and numerical order of their street addresses. (Kathy Jones of 1 Nelson Lane would be listed under "Nelson Lane," not under "Jones.") This enables salespeople to plot out their door-to-door routes, knowing in advance the names of the people in each house. With this kind of directory, a reporter can easily obtain the names and phone numbers of a person's neighbors and interview them over the telephone. A reporter can also survey a neighborhood and see whom the subject of an investigation lives near.

Directories listing an area's phone numbers in numerical order are also published. In these directories, each number is followed by the name and address of the person or firm to which it belongs. A reporter who obtains the phone numbers a person or firm dials regularly can easily use such a directory to find out the names and addresses those numbers represent (see Telephone Records in this chapter).

Crisscross directories are often published in the same volume as city directories. (See City Directories in this chapter.)

Death records

Death certificates, especially in cases involving foul play, can often be obtained from the county medical examiner in the jurisdiction in which the death occurred. Their primary value is that they indicate the time, place, and cause of death, as well as, in most cases, age of the deceased at death; date and place of birth; social security number; whether the person served in the armed forces and some specifics of that career; whether the person was dead on arrival or died in the emergency room; outpatient or inpatient status; date of admission to the hospital; marital status, and name of the surviving spouse; race; last year of school or college completed; title at work; name of employer and employer's type of business; father's full name; mother's full maiden name; name and address of the person who informed the hospital of the death; burial instructions; date the body was removed for burial or other disposition; place of burial; name, address, and registration number of the funeral home; name, signature, and registration number of the funeral director; name, address, and signature of the physician involved; exact period during which the physician attended the deceased; date the physician last saw the deceased alive; immediate and longer-term causes of death and how long the deceased suffered from each; whether an autopsy was performed and by whom; details of any accident or homicide involved; place such an accident or homicide occurred, and so on. And death certificates are often only one page long.

Obtaining a death certificate is easier when the deceased left a will and real estate is involved, because copies of the death certificate are often then filed in the grantor-grantee index along with the deeds and mortgages. (See chapter 7.)

Debt records

See Uniform Commercial Code Records in this chapter.

Driver's license records

Driver's license records, available from state secretary of state offices or motor vehicle departments, are treasure troves of information for investigators. In some states an investigator can send a filled-in request form to the motor vehicle department, along with a small fee, and receive in return such information as a driver's age, height, weight, eye color, and type of license; whether the license has ever been suspended or revoked; whether the driver needs eyeglasses or a hearing aid or is physically handicapped in any way that requires special controls; and whether the driver has ever received speeding tickets, been involved in an accident, been confined or treated in a mental institution, or been sent to jail. Skeptics have been known to say sneeringly, "Nah, nah, nah, you'll never find out if someone's been confined in a mental institution, because health records are private." Sure they are, but driver's license records aren't. Remember, if you can't get the information from the primary source, try a secondary source.

Expense account vouchers

A lot of people serving in paid and unpaid public positions, such as on school boards or park commissions, come to feel quite strongly that the public owes them something more than a salary or gratitude for their efforts. So before voting to build the new high school building in Pile o' Snow, Vermont, they find it necessary to inspect Hollywood High School — in January. They take their spouses along, fly first-class, and put the whole bill on their expense account. Boards and commissions also tend to hold meetings in good restaurants and let the taxpayer pick up the tab.

Financial information about a corporation or government agency

If a newspaper or broadcast station is willing to spend the money, a journalist can request a Dun and Bradstreet report — a rather complete, commercially prepared financial and credit report on a firm — through the news organization's business department. Or to gather financial information about a company or agency, check its budget (its predicted income or expenses), issued prior to its fiscal year; its periodic financial report (the end-of-fiscal-year report); and its audits (financial reports prepared by an outside agency). See Audits and Consultants' Reports and Business Records in this chapter; *How to Read a Financial Report,* from Merrill Lynch, Pierce, Fenner, and Smith (free); and *How to Understand Governmental Financial Statements,* from Price Waterhouse (free).

Financial information about an individual

A journalist can gather the financial information about an individual known as net-worth information by checking the local assessor's office for the worth of the house owned by the subject of the investigation, and by snooping around and finding out how many cars the subject has, what kind of clothes the subject wears, and what the subject does on nights on the town. The reporter can also find out if the subject has a boat or an airplane because both must be licensed in most states.

Be careful about drawing hasty conclusions from net-worth studies, however. Simply showing that people are wealthy beyond their public salaries does not show that the extra money was made illegally or immorally. We know of a police officer who legally inherited a multimillion-dollar fortune. When he drove a Corvette to the police station, nobody said anything. But a few years later when he traded it for a Jaguar E-Type, he was told that the new car would have to go because it looked too much like he was on the take. So he bought a ratty Dodge station wagon.

Government directories

The *U.S. Government Manual,* issued annually, lists all federal agencies, officials, and branches. Most states issue similar manuals, some of which include biographies of officials and legislators. Also helpful is the three-volume *Congressional Source Book Series.* The first volume, *Requirements for Recurring Reports to the Congress,* lists the reports that every federal agency and department must send to Congress. The other two volumes list equally informative reports.

Gun registration

In one sense at least, right-wing organizations opposed to gun-control laws are right. Requiring people to register their guns does tell the government where those guns are located and thus allows greater government surveillance of the life of its citizens. But because gun registration records are usually available for the asking, these laws also allow investigative reporters to find out which public figures legally own guns and which of those people who say their guns are registered have actually purchased permits.

Income tax forms for individuals

Tax forms are most easily available from the taxpayer. Many officials, such as New York City mayor Ed Koch when he was in office, make them available routinely. Some reporters demand income tax information from the taxpayers themselves as a way to force other admissions, or vice versa. For example, a reporter confronting someone with an allegation of bribe taking should ask to see income tax forms to prove no bribe was taken. If the person refuses, the reporter should pull the same stunt with the alleged briber but should accuse that person of taking rather than giving the bribe. The law requires that illegal income be reported on tax forms, so the alleged briber may turn them over to prove no bribe was received. Then the reporter should check whether the alleged bribe was reported as a business expense. But if obtaining tax forms from the taxpayer is barred by investigative circumstances, other sources exist, including the Internal Revenue Service.

Getting somebody else's tax records from the IRS is considerably harder than getting one's own, but it can be done. The *Providence* (R.I.) *Journal* published information from President Nixon's tax returns in 1973. Obviously, some people who work for the IRS are willing to supply tax returns or the information from them, under certain circumstances. The problem lies in finding those people. A group of IRS agents are reliably reported to have threatened to arrange for the publication of former U.S. attorney general John Mitchell's tax records unless he stopped obstructing their investigation of former federal court of appeals judge Otto Kerner. The same sources said the threat worked.

Even the IRS agents who will not show a reporter a certain person's tax returns can be helpful in other ways. Many of them will gladly tell a reporter which are the more corrupt government agencies in the jurisdiction and will provide hints on where corruption can be found.

Other sources of tax forms are people the taxpayer may have provided with copies, such as an accountant, or people or organizations the IRS may have provided with copies, including the following:

The president and some members of the White House staff.

Other government agencies that use the returns primarily for statistical purposes.

The police and other law enforcement agencies, which use the returns for tax prosecution as well as for the prosecution of other crimes.

Congressional committees, whose members have a ready-made excuse for demanding tax returns: to study them to prepare future tax legislation more intelligently.

State governments, which receive the federal returns so they can determine if their residents are paying the proper state taxes. Critics have argued that the federal government should give the states only that information relevant to this task rather than forwarding entire returns to state bureaucrats.

The courts are a major source of income tax forms, because judges often need to know the details of a person's income to determine guilt or innocence, how much should be paid or given up as part of a divorce settlement, or how an estate should be divvied up. Therefore, people with divorce, civil, criminal, and small claims cases in court are often required to file copies of their income tax returns with the court clerk, and investigative reporters and others often may examine them. The executor of the estate of a deceased person is also often required to file copies of the person's income tax returns with the clerk of the probate court handling the estate.

Naturally, the court with the largest lode of U.S. income tax information is the U.S. Tax Court, where people go to dispute the IRS's judgment on what taxes they owe, what penalties they must pay, and so forth. The tax returns are central to this process and must be filed with the court, which makes them available to the public at its Washington, D.C. office. Also available is testimony in tax cases, additional financial information submitted to the court, and other information.

Legal newspapers

In most major cities, a commercially published legal newspaper lists the day's name changes, business bankruptcies, suits filed, assumed names requested, births, marriages, divorces, and so on. A quick glance at this publication every day often pays off.

Legal notices

Most public agencies are required by law to publish legal notices in newspapers of general circulation in their area when, for example, they solicit bids, issue bonds, begin public projects, or hold hearings. Copies of legal notices are generally on file with the newspaper that published them and with the government agency that arranged for publication. Collusion and conflict-of-interest stories can be buttressed with evidence of the deliberate omission of legal notices with the intent of aiding particular individuals involved. In some jurisdictions it might be wise to learn how the papers in which the notices appear are chosen. Find a small newspaper publisher who is benefitting from $400,000 a year in legal advertising and you'll probably find a newspaper not all that critical of the agency tossing that business its way.

Marriage records

Applications for marriage licenses are usually on public file in the jurisdiction where the marriage took place. As with birth certificates, the reporter must know the approximate date of the marriage and the jurisdiction in which it occurred in order to see the application. As with birth certificates, a suspicion of nepotism is the major reason for going after a marriage license application. If a reporter suspects an official of having in-laws on the payroll, and if the official has no children, there won't be a birth certificate on which to find his wife's maiden name. But her maiden name will appear on the couple's marriage license application. The reporter will also have to look up the official's sisters' marriage certificates for complete in-law information.

Military records

Records of active service personnel are available from the Pentagon. Former service personnel can be located through local Veterans Administration offices or through the U.S. Army Personnel Center in St. Louis. The *Army Register,* the *Air Force Register,* and the *Register of Commissioned and Warrant Officers of the Navy and Marine Corps* list each commissioned officer by name, serial number, date and place of birth, and date of induction. These directories also list retired officers and are helpful in locating people who are no longer in the service.

Classified military records are sometimes available from friends in the Pentagon, from friendly congressmen, or from the employees of congressional committees. Classified records are also occasionally available from unexpected sources. One Chicago reporter was able to verify reports that the Nike missile bases in the city's lakefront parks were or had been armed with nuclear warheads when he was provided with evidence by a band of wandering native Americans. The leaders of the group had been trained by urban organizer Saul Alinsky and had occupied an abandoned missile emplacement to protest a housing shortage. In one of the underground silos, they found a technical manual on how to install and activate the missiles' nuclear warheads.

Motor vehicle records

There are at least three sources for state vehicle records: the secretary of state's office or state motor vehicle department, the local or state police, and the state or county prosecutor's office. Many newspapers, magazines, and radio and television stations attempt to maintain a reliable contact in one or more of these agencies so they can find out over the telephone who owns a car with a particular license plate.

In some states the distribution of this information is routine and systematized. In those states a reporter can send a small fee to the department of motor vehicles along with a form on which he has filled in a car's license-plate number, year, and make. The department will reply with the name, address, driver's license number, and date of birth of the car's owner. Sometimes this information indicates that a politician doesn't live in the district he represents or that a civil servant doesn't live in the city that requires him to live within its borders. Vehicle records are also necessary in tracing autos that are towed away.

Some secretary of state's offices, state motor vehicle departments, and Uniform Commercial Code offices also record purchase agreements on new cars. That information can be useful. Perhaps the records will indicate that the city purchasing director got a price break on a personal car from the auto dealer who always seems to be the low bidder, by a small margin, on city contracts. A reporter can find out the dealer's true cost on a car with options by calling the auto manufacturer's public relations department.

Museum records

Museums are public or quasi-public institutions in many cities, and itemizations of their collections are usually available through the museum's registrar. This information might be considered of interest only to art critics except that in some jurisdictions, museum officials — seeking bigger budgets — lend out works of art to public officials with pull. A reporter discovered that a Diego Rivera watercolor, owned by the Detroit Institute of Art and susceptible to damage from overexposure to light, had been hanging for eleven years on the sunlit wall of the office of an assistant county clerk whose boss was influential; that a former Detroit mayor, on leaving public life, had taken two of the museum's paintings with him to his new out-of-town residence; and that the city's current mayor, Coleman Young, had stacked a valuable statue lent by the museum among a pile of dirty coffee percolators and cups in the process of redecorating his office. The story also pointed out that although the ostensible purpose of the lending program was to increase public access to art, many of the works were in private, inner chambers of judges where only a few attorneys got to see them. As a result of the story, the artworks were recalled to the museum.

A *Washington Post* reporter investigated the gem and mineral collection at the sacrosanct Smithsonian Institution in Washington, D.C., in 1983 and discovered that donors' wishes that gems never leave the museum were routinely violated and that gems were being sold secretly from the museum's own display cases. He also uncovered massive tax abuse among the donors: One contributor purchased a gem for $750 and donated it to the museum. He then claimed a $1.1 million deduction for it on his federal income tax return.

Newspaper libraries (formerly known as morgues)

Obviously, a newspaper library is the most convenient place to begin an investigation. Reporters have discovered that it's wise to check there for the names of everyone even peripherally involved in an investigative story. Clippings or photographs, innocuous in themselves, may link the subject of the story with people who were, for example, convicted of fraud after the picture was taken and thus may add a whole new dimension to an investigation.

Payroll records

Personnel departments at most firms will confirm or deny—often over the telephone—that a certain person is on the payroll, unless that person is secretly employed as part of a corrupt arrangement. Civil service departments in many cities will provide similar information. Reporters sometimes encounter resistance when they try to photocopy payroll records, but remember that a public payroll is a public record, exact salaries included. The only exceptions might be the payrolls of agencies like the CIA.

Once a reporter has obtained a copy of a public payroll, it can be used to begin a number of investigations. City payrolls are nice to have around to check against police arrest blotters, business fraud indictments, and lists of people seen hanging around with known criminals. (The ordinary investigative story about almost anything is much improved if it can be discovered that its subject is also, say, a city attorney.) Payrolls can also be compared with lists of campaign workers. Or a reporter might check the various departments to see if as many people work there as are listed on the payroll. If eighty are listed, and the reporter can only find seventy-seven, somebody might be signing phony names to phony checks and cashing them. The next step is to look at the canceled payroll checks and see who's cashing them.

Detroit Free Press reporter Jim Neubacher once heard rumors that a woman named Glenda McGuire had a job with Michigan governor William Milliken's administration but that no one ever saw her or knew what she did. Checking the payroll was easy. He found out that McGuire had been hired by the governor's office as part of his unclassified staff and that she served as one of the governor's eight personal aides at a salary of more than $18,000 per year.

Neubacher's first task was to find out where, if anywhere, McGuire worked. He went to the governor's Detroit office and asked to see her. He was told she worked in Lansing. In Lansing he was told that she worked in Detroit. Finally, a governor's aide told Neubacher that McGuire did interviews for a research report that would give Milliken "insight on public attitudes," particularly among blacks. Neubacher was told that McGuire worked out of her Detroit home and had no office, desk, phone, or state car.

Neubacher asked to see any preliminary reports or memos — anything — pertaining to her project. Nothing could be found. But the aide to the governor said he talked with McGuire regularly. Neubacher asked who McGuire was interviewing, and the aide couldn't come up with a single name. Neubacher asked the aide to ask McGuire for a representative list of fifteen or so names of persons she had interviewed. Eventually Neubacher was given the names of eleven alleged interviewees, including a young man McGuire grew up with, McGuire's sister's boyfriend, and the principal of the school where her sister taught. Neubacher contacted them; none of them remembered any interview, although six other persons on the list did remember brief telephone conversations with a woman from the governor's office. When Neubacher finally interviewed McGuire, she had a Lansing office that appeared all of a sudden because she said she had finished interviewing and was ready to write her report.

In his story, Neubacher reported that McGuire was being paid more than $18,000 a year by the taxpayers to do practically nothing and that she was given the job because her boyfriend, a Detroit judge, had helped the governor during his reelection campaign. Neubacher was able to substantiate the latter part of his story by linking McGuire to the judge through motel registrations and real estate records (McGuire had lived in a house owned by the judge) and by linking her hiring to a closed-door meeting between a Milliken aide and the judge.

Private organization records

Among the private agencies with extensive files are public service law firms, Ralph Nader–type groups, ecology and consumer organizations, trade associations, political parties, the League of Women Voters, and civic watchdog organizations. Also, many community, ethnic, and even ecclesiastical organizations keep voluminous information on their enemies and often have full-time investigators. Most of these groups will routinely cooperate with a reporter who can convince them that their enemies are the same. In doing a story about a glue magnate who bribed a zoning board, it would be as foolish to overlook the ecology groups, glue workers' unions, and public-interest law firms involved as it would be to ignore the city planning and zoning records.

Professional, business, and trade directories

The *Dictionary of the American Medical Association* supplies a state-by-state listing of medical schools, hospitals, and physicians, including each doctor's date of birth and medical school attended. The *Martindale-Hubbell Law Directory* lists lawyers by area and includes a biography of each, which sometimes includes the law school attended and the major clients represented by individual law firms. This could lead to some important stories if a lawyer has taken out stock or part ownership in a firm in return for legal services — a common practice — and later accepts a judgeship or a regulatory agency position without getting rid of that stock. What if a case involving the firm comes before the judge? The directory also sometimes comments on the competency of the lawyers it lists. (A copy of the original bar exam application of every lawyer, compete with background information, is on file with the supreme court clerk in the state where the exam was administered. Notaries public must also file personal information with state officials, usually either the secretary of state or the governor.)

Many business and trade organizations also publish directories of their members.

Religious directories

Religious organizations frequently publish directories of their membership.

School records

Most schools and colleges will tell any caller, even over the telephone, whether a certain person was ever a student there, the dates of entrance and departure, and the degree awarded. Although a vast majority of America's schools are publicly supported or aided, school administrators seem to consider all other information on their students confidential; sometimes the law supports them in this. It's even difficult to find out who has applied for admission to a particular school, although politicians sitting on academic boards of directors have been known to help unqualified but intimate associates be admitted without public notice being taken. If a school refuses to reveal even the most basic information about its students, a quick look at the appropriate yearbook will close the information gap. Most schools keep their old yearbooks on file in their own libraries, which are often open to the public.

Much other information about a school is public, including students' scores on standardized tests (available from the state education office), the racial composition of the students in each school district (available from the U.S. Department of Education), and accreditation reports (available from the various accrediting associations). It also makes sense to treat schools as businesses or as major purchasers of business servicers (which they are) and check their bids, contracts, and purchase orders for possible conflicts of interest, such as school board members who sell to the schools they have jurisdiction over. Diploma mills also make good stories; investigating such an institution directly and checking it with the appropriate licensing and accreditation agencies usually turns up something interesting.

Securities and Exchange Commission records

The Securities and Exchange Commission (SEC) has a long list of dos and don'ts for those who buy and sell stocks. Reporters investigating stock fraud must familiarize themselves with these rules. The agency also makes available the Form 10-Ks, which every company selling stock to the public must file annually with the SEC. The 10-K contains voluminous information on the company that files it, including such gems as major lawsuits pending against the firm, changes in the company's financial standing, and details of its sales, revenues, and dividends over the preceding year. The SEC also regularly records a large number of stock transactions and publishes the *Directory of Corporate Ownership*. A commercial publisher, the Washington Service Bureau in Washington, D.C., produces the daily *SEC News Digest,* which includes a list of individuals who have just bought large amounts of a company's stock. By looking through current and back copies of both publications, a reporter can often discover who controls many corporations and the names of the front men or nominees used by stock owners for stock purchase. If, for example, a reporter flipping through the *SEC News Digest* finds that the mayor has purchased a large block of stock in Amalgamated Consolidated in the name of his lawyer, Harold DeComing II, it may be a good idea to see what local property is also listed in DeComing's name. Perhaps it's the land the mayor wants the new city hall built on.

State regulatory records

State regulatory boards are required to keep up-to-date files on all the members of the profession or trade they are charged with regulating. Most of these records are public; others may be pried from recalcitrant officials or other sources. In various states realtors, physicians, nurses, attorneys, architects, funeral directors, hairdressers, barbers, TV technicians, and others are regulated by state boards. A person who is not listed with the appropriate board is probably practicing illegally.

Telephone records

Although most telephone companies seldom give out unlisted telephone numbers or disclose the amount of someone's telephone bill, phone officials will sometimes tell reporters in what geographical area an unlisted number is or is not located. (Maps showing the location of all numbers beginning with the same three-digit sequence are printed in the front of most telephone directories.) Although phone companies don't give the information out to reporters, the companies do keep records of billable calls made; if they didn't, they couldn't bill their customers. Therefore, it is possible to obtain these records, or bills, from cooperative employees inside the company or through a government agency with subpoena power.

It is also possible to obtain these records by trickery. At least one reporter we know would stoop so low as to call the telephone company business office and, posing as the person being investigated, say that he didn't recall making long-distance calls that had been charged to him. He would then ask the phone company to check the numbers and dates of the calls and report back. (The same gambit is sometimes used by reporters who wish to check on the money a person has borrowed. They simply call the credit company to reconfirm the loan. A similar technique can be used to check someone's airplane reservations; see Airline Manifests in this chapter.) Obtaining such information from the phone company, however, works both ways. So an experienced investigator who is intent on protecting his or her identity or location should call from a remote pay phone or from the paper's subscription department rather than from a home or desk phone.

Remember also that if nobody knew a person's unlisted phone number, nobody would ever call that person — and there would be little reason for that person to have a telephone. The trick in getting an unlisted phone number is to find the person's friends and persuade one of them to provide the number. Some reporters will tell the friend, especially if it's the truth, that a possibly damaging story concerning the unlisted person is about to be printed or broadcast and that the reporter needs to talk to the subject immediately to find out if the story is true. At worst, the friend may call the person and relay the information.

If the reporter is lucky, the person may then call the reporter from the unlisted telephone. If the reporter's phone is equipped with a caller identification system, the reporter will then have the unlisted telephone number. (In the late 1980s, telephone companies began offering their customers such systems, which, if not blocked by the caller, would display the phone number of the caller on the screen of a device attached to the recipient's phone.)

Trade publications

Because the editors of trade publications assume that their readership is restricted, the publications are often loaded with inside information. Duane Lindstrom, former research director for the Chicago organization Citizens for a Better Environment, unearthed a number of major land-use scandals by regularly perusing local real estate trade publications. Every now and then a rather brazen developer would indicate that an upcoming project had investment advantages that others lacked, such as exceptionally low or nonexistent property taxes. Stories about such a situation in a general-circulation newspaper would be read with intense interest by the heavily burdened property-tax payers nearby.

Uniform Commercial Code records (or chattel mortgage records)

Uniform Commercial Code forms are filed for the benefit of private businesses, such as collection and lending agencies. If the records are kept in a reporter's jurisdiction — they're often kept at the county level as well as in the secretary of state's office — the reporter need only know the name and sometimes the address of the person being investigated. Then the reporter can request copies of a form the person filled out and signed each time he or she purchased something wholly or partially on credit. The forms are useful in obtaining a copy of someone's signature or in comparing assets to income. For example, a person who lives in a $150,000 house, paid $100,000 cash, financed the other $50,000, and is only a deputy assessor may be on the take. But a deputy assessor who lives in a $35,000 house, put $5,000 down, and financed the other $30,000 may be honest after all. Or suppose a reporter investigating the city treasurer discovers that that official was granted a 7 percent mortgage at a time of 8½ percent mortgage interest rates. If the city deposit records indicate the treasurer deposited a lot of city money in that same bank at the same time, also at a low interest rate, the reporter may have uncovered a sophisticated bribe.

Interest-free deposits are a popular medium of exchange. A Blue Cross and Blue Shield organization in one state was found to be putting members' money in interest-free accounts in the bank of one of its board members. No interest had been paid on the deposited funds for 28 years.

Vanity directories

Unplumbed depths of personal information on thousands of prominent and not so prominent people await the enterprising reporter who looks in the latest edition of any of the vanity directories, which are on the shelves of most major libraries. They include the *Social Register, Burke's Peerage, Who's Who* in its various versions (for example, *Who's Who in America* and *Who's Who in the West*), *American Men of Science, Contemporary Authors,* and others. The value of such directories, however, is limited in that usually only information furnished by the listed person is printed.

Voting records

In most jurisdictions a person registering to vote must give his or her full name, present and previous address, home telephone number, social security number, party affiliation, and mother's maiden name. This information is stored on file cards with the jurisdiction's election officials. Whenever that person votes, an *X* is marked on the file card next to the date of that particular election. Reporters will find it easy to become friendly with the election officials who control these files by encouraging their publication or station to play up stories about voter registration deadlines and other matters important to the officials. Then it is easy to persuade them to give a reporter access to the voter records. In many jurisdictions even friendliness is unnecessary: The general public is routinely allowed access to voter registration files.

The information gleaned from these files is frequently of use in non-election-related investigations. However, election stories can result from a perusal of these files when, for example, a reporter knows someone's real address and discovers that the person is claiming a false address for voting purposes—a crime in almost any jurisdiction. Reporters have taken the trouble to go over the voter registration records for one precinct and then interview people whose records indicate they voted in the previous election. If a significant number of voters say they didn't vote in the election, but they were marked present and voting on their registration cards, somebody may have been voting for them. Voting in someone else's place is both a crime and a tip-off to a good story.

Welfare records

In many jurisdictions, a reporter can find out informally from the local welfare office if a particular person has been on welfare and for how long, but other information—such as the levels of payments and the reason the person went on relief—must be pried out of a caseworker. If a reporter finds a talker, it is useful to remember that welfare records are also a good way to find out who's related to whom, where people previously lived, and where they were born—information a reporter needs to locate birth, marriage, or criminal records.

A surprising number of journalists are of the opinion that nothing genuinely derogatory can be found in records available to the public. But the truth is that most corrupt persons believe that no one will ever look at the public record forms they routinely fill out. In most instances, they are right.

Federal Communications Commission records, for example, contain the case of a lawyer's advising a corporate client that he had to file potentially damaging information but he should overload the file with trivial information so that reporters would be loath to sort through it all. A certain Chicago tax assessor believed that his assessing system—based on factors involving a building's original cost, age, occupancy rate, and relative profitability—was so complicated that no reporter would have the nerve to charge that it was being applied unfairly. His presumption proved accurate for quite a while: From 1934 until 1970 the story went unwritten.

Experienced reporters realize, however, that evidence of wrongdoing often is contained in public records simply because the persons involved have no alternative but to file it in public record offices. Although public records research is often fruitless, on some occasions every record touched reveals something relevant to an investigation. Take as an example the Detroit reporter who was investigating allegations that the Detroit police department's auto recovery bureau and a towing firm on contract to the bureau were falsely designating relatively new cars as abandoned, then towing them off and selling them for the towing firm's financial benefit. The reporter's first step was to look up the company in the assumed names office. The firm was incorporated, so the names and addresses of its officers and directors were on record, as well as the names of some of the stockholders in the firm. Earlier annual reports, filed in the same office, provided the names of previous officers, directors, and stockholders.

The names on file didn't mean anything to the reporter, so he looked them up in his newspaper's library. The old clippings he found indicated that one of the firm's founders had been indicted by a federal grand jury for conspiring with an alleged Mafia leader in an illegal gambling operation. Another clip indicated that the towing firm's president had been convicted years before of receiving stolen property, a felony.

Knowing that in Detroit, towing firms are required to hold city licenses, the reporter looked up the firm's license application in the city license bureau. On the application filled out by the convicted felon, president of the firm, the question "Have you ever been convicted of a felony?" was left unanswered. But the form had been approved anyway, in writing, by two Detroit police detectives. At this point the reporter should have been sufficiently suspicious of the policemen to check the names of the firm's officers against the police payroll, but he didn't think to do so.

After his check of the towing firm's incorporation papers, but before writing his story, the reporter went back to the assumed names office for a recheck. There he discovered that the records he had previously examined were out on loan to two persons who had left their business cards where the records had been. Those cards identified the two as an agent of the IRS and an agent of the police department's self-investigation unit. So the reporter was able to write in his first story that the firm was alleged to have misdesignated cars as abandoned and towed them away for a profit; that it was owned by a former felon who, in violation of city ordinances, had submitted an incomplete license application; that one of the founders of the firm had been indicted for conspiring with a man named as a Mafia leader at a U.S. Senate hearing; and that the towing firm was being investigated by the IRS and the police department.

After the story came out, the reporter, working on a follow-up, called all the current officers of the firm to get their reaction to the first story. One of them, apparently not the craftiest person in the world, blurted out over the telephone that he had been on the police department's auto recovery bureau (which designated cars as abandoned) when he bought a part interest in the towing firm and that the firm had not been contacted by the police department to tow away any cars until after he became one of its owners. He also said he saw nothing wrong with his course of conduct because the superintendent of police had known about it all along. When questioned, the superintendent said he didn't remember anything about it, but the follow-up story made interesting reading nonetheless.

It made especially interesting reading because the reporter, acting on a tip, did what he should have done before writing his first story: He checked his newspaper's library for the names of the two detectives who approved the towing firm's license application. There he discovered that one of the detectives, after approving the application, had been indicted for accepting a bribe in another auto case. That information was duly noted in the follow-up story. After a second follow-up the auto recovery section of the police department was reorganized, and the towing firm lost its city contract.

The reporter's only regret about these stories was that they incorrectly identified the Detroit police department's self-investigation unit as the Special Investigation Bureau. The correct name for the unit at the time the stories were written was the Internal Affairs Bureau. The name of this unit may have been the only fact that the reporter didn't check several times, because he blithely believed himself familiar with the names of the various police units. In investigative stories it's almost always the fact you think you know and don't bother to check that turns out to be wrong.

CHAPTER 7

Zoning, land use, and property tax records

Zoning

Zoning is a strange and wondrous thing. The value of land can be made to rise and fall like a roller coaster simply by changing the little numbers on a zoning map. Zoning was conceived earlier this century to prevent commercial structures from being built in residential neighborhoods. Houston, Texas, however, which has no zoning ordinances, looks pretty much like any other American city. The rich live in one neighborhood, the poor in another. The drawing rooms of the mansion district have not been remodeled into taco stands.

One of the effects of zoning has been the creation of a class of wealthy zoning officials and land speculators. When the uses permitted on the land go up, so does its asking price and value—until the zoning is changed again. The possibilities for graft in zoning are one of the major marvels of modern malfeasance. According to Dan Paul, a Miami attorney who wrote the Dade County (Florida) metropolitan charter, "Zoning is the single biggest corrupter of the nation's local governments."

Zoning is a complex subject, and its jargon consists of no household words. We suspect that for these reasons most reporters are leery of getting into it. With all the land-use symbols involved, such as B3 and R2A, zoning stories are generally unread by anyone, except perhaps the family that finds itself living next door to a new cyanide plant.

But there are great and good stories in zoning, to be had almost for the asking. In some zoning scandals reporters may find no money changing hands. Often, well-intentioned city fathers are bullied into bad zoning decisions by the relentless pressure to increase the city's tax base. Public officials are susceptible to corporate threats to locate in "friendlier climes" if they are not granted the zoning variance necessary to build their sulfur dioxide factory upwind of the tuberculosis sanato-rium. Municipalities are played off this way, one against another, and wind up bargaining away either their tax base or their environment.

The term "zoning variance" should make the alert reporter take notice. What it means, generally, is that despite the advice of the profes-sional planners who thought an area should be restricted in use or build-ing size, the politicians in power decided to permit different, sometimes even incompatible, uses and structures. The questions to be asked are these: Why was the area zoned one way in the first place, if variances were to be granted? How is it decided who gets the variances?

In a lot of zoning changes, it appears that lightning has struck. The numbers on the zoning map are changed, and land that was worth 10 cents a square foot on Monday is worth $2 a square foot on Tuesday. Consider the case of the peon's assistant who spends his entire life plow-ing eighty acres with his fingernails and wakes up one morning to dis-cover that encroaching suburbs have raised his property taxes to the point that he can no longer afford to farm. Two days later someone offers him four times what he thinks the farm is worth, and happily he sells the land. But the developer who bought it has the connections, energy, and the nerve to get the little numbers on the maps changed, and in a short time the farm is rezoned from R1A (which permits only single-family residences) to C5A (which permits limited nuclear wars.) It is then worth four times what the developer paid.

Reporters interested in zoning stories don't have to wait for the local inside dopesters to tip them off. They can just look at recent major changes in their areas. If they go back any further than recent zoning changes, they will find themselves conducting their interviews in Miami, Palm Springs, and Rio de Janeiro. Wherever a large upgrading oc-curred, someone made a fortune.

To start a zoning investigation, the reporter first needs to find out who owned the land and benefited from the variance. Whose campaign did the owner support? The reporter also needs to find out who was on the various boards that recommended or approved the change, what they did for a living, what land they owned, who they bought from, who their relatives are, and who their relatives worked for.

Next the reporter should interview the people who were or will be adversely affected by the zoning change. The best approach is to knock on doors in the affected neighborhood, let people know about the inves-tigation, and enlist their aid against a common enemy. It shouldn't be too hard to get them to ask around and call if they hear anything. There is no such thing as an airtight conspiracy: Someone has talked, and tracks have been left. Secretaries not party to the action know about the deal and whatever secret alliances may be involved. So, probably, do various municipal employees, real estate brokers, tax assessors, or even the local bartender. Perhaps a hundred people are in a position to provide important information. Surely one of them will talk about some part of it. Then it is only a matter of using that information to deduce the broad outlines of the deal and bluff the various officials and developers into admitting the details.

In most communities proposed zoning and city plan changes must be discussed at one or more hearings to which the public is invited to voice support or raise objections. In such cases an advance notice describing the proposed change is usually published in a general-circulation newspaper. Sometimes, however, zoning officials run an inaccurate notice or neglect to run any notice. In at least one case the published legal notice said a small shopping center was proposed when, in fact, the zoning board had planned to approve and did approve a large shopping center. (See Legal Notices in chapter 6.)

Land use

In some communities the practice of planning future land use has as much or even more effect on corruption as zoning. As planning becomes widespread, reporters will have to study proposed changes in land-use plans as well as in zoning. Planning is what is done before zoning. A plan amendment, or a new plan for a certain area, records the local public body's statement of intent for future zoning. By planning an area for high-rise offices, officials are saying that when a developer actually comes along and requests that the zoning in an area be changed to permit high-rise offices, the request is likely to be granted.

Planning has come to wield the force of law because the courts are tending to hold city commissions or planning commissions to the plans they set out. If a developer buys land planned for high-density residential use but is denied high-density residential zoning when he is ready to begin development, he can sue for the requested zoning and in some jurisdictions can win in nine cases out of ten.

That being the case, the replanning of land has a substantial impact on its value. Yet we know of no state where an upgrade in the planning designation alone increases the taxes. This presents unscrupulous public officials with the opportunity to increase the market value of their own land or that of their associates without increasing the taxes on the land. Consequently, although good planning is a definite aid to the orderly and aesthetic growth of an area, it presents great temptations. The power of planning encourages shady public officials to perform any one of a number of dishonest acts:

Public officials—including mayors, city council members, planning commissioners and staffers, assessors, and city attorneys—may participate in the rezoning or planning of their own land. They may openly announce they own the land, or they may own it (or own shares in the companies that own it) secretly. Either way, their participation in the redesignation is a conflict or interest. They should not participate in any decisions affecting the value of or taxes levied on the land. That includes discussions of or votes on zoning, planning, sewer assessments, streetlights, utilities, roads, zoning variances, or site plan approvals.

Public officials may accept campaign contributions, gifts, stock options, stock, or money from developers favored by their votes. It should make no difference to a reporter whether the vote comes before or after the money is paid.

Public officials may use their votes or influence to increase the value of land owned by their business partners, relatives, or friends. The scrupulously honest official will abstain from all such votes or discussions.

Public officials may rezone or replan land for developments in which they later come to hold a direct or lease-hold interest. For example, a developer who plans to lease part of a shopping center to a local businessman who is also a city commissioner is in an excellent position to encourage favorable zoning by offering a lucrative lease arrangement.

Public officials may benefit from inside knowledge. Most commonly they buy land or advise associates to buy land in an area they expect to be upgraded by zoning or planning changes. (Before the expected changes are publicly known, the land can be purchased for a fraction of its future value.) Corrupt officials can also purchase lands or buildings they know or have good reason to believe are about to be purchased by a public agency. This practice also produces healthy profits for the officials, at public expense.

A cautionary note: When doing zoning and planning stories, reporters should take extreme care to read the fine print in the local zoning ordinance. In one township, R1 may permit up to fifteen housing units per acre, and in another, the classification may make no mention of density at all. In some exclusive suburbs a person must own an acre of land for each bedroom planned in a new home. Obviously, a reporter must be certain of these nuances before accusing someone of engineering the grandmother of all boondoggles. Good sources for interpreting the detail of zoning machinations are law professors who teach zoning, urban-planning firms, and the zoning staffs of nearby, honest cities.

Property tax records

The property tax section may seem to be the most boring place in the hall of records, but consider for a moment some of the things a reporter can learn there:

Who pays the taxes on a certain parcel of land, and hence who owns it or at least knows who the real owner is

The past and present zoning of the land

Which $30,000-a-year public officials live in $1,150,000 homes

Whether a person's taxpaying address and voting address are the same

Whom someone bought a house from and, often, at what price

Who the real estate broker and lawyers were and who holds the mortgage on the house

Whether the local bowling alley is listed as a public school and is thus exempt from paying taxes

The approximate value of urban renewal land before and after the bulldozers got to it

Whether the county assessor is paying his or her own taxes

Whether big campaign contributors are being fairly taxed

Property records and property tax records are easily inspected. Remember, if a real estate person needs a record, you can get it. Property record offices are generally swarming with lawyers, title searchers, and realtors, and reporters often go unnoticed in the shuffle. The main difficulty lies in correctly converting street addresses or intersections into the appropriate parcel-numbering system or legal description, and vice versa.

Legal descriptions of land, always highly abbreviated, read something like this:

Lot 3 or parcel 12 of the NW Sec. of the SW quarter of Eyesters
Beaver Gardens, T2N, range 11E, Hapless Twp.

That's if the reporter is lucky. Some legal descriptions are a series of surveyor's notations that ramble on for hundreds of words and delve into arcs, tangents, secants, and all the horrible things the average reporter has forgotten since flunking high school trigonometry. The reporter either has to call for help or buy a tract map and a degree wheel and carefully trace the lines described. Until a reporter gets good at this, it is wise to have one of the clerks demonstrate how it's done, or even to visit the house-numbering offices, established in many jurisdictions, that convert legal descriptions into street addresses for a small fee.

Assessor's offices, treasurer's offices, and tract indexes use an elaborate system of maps and cross-indexed binders or electronic filing systems to help researchers locate land. The maps bear land identification numbers that refer to pages in tax books and to individual lots. Some offices charge a fee for their help, but most will provide the information without charge, particularly for reporters. Relying on the clerks without checking their work can be risky, though. If a reporter gets just one of dozens of numbers wrong, it is possible to wind up describing the wrong property or accusing the wrong person of property manipulation.

The first time a reporter delves into property tax matters, it usually takes a few hours to learn how the whole system works. After that, the research becomes fairly routine. In general, property is assessed at some fraction of what it is really worth. Generally, what it is really worth is determined by its fair market value (what it would sell for). For a building, the assessment is based on its replacement cost (how much it would cost to build another structure like it), some multiple of the annual income it produces if it's a commercial building, or some combination of the two.

The most common mistake reporters can make in mentioning a property's value is to confuse the assessed value with the real value. In some states all properties — houses, factories, stores, and vacant land — are assessed at the same fraction of the fair market value. In other states the fraction varies with the type of property assessed. Houses may be assessed at 50 percent of market value, office buildings at 20 percent, and land at 10 percent, for example. In some states the market value is further reduced by various depreciation factors. An office building that is half-abandoned, for example, will have its assessment further reduced by, say, 40 percent. The way to avoid any possible confusion is to call an assessor over, point to the number, and ask, "What is that?" Then the value of the land can be attributed to the assessor's office.

The opportunity for corruption and unfair taxation in different states is directly proportional to the complexity of the assessment procedure. In states that do not set a fixed percentage of real worth as the basis for assessment, little more than the assessor's discretion decides a property's taxes. The opportunity for corruption usually manages to overwhelm at least a few assessors. But even in states that require that all property be assessed at half of market value, for example, it is still the assessor who determines what the market value of the property is, and that leaves enough room to permit corruption. In most states a state agency also applies an equalization factor to the assessments made by various county officials. This is to prevent a county from paying less than its fair share of taxes if its assessors set unrealistically low values for the property.

The formula for determining a property's taxes, then, is

$$(Vm)(Va)(Ef)(R) = T$$

where Vm is the market value; Va is the fraction of market value used or imposed by law; Ef is the state equalization factor; R is the tax rate; and T is the amount of taxes due on the property. For example, suppose a house under investigation sold two years ago for $48,000. Last year an almost identical house down the block sold for $49,000. It would be reasonable to estimate the current market value (Vm) at $50,000. Either state law or current assessment practice in the jurisdiction specifies that homes are assessed at, say, 60 percent of their fair market value. That means that the assessed value (Va) of the home in question is 60 percent of $50,000, or $30,000. Because the state has decided that assessors in the county or township where the house is located assess property too low, there is a state equalization factor (Ef) of 1.2. The $30,000 assessed valuation is then multiplied by the equalization factor to obtain a $36,000 state-equalized value. That figure is then multiplied by the tax rate (R) to determine the amount of taxes the property owner should pay. If the tax rate (R) is $70 per $1,000 assessed valuation, the tax liability should be $2,520. If the local assessor has arrived at a substantially different figure, something is wrong.

In most large cities, private companies publish books showing land values in the city and suburbs. It is often useful to compare what these books say property is worth with what the local assessor says. These books, like the blue and red books of used-car prices, derive their figures from surveys of recent sales. Wide discrepancies in the assessment of selected parcels may show that an official is underassessing friends or overassessing enemies. If the book is not available at the city hall or county building's reference library, a copy can often be borrowed from a large real estate firm, bank, or savings and loan association.

The assessment of buildings is more complicated than the assessment of land, making it more time-consuming for reporters or prosecutors to arrive at an accurate, independent appraisal of a building's worth. For that reason the crooked assessor is more likely to negotiate building assessments. What the reporter must do first is learn the complex formulas that assessors use to value the buildings. The formulas include such factors as replacement cost, square feet of floor space, gross annual rent, age, condition, and the recent sales price of similar buildings. It means little to say that an assessor is assessing everything in the county too high or too low, because the state will lower or raise the taxes by the appropriate equalization factor. What the reporter is seeking to find out is if the assessor is breaking rules to the advantage or disadvantage of particular buildings or land parcels.

Experienced investigators take extreme care with the basic research underlying such stories, because in essence the reporters involved are making their own assessment of the worth of the buildings—a fairly brazen enterprise—and a single mistake could invalidate the whole story. If possible, the wise reporter persuades a disgruntled employee of the assessor's office to help with the investigation or even persuades the publisher to finance an independent appraisal of at least one of the buildings the reporter thinks is underassessed.

Because property transfers are often used to conceal bribes, tax records are helpful insofar as they constitute a sort of government-approved property valuation. For example, if a businesswoman sells her home to a politician for $50,000, and the assessment records value the house at $70,000, it's a story. If the assessor's records show only a vacant lot or a row of small buildings where someone built a large factory two years ago, something newsworthy is happening.

The deeds in each jurisdiction's recorder- or register-of-deeds office or its equivalent provide citizens with a record of property ownership. (Mortgages and partnership agreements may also be recorded.) For various reasons, people are frequently reluctant to reveal what they paid for a house, a property, or a building. But the deed tells all. Often the price of the property appears on the deed. Sometimes the price doesn't appear, or the word "$1ovc" appears where the price should be. Officially it means "This property was sold for $1 plus other valuable considerations." Unofficially it means "Nah, nah, we won't tell you nothin'." But the deed reveals the price anyway. That's because although the great and glorious American Revolution was fought in part as a protest against the hated stamp tax, tax stamps are still in use today. That is, most jurisdictions levy a tax on sales of real estate, and no deed in those jurisdictions is certified unless tax stamps are affixed to the deed, indicating that the appropriate tax has been paid. And what is the appropriate tax? It depends on the sale price of the property, naturally. So all you have to do is add up the prices emblazoned on each stamp and then find out from a nearby clerk how much each dollar in stamp tax represented at the time of purchase in terms of the purchase price of the property. If each stamp sells for $10 and represents $10,000 of purchase price and four stamps are affixed to the deed, the property sold for $40,000. Simple? You bet.

Experienced property researchers usually commute between the office where the deeds are stored and the tract index. The information in the two offices is complementary, but the differences between the services provided are quite important. For instance, to find out who owns a certain property, the reporter can look up the address or legal description in the tract index and find the entire history of that plot: sales, purchases, mortgages, and so on, all the way back to the first entry for that plot, which will read something like "King of England grants to John Smith, Esq." The tract index, however, may not give indications of the amount of money exchanged in each transaction, nor copies of the deeds, divorce papers, death certificates, and other legal papers involved. For that information the reporter must take the index number of each transaction listed in the tract index to the deed room, where the various papers can be found and the tax stamps on the deeds translated into purchase or sale prices.

The grantor-grantee index or its equivalent is especially helpful if a reporter wants to find out what land a person or company owns, rather than who owns a particular piece of land. By looking up a person's name in the index, the reporter can discover all the property that person owns in his or her name in that jurisdiction — information crucial to planning and zoning investigations. The grantor-grantee index also directs an investigator to the relevant deeds, so if forgery or misrepresentation is suspected, a check can be made on the signatures of the principals involved, including notaries, lawyers, secretaries, spouses, and witnesses (who are often secretaries, friends, or associates.)

Tract index listings are sometimes surprising. A real estate company headed by Detroit mayor Coleman Young once owned some apartment buildings on the city's east side. A *Detroit Free Press* reporter checked those buildings in the tract index and discovered that the mortgage on the properties had been transferred from the life insurance company that originally held it to the U.S. Department of Housing and Urban Development (HUD), which insured it. The reason was that the mayor's company had not made any mortgage payments for months.

A secret of Chicago mayor Richard Daley's — that his one real estate holding was protected by a secret land trust run by an accountant who had received hundreds of thousands of dollars' worth of city business — was also revealed through tract index research. The reporter involved, Ed Pound of the *Chicago Sun-Times,* was curious about Daley's lifestyle. Daley lived modestly, almost humbly. He put a number of his sons through school but showed no signs of affluence other than a summer home in Michigan. So Pound went to the Michigan county where Daley had his summer home and looked it up in the tract index. He found that the title to the house was listed under the name of an Illinois corporation, Elard Realty ("El" from Daley's wife's name, "Elanore," and "ard" from Daley's first name, "Richard"). The corporation, a secret land trust aimed at concealing the real ownership of the property, was run by an old friend of the mayor's, the accountant who had received city business. Illinois and Florida are apparently the only states that allow secret land trusts; Michigan does not, so Daley couldn't bill his taxes to a trust number at a bank as he could have in his home state.

In addition to the public tract index and deed room, a number of private firms—mostly banks—keep similar records for much of the country. The title transfer records these firms retain often show the name of the broker or salesperson who handled the transfer. When contacted, the broker may reveal more details about the purchase—how long the property was on the market, the asking price, how long the buyer was in the market, and perhaps even some financial information on the buyer and the seller. If the broker balks, or if there is no reason to think the broker will talk, a reporter may be able to persuade someone at the assessor's office to make the call instead. Assessors make such inquiries routinely to keep abreast of changes in property value. Some reporters, finding both these options closed, are not above calling the broker and pretending to be from the assessor's office. Sometimes they even place the call from a phone in the assessor's office.

One thing to remember is that real estate and insurance brokers are licensed by the various states. An unusual number of public officials are real estate brokers and insurance salesmen, not because people with these vocations are attracted to public service but because people attracted to public office soon learn that their many contacts can be profitable if they are in a position to get broker's commissions. The commissions not only conceal bribes but also allow the officials to report bribes as income (thus keeping IRS investigators at bay) and explain them away to nosy reporters. Taking bribes in the form of commissions also can reduce any potential charges of bribery to a conflict of interest.

For example, if the Grave Stone Company wants the contract to pave all the parks in the city, the company president may buy his next home through a broker who happens to be the park commissioner. The broker–park commissioner will receive the commission on the sale of the home. The park commissioner will then recommend that the company be awarded the city's contract on the grounds that the low bidder, if there is one lower than Grave, lacks experience in park paving. When caught, the company president will deny it was a bribe, saying that he didn't even decide to buy the house until after the parks were already paved. He will say that if he never bought anything from anyone even remotely connected with his business, he would not be able to buy anything. Likewise, the park commissioner will deny it was a bribe. He will say that the reporters are just trying to sell newspapers through sensational stories that ruin people's lives and do irreparable harm to their families. He'll say he obtained a broker's license to have additional income so he wouldn't be tempted to wheel and deal with the taxpayers' money, and therefore the reporter has the story backwards. He will say that he has been paid commissions from lots of people who never did business with the parks department and that therefore he is a legitimate real estate broker. He may even offer a reporter a commission to show that they aren't such bad things.

Something else to watch for when mucking about in real estate records is whether a utility or a state-controlled or nonprofit corporation sells or leases any of its land, air rights, or rights-of-way. The land should be traced back to its original deeds, which are usually on microfilm, because in many cases the land was given or sold on the condition that it be used for specific purposes only. Such deeds or legislative acts generally contain a reverter clause, which requires that the land be returned to the public when no longer used for the purpose specified in the deed. Many states gave land to railroads and utilities (to "foster commerce and industry") with the proviso that the land revert to the state whenever the railroad or utility ceased to use it. At a time when many railroads are closing down inner-city switching yards and rights-of-way, they often sell the land illegally to developers. Most of the reverter deeds were drawn up a hundred years ago or more, and who remembers? Certainly not the railroad's lawyers.

In the preceding pages we have discussed records of real property: land and permanent improvements to it, such as paving, swimming pools, or buildings. Personal property is what sits inside the buildings or out in the driveways. It includes plant machinery, mink coats, Volvos, and all the diamonds stored in the shed behind Mr. and Mrs. Cartier's house. Some states tax personal property, and others do not. (Florida, for example, taxes and lists bank accounts.) If a reporter is investigating taxes in a state that assesses personal property as well as real property, it is important to avoid confusing the two. If, for example, the total of property taxes paid by the owner of a certain lot is $5,000 and the assessment is $100,000, a reporter would not want to report that the building is assessed at $100,000 until finding out if the assessment figure included the $50,000 diamond stored in the building.

Because so much of what is taxed as personal property is portable, taxpayers are often tempted to transport it somewhere else when tax time rolls around. When the county treasurer is asked why the county commissioner did not pay taxes on the diamonds in his jewelry store, the treasurer may say it's because the jewels were in the commissioner's other store, across the state line, until last week. Personal property taxes are hard to collect equitably. In Illinois the county sheriffs downstate sometimes resort to snatching cars from driveways to enforce the tax collection, but in the Chicago area the tax is not enforced at all.

CHAPTER 8

Court records, police records, and the law itself

Court records

Most of the subjects a reporter investigates are also dealt with by the courts on a semiregular basis. If a reporter is trying to find out what someone is worth, for example, it may be that a judge has already asked and compelled an answer to the question, and the information has become a part of the public record. People and corporations are charged with crimes and sued every day. Lawyers and prosecutors who go after each other's clients are often quite thorough and develop much information that reporters find extremely useful. This information is contained in court records.

Court records — consisting of civil suits, criminal indictments, other civil and criminal actions, and all the documents relating to them — are readily available to the public. In most jurisdictions the reporter should first visit the court index, which usually contains the names of litigants in civil cases and the names of persons charged with crimes; the docket, which contains records of all the actions in a particular case, such as arrest, trial, and verdict; and then the case file, which contains the actual documents produced by the case, including warrants, depositions (transcripts of examinations of witnesses held under oath but outside the courtroom), and often the transcript of the trial. The court clerks will usually explain anything confusing, and the court reporters and judge's law clerks are also, as a rule, helpful. This is particularly true in jurisdictions where judges are elected. Should a reporter run into the occasional clerk who is recalcitrant, a talk with the presiding judge, who actually controls the records, will generally straighten things out. Should the judge balk, the reporter need not give up. A complaint to the local bar association should bring the whole lot of them—judges, clerks, file cabinets, and toilet seats—to rigid attention.

In investigating a slumlord, for example, the records of the court that handles tenant eviction cases would be an important source of information for a reporter. The names of people the slumlord has evicted can be found there, along with the names of their lawyers and their witnesses. If the reporter wants to find out what property or companies a person owns, the court records could be checked to see if that person has been recently divorced. Whether or not the spouse contested the property settlement, a statement of assets and liabilities will have been filed with the court or with a court agency such as Friend of the Court. If the person secretly owns land he is rezoning or embezzled money when he was county treasurer, his ex-wife may even tell the reporter about it when contacted.

The federal government may have sued someone for unpaid taxes or even brought criminal fraud charges. Corporations are regularly sued by customers, competitors, or governments. Often corporations and land developers hire public officials who happen to be lawyers to handle certain matters for them as a way of repaying official favors.

People inherit money as a result of probate court hearings. Checking probate court records of such hearings is a good way to find out not only what people inherited but also who their relatives are. Because changing one's name is an effective but illegal way to escape debts and other unpleasantries, our nation's probate courts keep careful records of the petitions and court orders that effect such changes. (A judge's permission is required for a legal name change.) Various officials in various jurisdictions have been known to change their names, assume official posts, and then award contracts to firms bearing their old names and still owned by them, or to relatives who did not change their names. A check with the probate court records in the county in which the name change was approved often provides what the reporter needs: the old and new names and the date of the name change.

Petitions for and court decisions ordering the commitment of people to mental institutions are also in court records, as are bankruptcy petitions and the records and transcripts of bankruptcy hearings. Bankruptcy records are especially interesting because they almost invariably contain a listing of the complete assets and debits of a firm going into bankruptcy, thus allowing an alert reporter to discover which individuals or firms hold which interests in the bankrupt firm. The bankruptcy proceedings may also indicate any organized-crime participation in the ruination of the firm.

No matter what kind of information a reporter seeks from court records, however, a quick reading of the pleadings is rarely enough—even though the case may seem simple or innocent. The thorough investigator uses briefs and transcripts, if transcripts were made, to obtain the names of other litigants, witnesses, and lawyers involved and then interviews them. Information that might be useful to the reporter's investigation may have been ruled inadmissible in court and may not appear in the transcript. Some of what was ruled out may have been hearsay, or the judge may have thought that, though true, it did not pertain to the matter at hand. The information may be useful nonetheless to a reportorial investigation. Even the hearsay may be useful, so long as it isn't immediately printed but is treated as an unproved tip to be further researched and documented. Beyond that, any of the parties involved in a court action may have discovered additional information pertaining to the case since the day they appeared in court.

Court records not only yield information about people and corporations who may have been plaintiffs or defendants but can also be used to evaluate the performance of judges, prosecutors, and police agencies. Buried in these records are statistics that will show which judges give twenty-year sentences for minor crimes and which judges find 85 percent of the defendants who come before them not guilty. The records will show how many cases were dismissed because the arresting officer didn't appear to testify and which robbery detectives have the best conviction rate. They will show if the county prosecutor, campaigning for reelection on a law-and-order platform, has as good a conviction rate as his predecessors. Careful scrutiny of the records will show whether blacks are convicted more often than whites and whether the race of the victim seemed to have significant bearing on how justice was done.

Two investigators for the *Philadelphia Inquirer,* Donald Barlett and James Steele, once ran records of the Philadelphia justice system through a computer and found inconsistent sentencing, inefficiency, laziness, and racism at all levels. Their series of reports was best summed up by a cartoon showing a judge throwing a dart at a board divided into areas labeled "bail," "retrial," "10 to 25 years," "probation," "life," and "summer camp."

Reporters should also look into the hundreds of different kinds of quasi-judicial hearings held by local, state, and federal agencies. It is at these hearings that utilities apply for rate increases, haulers apply for permits, corporations apply for permission to pollute, quacks seek to continue practicing, and civil service violators seek to keep their jobs. Insurance companies, banks, and utilities are all licensed by state boards that hold public hearings. Crime commissions, hospital licensing boards, environmental protection agencies, water quality boards, tax commissions, public utility commissions, and intrastate commerce commissions also hold quasi-judicial hearings, complete with competing lawyers, and most of them keep public records of those hearings. If a reporter wants to find out how many doctors, nurses, druggists, and veterinarians have been licensed or prosecuted by the state, the various licensing boards probably have the information on file.

Police records

Basic arrest records include the defendant's name, age, address, and occupation, the site and time of the arrest, the name of the arresting officer, and the specific charge filed. The lack of a criminal record, however, does not necessarily mean that someone has never been arrested or convicted. (To be certain, a thorough reporter tries to persuade a friend in the police department to check with the FBI.) Perhaps the arrest took place in another jurisdiction. If the city police don't have a record on someone, the county or state police may. Frequently, calls to neighboring states or to a suspect's home state uncover outstanding warrants. (The availability of such information varies from state to state, sometimes in accord with the state's open-records act, if one exists.) Sometimes, too, people are able to get their criminal records expunged in court or have them removed by bribing a clerk. In at least some police stations the expunging of records involves nothing more than crossing out entries with a pencil. One enterprising reporter we know persuaded a friendly records clerk to hold a criminal court judge's criminal record up to a light to read the expunged arrests.

Experienced reporters, however, are careful in drawing conclusions from arrest records. Arrest does not mean conviction. And for a person who grew up in a bad neighborhood, particularly if he or she is black, it is not unusual — and not always an indication of criminal activity — to have an arrest record. Also, given the amount of plea bargaining that goes on in most courts, reporters are aware that a conviction for a misdemeanor may have precious little connection with the gravity of the crime actually committed. Finally, just because someone is sentenced to five years, a reporter cannot assume, without further checking, that the person served the full term. Parole may have been granted after only a year.

The law itself

Often a reporter needs information about the law itself. The law is kept in law libraries, which are generally associated with a local law school, the local bar, or even a governmental unit. Most law libraries admit only lawyers or law students, even though many of them are supported with tax money. Cynics have theories about that practice, but let's suppose those rules are there simply to keep the homeless from sleeping on the carpets. It means a reporter either must have a note from a lawyer saying the reporter is doing research for the lawyer or must bring a lawyer along while doing legal research. Until a reporter is thoroughly familiar with the process of checking statutes (laws made by legislatures) and case law (interpretations and rulings by judges), it is probably a good idea to have a patient, competent lawyer or law professor as a tutor.

The kinds of law most frequently used by investigative reporters can be found in one or two conveniently indexed volumes referred to as codes or compiled laws. In general, these are hardcover volumes containing laws enacted by legislative bodies and annotated with decisions of courts applying and interpreting the laws. Current inserts — paperback pamphlets — are regularly published to keep the volumes up-to-date as the legislative body adds, amends, or repeals laws and as courts issue new decisions. At the local level, however, the codes often contain only very limited references to court decisions or none at all.

Local codes also contain the charters granted by the state or adopted and amended by the electorate under a grant of home-rule power from the state. Charters function for cities much like constitutions function for states and the federal government. Most charters are quite specific, and public officials are sometimes caught violating specific charter provisions.

At the federal and state levels the codes include annotations of relevant court decisions and attorney general's opinions, along with the federal and state constitutions. These compilations at the federal level are the *United States Code Annotated* and the *United States Code Service*. Both contain the same law; they are simply published by different companies and are organized differently. Federal administrative regulations are contained in the *Code of Federal Regulations*. On the state level, titles of codes vary somewhat from state to state: *Alabama Code, Colorado Revised Statutes Annotated,* and *Michigan Compiled Laws Annotated* are some examples. Regulations issued by state agencies are sometimes available in a single set but sometimes are not available even in well-stocked law libraries. In such circumstances reporters must request the most recent regulations from the secretary of state or the responsible agency.

To locate law in a code, compilation, or administrative code, the subject word or descriptive word index should be consulted under all the possible headings. Indexes are often fallible; just because nothing appears under the most logical heading, a reporter should not assume there is no law on the point. Conflict of interest, for example, may be listed under the heading "adverse pecuniary interest." Also, be sure to consult the current inserts that update the index. Once a reporter has found what appears to be relevant laws in the index, they should be looked up in the accompanying volumes of the set. Before spending too much time reading long sections of laws, however, the current inserts and any other published pamphlets or recent laws should be checked to make sure the reporter has the last word on the subject. Current inserts are organized in the same way as the bound volumes; pamphlets of recent law are not. But both the inserts and pamphlets generally include cumulative tables showing which sections of existing laws have been modified by recent acts, as well as a cumulative descriptive word index for these acts.

After the current applicable law has been located and read, the reporter should tackle the annotations of court decisions that interpret the various sections. These usually are arranged under subject headings, but the headings tend to be somewhat technical. Therefore, a few annotations under each heading must be scanned to avoid overlooking something important. Finally, an investigator should check the current insert and any published pamphlets of recent decisions interpreting the pertinent sections of law. Only after taking all these steps can a reporter be reasonably sure the key statute wasn't repealed in the last session of the legislature or ruled unconstitutional in recent months.

As we have noted, constitutions generally are included with codes or compilations of law. A reporter should be sure the index being used also cites pertinent sections of the constitution. Most state constitutions are much more detailed in what they permit or prohibit than the U.S. Constitution. For example, often they will specifically proscribe conflict of interest and require that anyone found guilty of such a conflict be removed from office.

Administrative regulations and local codes generally are not annotated with relevant court decisions. The best way to find important court decisions in these areas is to consult with the local city attorney or state attorney general. Nor are administrative manuals and local codes kept as up-to-date as federal and state codes. Therefore, a reporter must quiz a well-informed administrative agency officer—not, we repeat, not the public relations person for the agency—to be sure the reporter has located the most recent information. City and county clerks can provide the latest word on acts passed by city or county governments.

Computer-assisted legal research systems also are available in law libraries and law offices. These systems can greatly assist a reporter's research task. However, access to these systems is limited, and use of the systems requires training. Thus, a reporter must seek out a helpful law librarian, law student, or recent law school graduate with access to a system.

The results of a reporter's research should be checked with a lawyer who has some expertise in the area. (Patent attorneys should not be asked, for example, whether rezoning a relative's ranch is a conflict of interest, or if campaign contributions in return for specific performance legally constitutes bribery.) Talking with a sharp lawyer may reveal that the reporter has been outwitted by some perverse indexer. Or a reporter may discover that a law doesn't mean what it seems to. It may be that a law made by judges without reference to a particular statute (common law) has an important bearing on the issue — and the somewhat simpli-fied research procedure outlined here will not lead a reporter to the relevant common law. If the above procedures were all there is to the study of law, anyone could pass the bar after a one-semester mail-order course. No responsible reporter would use anything unearthed in this way to pronounce someone guilty in a story. The reporter may, however, want to quote certain sections of the law in a story.

A reporter who takes the time to become familiar with whatever laws apply to the particular subject under investigation will be able to conduct a much more intelligent and useful discussion with a selected legal expert or experts. Ask a city attorney if a city official can moonlight and you will probably get a vague, virtually useless opinion. Ask the attorney if he or she interprets section 23, paragraph 4, to mean that a city assessor cannot be hired as a property tax consultant by a large company the consultant assesses annually and you will get a much more useful answer.

CHAPTER 9

Election fraud

Most elections held in this country are probably fair. Nevertheless the possibility of stealing an election is a temptation not always resisted by the unscrupulous. The election system is complex enough to allow those who would profit by its misuse to churn out an endless stream of new methods aimed at blocking the exercise of the popular will.

Sometimes people who should not be on the ballot get their names on anyhow. They may have filed their nominating petitions past the deadline. They may not have obtained sufficient petition signatures. They may have had ineligible people sign their petitions—people who aren't registered voters or who live in a different district. They may have forged some or all of the signatures. They may have coerced people into signing or circulating their petitions. Sometimes, for no good reason, candidates manage to get their own name at the top of the ballot, giving them an advantage over the opposition. Paul Powell, an Illinois secretary of state who left $400,000 in shoe boxes in a hotel closet when he died, made a habit of putting his friends at the top of the ballot. Even when other candidates spent the night in line to be the first to file for office, Powell's friends would mail in their petitions, and Powell would simply open the mail before he opened the doors. Who could say otherwise?

Sometimes people are improperly barred from the ballot by election officials. The common practice is for the party in power to accept the nominating petitions of their colleagues without question but to go over the opposition's with a fine-tooth comb. Even if they don't find technical violations, they sometimes disqualify legitimate signatures and leave it up to the candidate to pursue a long and costly court fight. For example, one candidate was ruled off the ballot because the people who signed his petition didn't include the abbreviations "St." or "Ave." in their addresses.

Just seven hours before the deadline for filing nominating petitions in one local election, Chicago mayor Richard Daley changed his mind about who would be the Democratic machine's candidate for county prosecutor. Daley had originally reslated the incumbent, Edward V. Hanrahan, who had just been indicted for obstructing justice. When other candidates on the Democratic machine ticket complained that the indictment was hurting their own campaigns, Daley finally decided to dump Hanrahan and replace him with Chicago's chief traffic court judge. To do so, he needed about twelve thousand signatures in a hurry. But Daley had nothing if he didn't have the largest, most resolute army of loyal patronage workers in the country. By 10:00 A.M., the petition blanks were off the presses, and a thousand had been distributed by 11:00 A.M. Shortly after 3:00 P.M., the petitions, containing more than twenty thousand signatures, were filed.

What is even more remarkable is that some of the signatures were genuine. At least half were forgeries: The names on some of the petitions were signed in alphabetical order; on others, every fifth or sixth signature bore the same handwriting. Hundreds of names were misspelled, others were listed with the wrong address, and one sheet was almost all in the same handwriting.

The next day, *Chicago Daily News* columnist Mike Royko, one of the nation's top investigators, explained how they did it. The freshly printed petitions had been taken over to city hall and "round-tabled." Five or six city employees—all of whom owed their jobs to the machine—sat around a table and passed petition blanks and voter registration lists in a circle. Each person copied every fifth or sixth name from the registration list. That way, the forgeries weren't so obvious.

The following day the Board of Election Commissioners office was jammed with reporters trying to catch up with Royko and with lawyers for other candidates trying to find someone to subpoena. The story was easily verified, even though the city workers denied everything. Reporters simply looked up the names on the petitions in the phone book and called people who allegedly had signed the blanks. Some were amused, some were angry, and some were frightened they would go to jail for signing something they hadn't signed.

The less sporting of the reporters tracked down the city workers whose names appeared as petition circulators and asked such rude questions as "Tell me, how did you manage to get all those people to line up alphabetically?" It was all good, clean fun, of course, and nobody got in serious trouble, because in Cook County the mayor names the judicial candidates. But it made good reading, and the mayor's candidate was defeated in the primary.

Another common, but rarely reported, type of election fraud takes place long before the voters get into the polling place. That is using federal employees to circulate petitions, ring doorbells, and raise money. The Hatch Act, which outlaws such activity, was written to prevent incumbent officeholders from using the vast federal bureaucracy as a campaign staff. It also applies to employees of federally funded, locally administered programs. Put simply, the law prevents local politicians from using federal grant money to build patronage armies.

Catching federal employees who are working elections is easier said than done. The petition forgery scandal we have discussed led two Lerner Newspapers reporters to the largest Hatch Act violation scandal in the history of the U.S. civil service. One of the reporters had put together a list of the people who had done the forging and was in the process of trying to see if any of them felt pressured or intimidated to break the various election laws. The mayor had long maintained that his precinct captains and other election workers served out of loyalty to the cause. But every now and then a city worker would complain about the long hours of precinct election work required to keep a job or get a promotion.

Precinct captains had never been interviewed on a large scale because the Democratic party closely guarded its list of campaign workers and nobody thought to check the names of those who circulated the party's nominating petitions. One of the names on the list the reporter was about to begin calling was Saint Joseph Smith. At the next desk sat the paper's urban affairs reporter, Roger Flaherty, happily thumbing through the office phone directory for the federal Model Cities agency, which he had been trying to obtain for more than a year.

The first reporter, a person deeply committed to trivialities, said, "It's quiz time, dummy. Who was St. Joseph Smith?" Flaherty was about to look up with his usual pained expression when he noticed that a Saint Joseph Smith was listed as a Model Cities employee in the agency directory, a coincidence he gleefully announced. If the Smith in the directory was the same Smith who circulated the nominating petition (and not the Joseph Smith who founded the Church of Jesus Christ of Latter-day Saints), he was in violation of the Hatch Act. The reporters called Smith's home, and his wife gave them his office number, the same one that was listed in the Model Cities directory. Then the first reporter began reading names from his list while Flaherty looked them up in the agency directory. Within an hour, they turned up about twenty violators of the Hatch Act. Not bad for a day's work: The *Chicago Tribune*'s previous investigation of the Model Cities program had unearthed only one Hatch Act violator.

The next step was to compile the names of everybody who had circulated petitions for candidates in the last two elections to find out who the city's election workers were. Then the reporters needed to check the list against more than just the telephone directory of one agency. They needed a list of all the employees of federally funded, city-administered programs – the city payroll. So one of the reporters visited the city comptroller. The comptroller knew without asking why the reporter wanted to see the payroll and tried to discourage him by pointing out that there were more than twelve thousand names on the unalphabetized list. The reporter said he wanted to look it over anyhow; he had turned up a number of relevant names by comparing the petitions with the Model Cities directory, but he didn't want to accuse anyone who was innocent.

The comptroller consented, apparently certain that the one reporter, in the two hours that remained before the office closed for the day, couldn't find more than two or three names in such a long, unalphabetized list. To this end, the comptroller refused to sell the reporter a computer printout of the payroll or permit him to photocopy the printout, saying that the city could not give out such information. The reporter, however, could copy down by hand whatever information he found. Rather than brawl over the details and risk not seeing the list, the reporter said he had another appointment to get to that afternoon and would be back in the morning. The comptroller said he would be out of town the next day, but because he had already committed himself, he called his assistant into the room, introduced the reporter, and said, "Show him any of the payroll he wants while I'm gone tomorrow, but no Xeroxes – and don't sell him a printout."

The reporter made small talk until the assistant left, noted which way he went, then excused himself. He found the assistant and said casually, "We'll be in about eight-thirty in the morning. We'll be glad to work in the hall so we won't get in your way if you can set us up with a couple of tables." The assistant comptroller, thinking his boss had okayed the plan, assented. The following morning, the two reporters and three typists showed up with five portable typewriters and eight reams of paper. Before the day was out they had copied the names and social security numbers of 7,000 of the 12,600 federally funded workers.

They no longer had any reason to keep secret what they were looking for. The reporters openly canvassed every political source they had for any lists of precinct captains and campaign workers who had happened to circulate petitions. They got about five hundred such names through Operation Eagle Eye, a civic organization that had staffed a number of polling places during the previous election. Each poll watcher, it turned out, had noted the name of the Democratic precinct captain who had worked each precinct the day of the election.

Next the reporters took both lists, of the workers and the employees, to the Better Government Association, another civic watchdog group, whose staff laboriously alphabetized one of the lists. Then the reporters read names from one list to fifteen or twenty volunteers sitting around a large room, each with three or four pages of names from the other list in front of them. Every time a name was found on both lists, a volunteer yelled "Bingo!" That raised the total of apparent Hatch Act violators to about one hundred. A story could then be written charging the city administration with using Model Cities funds to provide jobs for loyal campaign workers. The story noted that because neither the payroll nor the political list was complete, there were undoubtedly many more Hatch Act violators.

The local U.S. attorney's office passed the story on to the civil service in Washington, which began its own investigation a few weeks later. In a two-day weekend blitz, catching the workers at home and away from their supervisors, civil service agents from five other cities got about seventy-five of the payrollers to sign depositions admitting their guilt. Then the civil service subpoenaed the entire city payroll, increasing the total number of suspects to more than two hundred.

The week the civil service hearings were announced, the city comptroller was fired. (That same week, however, another reporter had bluffed him into admitting that Mayor Daley had ordered him to transfer the city airport insurance to the mayor's son.) The first batch of Hatch Act violators brought to trial were building inspectors. Two days after the trial began, the home of one of the reporters was visited by three city inspectors, and he was hit with $3,800 worth of code violations. But that's another story.

The Chicago Hatch Act investigation was a success for a number of reasons, not the least of which was luck. But had the reporters not understood the details of the Hatch Act, particularly that it applied to locally administered programs, the investigation would never have been started. There is no substitute for knowing the law.

That is also true for most unreported election frauds. They go unreported largely because few reporters take the time to familiarize themselves with local election laws. The easiest way to learn election laws is to get a copy of the brochures published by the local election agency to educate its election judges. They are written in simple language and are amply illustrated. They should be read far enough in advance of the election that a reporter can get explanations for anything that is not clear.

Before an election, a reporter should also get a copy of the local election board's voter canvass in precincts where fraud is suspected. It is a good idea to spot-check the list by ringing doorbells to see that everyone ruled eligible is still alive and kicking and living in the precinct. Then the reporter can wait for election day and see how many of the dead and gone come back to vote. Although it could be argued that a person should not be discriminated against just because he or she was unfortunate enough to expire the week before the election, it is still against the law for a dead person to vote, and any reappearance should be reported.

A number of irregularities should be watched for in the polling place. Physically handicapped, blind, or illiterate people can ask whomever they want to help them vote, be it their mothers, the precinct captain, or Rasputin, although in some states neither the employers nor the union officers of such voters are allowed in the booth with them. But in some states a voter who is unsure how to mark the ballot or work the levers on a voting machine must be accompanied into the booth by an election judge from each party. Sometimes in elections involving long ballots the precinct captains get people to invite them into the booth on the pretext of illiteracy. That is also illegal. The impaired voters must sign cards attesting to their disability, and even if they can't write, they are required to make their mark, usually an X, on the card. That is where experienced reporters keep a sharp eye out to see that the signature matches the one in the registration binder and that the voter has adequate identification if challenged. Generally, the word of an election official who recognizes the person is considered adequate identification. To watch for ghost voting, the reporter must stand in a place where the signatures can be compared. If the ghosts are unable to spell the name of the person they are ghosting for, something's up.

Election-scarred reporters watch closely for people who vote "early and often." The reporters check the counters at the rear of the voting machines before voting begins to make sure some candidate isn't starting out with a one-hundred-vote edge. They also watch for bribes, particularly in poor precincts. Bribes are given not so much to get someone to vote a certain way (as most people believe) but to get loyalist troops out to vote. Campaign workers will generally not attempt to bribe people to vote a certain way for two reasons. First, that involves the risky proposition of offering bribes to people planning to vote for the opposition. Second, unless the polling place is really up for grabs, a precinct captain has no sure way of knowing for whom someone voted.

The *Chicago Tribune* won a Pulitzer Prize during the 1970s for a series on election fraud in which a reporter was secretly hired as a clerk at the Board of Election Commissioners. The paper also persuaded a Republican party official to appoint a number of other *Tribune* reporters as election judges in precincts where votes were said to be regularly stolen. In one polling place three of the journalists reported that voters were being given bags of groceries. When the three were questioned before a grand jury, however, each said another had actually seen the bribery. The moral here is to be sure you are seeing what you are seeing, and not what someone else says you are seeing. Incidentally, the paper kept the Pulitzer.

Another popular method of winning elections when paper ballots are used is chain balloting. Here a party worker gets a blank ballot, generally from someone who comes in early and asks for assistance. The ballot is filled out to the party worker's satisfaction, but instead of being deposited in the ballot box, it is given to the next friendly voter who comes in to vote. The second voter deposits the marked ballot and passes the blank one to the precinct captain, generally outside the polling place. Every time friendly voters come along, the process is repeated. This system guarantees that friendly voters vote the preferred way, especially on long and complicated ballots. It is a difficult practice to catch. Sometimes a reporter can see the ballot passed; other times a careless voter will pocket the unmarked ballot in plain view. In all cases, however, the number of ballots cast at closing time will equal the number of voters, because the precinct captain will vote last and drop two ballots in the box.

Just seeing a voter take a ballot from the precinct captain, stick it in one pocket and pull another ballot out of another pocket doesn't make much of a story. What a reporter really needs are names, dates, instances, and confessions. Some reporters would advocate catching the voter outside the booth, after he or she has voted, and reciting the penalties for election fraud to persuade the voter to turn state's evidence on the spot and give up the blank ballot. That ought to produce an interesting reaction. Then these reporters would advise taking the ballot over to the precinct captain and telling him that six people have told them what the precinct captain has been doing. The reporters would ask why the captain did it, what's in it for the captain, if the captain was forced to do it, and by whom.

Sometimes elections are stolen because extra ballots are printed, marked, and substituted for legitimately cast ballots. This can be done any time from before the polls open until shortly before the results are turned in. One reporter we know found a bunch of blank ballots in the gutter outside a polling place. Nobody seemed to know where they came from, and the reporter still gets a faraway look in his eye when he thinks about it. Obviously, something was going on, but neither he, nor we, know just what. But it must have been a doozy.

The simplest way to steal elections is to miscount the votes. This is hard to catch, because if a newspaper reporter is leaning over shoulders while the votes are counted, they will be counted accurately. Voters could be polled, once the election is over, but many probably would not talk, some might lie, and there is no guarantee the lies would be self-canceling. One solution, used by the *Chicago Tribune,* is to have reporters appointed as election judges.

One party is often able to steal votes in the presence of the other party's election judges because those judges often do not really belong to the other party. If they do, they are paid off. In a few cases the dominant party's workers are able to outsmart or intimidate them. But in most cases they are wolves in sheep's clothing. This comes about because in many rural or suburban areas there are not enough Democrats to supply the requisite number of judges in each polling place, and in many inner-city areas there are not enough Republicans to go around.

In an inner-city area, for example, the Democrats will give out a certain number of patronage jobs to the Republicans. The grateful Republicans, hired as judges, don't make waves on election day. In other cases the election judges are just not alert. It is difficult to find people who will miss a day's pay to work eighteen hours in a polling place for the pittance generally paid election judges. Consequently, many of the judges, particularly of a minority party, are the aged, the unemployable, the apathetic, or the inebriated. A hustling precinct captain can take over and run such polling places.

Journalists observing such polling places should watch out for themselves. Emotions run high, and it is not unusual for reporters and photographers, especially photographers, to take a beating. Reporters may be challenged on many things they want to do in a polling place, particularly if something sneaky is going on. And in most jurisdictions an election judge can have a reporter arrested or removed from the polling place, with or without cause. The experienced reporter tries to avoid disputes that end this way, because that's exactly what crooked officials want. Our best advice is to sit back and work crossword puzzles, simple crossword puzzles. The idea is for the reporter to look stupid or bored and not to let a campaign worker catch the reporter focusing on anything unusual while it is happening. To be really convincing, the reporter might show up late and smelling of liquor.

If the reporter successfully avoids attracting attention, however, he or she will be faced with a rather sticky ethical problem. There they are, stealing votes right and left. It may be possible to try to stop the stealing, but then the reporter is making news, not discovering it. So he or she might decide to let the corruption proceed and write a story about it, secure in the knowledge that the exposé will have a more salubrious long-range effect on election-day honesty than the temporary reform of one precinct. But the problem with that approach is that the reporter, if appointed as an election judge, displaced someone who might have prevented the vote stealing. So silence makes that reporter an accessory.

Another aspect of election fraud is campaign fund-raising. Fund-raising laws sometimes do not require disclosure until after the election is over. So even when fund-raising fraud is exposed, it is too late. Fund-raising laws vary from state to state, however; the wise reporter will carefully study the appropriate state law. The best way to learn the ins and outs of the fund-raising law is to talk to the chief fund-raisers for both parties. They'll be glad to tell a reporter what the other side can't do and how to catch the other's violations. (See Campaign Contribution and Expenditure Records in chapter 6.)

Campaign fund-raising methods include selling advertisements in magazines published by the party. The ads cost a fortune, nobody reads them, and the merchants who buy them know that nobody reads them. In some areas these "ward books" constitute a virtual shakedown of the local merchants. They are often used to build war chests in off years, when there is no election, making it much harder for the reporter to find out how much money a candidate has spent. Another trick is to use official stationery, or stationery that looks official, for fund-raising. One sheriff was caught sending out letters — on sheriff's office stationery — that promised voters that if they donated money to his cousin's campaign for coroner, they would get a deputy sheriff's badge and the right to carry a gun. A clever fellow, he even offered to give a reporter a gun permit. The offer was recounted in the reporter's story.

Once a reporter investigating campaign finances has compiled a fairly complete list of campaign donors, fund-raisers, and benefit-party hosts, the people will have to be identified. Are any of them on government payrolls? If they are businesspeople, do their firms handle city contracts? What has happened with any land they own or owned? Anytime a local election is held in conjunction with a federal election, it becomes a violation of federal law to coerce government workers into making contributions or to make working in a campaign a condition of employment.

A large source of campaign contributions are the various lobbies and lobbyists. Lobbyists are so named, it is said, because they stand in the lobbies of state capitols handing out $20 bills to passing politicians.

Many states require lobbyists to register, and the registry book in some states includes a lobbyist's picture as well as background information. A good way of ascertaining how much money any particular pressure group donated during an election is to talk with those who didn't get any of the money and with opposing lobbyists. Lobbyists always seem to have copies of the opposition's mailings and fund-solicitation documents. If a reporter wanted to find out how much the automakers gave congressional members during the last election, a good place to start would be with Ralph Nader's group.

Election fraud also takes the form of "dirty tricks" directed at one's opponent, not good-natured or obvious pranks but tactics that portray a candidate as saying and doing things he didn't or as having friends and supporters he hasn't.

In many cities, welfare recipients are threatened with loss of their benefits if they do not get out and vote a certain way. They are told that somehow or other the precinct captain will know how they voted. (We'll partially qualify our previous statement that there is no real way party workers can tell how a person has voted. It has been charged that a popular make of voting machine sometimes emits different noises depending on which straight ticket lever is pulled. It is said that a precinct captain with a good ear can listen to a few votes and distinguish among the various clicks. We have tried it ourselves, however, and have not been able to distinguish the sounds. It is possible, of course, to tell when a voter is splitting his ticket by the amount of time spent in the booth and by the shuffling of his feet, visible under the curtain.)

The threat that a person will lose his or her welfare benefits should not be confused with the political charge that if an antiwelfare candidate is elected, all welfare recipients may be hurt. The first is coercion; the second, just politics. It is illegal to threaten individual voters with a cut in their benefits if they do not vote for a certain party or candidate. The best way to keep an eye on these tactics is to have some friends who are welfare recipients. Ringing doorbells the day after the precinct captain has been around will probably fail. It's foolish to expect people to risk their welfare checks by talking to reporters.

The phony heckler or the embarrassingly obnoxious sympathizer is probably the most sophisticated of the dirty tricksters and the hardest to catch. Generally, a reporter sent to cover a political rally is kept busy recording the speeches and doesn't have time to find out whose side the various shouters and demonstrators are really on. But anytime someone is so severely heckling a speaker that the speaker is getting the audience's sympathy, a reporter should be suspicious. And anytime somebody particularly obnoxious makes a big show of supporting a speaker, it is a good idea to try to find out whose side that person is on. The same goes for campaign literature that smoothly backfires.

Whenever a politician is being hurt by supporters or helped by opponents, a reporter is on to an exciting story. For example, if a candidate is known to support abortion, and a number of supporters show up with placards reading "Elect D. Encee—Legalize Euthanasia," dirty tricks may be going on. After the rally, a reporter should follow some of the "supporters" to their cars and get their license numbers. If necessary, the reporter could follow them home or to party headquarters and persuade someone else to identify them. The next step is to call the opposition's party headquarters and ask for them. If the "supporters" appeared at a Democratic rally, and the next day the person who answers phones at Republican headquarters knows who they are and takes a message for them, it could be the beginning of a good story.

Some reporters would advocate other methods of discovering the true identities of the cast members of these political dramas. It is possible to ask them who they are, have a cop bust them, get them to sign a petition, or have them photographed and then show the pictures around. It's even possible to take a picture into various party headquarters and try to find "the person who saved my child's life." Maybe it won't be possible to find out who the mysterious demonstrators are, or maybe they'll turn out to be just crazy people, but little will be lost trying.

Another election trick of growing popularity is to attempt to plant a phony story in the newspaper. In 1988, aides to Republican presidential nominee George Bush and President Ronald Reagan attempted to plant a phony story in the press: that Democratic presidential nominee Michael Dukakis had undergone psychiatric treatment for depression after the death of his older brother in an automobile accident in 1973 and his defeat five years later for a second term as governor of Massachusetts. Bush's backers assumed that successful germination of such a story would hurt Dukakis with an electorate touchy about the mental health of its presidential candidates (although many argued that if Dukakis had sought such aid, he deserved praise for doing so). Bush's backers succeeded in planting the story, most prominently in Rev. Sun Myung Moon's *Washington Times,* and Reagan referred to Dukakis as "that invalid" at a news conference. Dukakis and his physician denied the story, no proof of the allegation was ever brought forward, and the incident blew over, but some damage had been done.

Most reporters will listen to a phony tip and check it out. Finding it false, they will discard it and go on to the next story (although in the Dukakis case the *Boston Globe* published the story before the *Washington Times,* and Reagan made it a major issue, on the flimsy basis that a

Boston Herald reporter had asked Dukakis about the rumor and Dukakis hadn't explicitly denied it). But the fun thing to do is to go back to the source and to those who may have published the phony story and ask a few careful questions. Find out whose idea the phony story was, how it was dreamed up, and why it was done. Was it done in fear of losing? Was anyone convinced it was true? Will a retraction of the tip or the published story be forthcoming? If not, why not? If a reporter pursues this line of questioning, it will probably yield a far better story than the original phony one.

PART III

Techniques

CHAPTER 10

Approaching and interviewing sources

Although many stories can be documented in their entirety without once leaving the record rooms of a government agency, most cannot. In addition to learning the paperwork, a good investigative reporter must learn to deal with people, all kinds of them. It's as necessary to decide which people should be interviewed first as it is to decide which files should be explored first. The reporter who stops to reflect about a story before rushing off to interview the first person who comes to mind may be able to gather and arrange all the facts mentally in a way that will make the missing details more readily apparent. It may be hard to explain to an editor why a reporter, on the verge of a major journalistic achievement, is sitting and staring blankly at the ceiling. But the reporter should stare anyway. Fifteen minutes of reflection may save days of digging. If nothing else, forethought will make the finished investigative product more readable.

Some reporters begin by writing a preliminary draft of the story, leaving blanks in the appropriate places, to give them a clearer idea of the information they need and to prevent them from wasting time unearthing facts they may not use. This technique can backfire, however, by blinding a reporter to the need to kill or reinterpret the story later, in light of new or contradictory evidence. Underestimating the importance of unanticipated discoveries is another pitfall of this approach.

Of course, some preliminary organization is crucial. Part of the plan should cover the order in which the reporter wants to gather evidence. In most cases, it's a good idea initially to verify that part of a story least likely to tip off the subject of the investigation. And in most cases that means going to clips, other reporters, libraries, and file cabinets first. Even if the reporter talks to sources who aren't particularly close friends of the subject, they might pass along word of the reporter's interest anyway, hoping the subject may return the favor someday. The subject's worst enemies may present the investigator with other problems, such as exaggerating the subject's sins.

Reporters find that in some investigations, they are unable to determine which of their sources are only sources and which are both sources and possible subjects of investigations themselves. Journalists find they must return to each source several times, mixing the techniques of confronting the subject of an investigation with the techniques of interviewing a source, in an attempt to determine the truth about what each person is saying about each of the others.

Some reporters find it more effective to confront their subject before they talk to the subject's colleagues. That way, they're more likely to catch the subject unaware and increase their chances of extracting the full truth. They would then interview everyone else and gather any other information that will add to the scope of the story and make it more lively. A tactful reporter can sometimes return to an investigative subject for a second interview and dig for additional details, once the basic story has been drawn out of the first interview.

Obviously, different sources are best approached in different ways. In most instances, one does not approach a businessman who has little press contact in the same way one would approach an experienced politician who has dealt with reporters, including investigative reporters, for decades. Nor does an experienced reporter use the same methods and techniques in interviewing friendly and unfriendly sources. Most of the time, however, a reporter doesn't know with any certainty just what side of the controversy a potential source is likely to be on or how much experience that source has had with the media. So the reporter broaches controversial topics circumspectly, and slowly and carefully feels out the source's prejudices as well as the extent of the source's knowledge and experience.

Nevertheless, some generalization about classes of sources can be made. Public officials, both elected and appointed, often consider press relations a sort of game, complete with rules and a scoring system. If they feel themselves falling behind, they will try to score enough points to catch up. Although some will take public embarrassment or even public setback good-naturedly, many more will not. The familiar motto of the Boston Irish politicians is "Don't get mad — get even."

As we've already mentioned, the Michigan state senate tried to get even during the 1970s by building a wood-and-glass cage for the legislative news corps. Reporters were to be locked in it from fifteen minutes before a senate session began until fifteen minutes after it was gaveled to a close. The senators said the cage was needed because a number of stories written by uncaged journalists had angered individual senators. (The cage was finally dismembered when the news corps refused to use it and sat in the public galleries instead.)

Businesspeople, as opposed to politicians, are often deadly serious in their dealings with the press and are generally guarded by horrendously overpaid public relations advisors. Getting an appointment with a businessperson can be as hard as conducting an entire interview with a public official. But businesspeople generally read newspaper exposés less carefully than politicians and consequently are more likely to blurt out statements that would give the average politician heart failure. This is especially true in cases involving the payment of money to politicians and others. Businesspeople are used to paying for goods and services and often ignore the ethical or political questions involved in such payments.

For example, Dave Johnston, now a reporter for the *Los Angeles Times,* was once gathering information for a story about a foundry that was constantly accused of severe violations of state pollution regulations. When he was informed by one of the foundry's neighbors that a certain state representative was active in many forums defending the foundry and was possibly on its payroll, Johnston decided to bluff a little. While touring the foundry with the plant manager, the reporter asked, "What are you paying him [the state representative] for?" The manager replied, "Well, we paid him to [pregnant pause]. We paid him as a financial consultant." The upshot of the manager's comment was that the "financial consultant" was censured by his colleagues in the legislature and trounced in the next election.

Professional people, such as planners, accountants, and social workers, differ in many ways from both businesspeople and politicians. They are often more loyal to their professions than to their superiors and thus are top-notch sources. A professional who believes that recommendations are being ignored or distorted for political reasons or who thinks that he or she is unfairly shouldering the blame for a bad decision may well want to talk about it. But not all professionals, even those who feel betrayed by politicians, will talk to reporters. It's up to the reporter to find the ones who will.

Some reporters request an interview with a professional on the grounds that they need a quick but thorough education in a particular field. The reporters probably do need such grounding, even if getting it isn't a pressing concern. During the interview the reporters express no opinions until knowing what the source's opinions are. They portray themselves as friendly fellow professionals. They talk about how much they admire the good examples of work done in the interviewee's field and the comradeship they feel with people like the interviewee who struggle mightily against the awful forces of bureaucracy — struggles not unlike their own with the newsroom bureaucracy. They concentrate on what the interviewee is saying, picking up the nuances, showing understanding, and nodding sympathetically. They tell the person that they almost entered the same field once and sometimes wish now they had. Finally, they hint that it is too bad that the hallowed principles of the profession are so often compromised by expedient, greedy, or cowardly politicians.

If, after all this method acting, the source doesn't appear willing to talk, wise reporters wait for a graceful interval and then leave. Later they try one of the individual's colleagues or someone else in the same professional field. In general, it is a good idea not to press the first potential source to the point that the journalist's interest will be reported to others.

If and when an inside source can be found who admits being some sort of good-government, anticorruption fanatic too, the reporter should guardedly lay out the cards, tell the source who or what is under investigation, and ask for help. If the source is on the reporter's side, the more the source knows, the more help the reporter will get. If the source is afraid of being fired, the reporter may suggest that the subject of the investigation is in so much trouble, or soon will be, that he or she won't be able to demote a janitor. It might be wise to add that the reporter's newspaper (or magazine or TV station) is not without influence and that, should the crunch come, the reporter is friendly with public officials in other areas who would only be too happy to provide an honest hardworking person with an equal, perhaps even better job. After all, if someone helps with an investigation and is fired or harassed because of it, there is no reason why the reporter shouldn't help the source find other employment.

Some reporters pretend to be someone else when interviewing sources. Stories are told about the reporter who calls the scene of some tragedy and tells the voice at the other end, "This is Coroner O'Bannion. How many dead ones you got?" After a pause, according to the story, the voice replies, "No, *this* is Coroner O'Bannion. Who the hell are you?" Often reporters use their own names but imply they are someone else: "This is Jones calling from headquarters. Who'd you arrest out there?" The legendary Harry Romanoff, former city editor of the defunct *Chicago Daily American,* once managed to interview the mother of mass murderer Richard Speck by pretending to be Speck's attorney. Some slightly more ethical reporters don't hesitate to pose as students during interviews to shield their purpose with the protective mantle of academia. These ruses are questionable and in some instances illegal.

Ethical questions aside, however, even a crooked reporter's self-interest might not be served by pretending to be someone else. Sources tend to tell fewer lies and exaggerate less when they're talking to journalists, who may print or broadcast what they say, than when they think they're just gabbing with a student or acquaintance. So the reporter who pretends to be someone else may not end up with the truth.

One newspaper reporter a few years ago began to investigate a tip that a mayor's aide in his city had been treated to an expensive gambler's junket to Las Vegas by a company doing substantial business with the city. Part of the investigation was on an ethical level with the Watergate break-in. The reporter enlisted the aid of a colleague, and the two stayed late one night in the paper's city-hall bureau. While one coaxed the janitor into inebriation, the other entered the aide's office and rifled his desk, searching for airplane ticket receipts, thank-you letters, or anything that might have proved the company's financial sponsorship of the aide's junket. He found only telephone message slips indicating that a company official had called the aide immediately before and immediately after the trip was taken. Further investigation was obviously necessary.

The reporter telephoned the manager of the hotel where the pair had reportedly stayed in Vegas. The reporter identified himself as a state police officer who wanted to know whether the men had stayed in the hotel and who had paid the bill. To the reporter's dismay, the hotel manager announced that he was a recently retired trooper from the reporter's state. He began asking questions about the new kinds of handguns and a new organization plan in the works for the force. He also inquired about his former colleagues. The reporter knew something about the force and was able to chat along for a while, but in the end the manager would not reveal who had financed either the junket or the hotel stay, and the story was lost. *Caveat investigator.*

Another investigator might have pretended to be a police detective intent on arresting the two vacationers for passing bad checks. When told that two of his former guests had been fraudulent check artists, the manager would have summoned their payment record. No, he would tell the reporter, the check had not bounced. The reporter would sound puzzled and then ask which of the two had written the check—the answer to that question being the sole object of the call—and the manager would name one of the two. The reporter would end the conversation by saying, "Oh, he writes legitimate checks. It's the other one who passes rubber money." Then the reporter would know who paid for the trip.

There are many other ways to worm information out of sources, some deriving from the mundane experiences of the average person's daily life, others from police interrogation manuals, Len Deighton novels, and Dale Carnegie courses. Some reporters time their calls to catch the source at a less tension-filled time than during the nine-to-five business day. Sometimes they call in the evening, after the source has had a chance to go jogging and unwind, or early in the morning, before the source has had a chance to wake up and do aerobics.

Some investigators, knowing that many people see reporters as beaten-down subjects of tyrannical editors, attempt to elicit sympathy and information by explaining that they are subjecting a source to an interview only because "my editors forced me to come over here and bother you for no good reason." Or they may beg for help: because they don't understand what's happening and are terribly frustrated by their own ignorance and incompetence; because they have a spouse or children to support and will be fired if they return without a story; or because they're new in town. (Considering the professional mobility of many reporters, this could be said with some truth every other year or so.)

If a reporter is unable to elicit sympathy from a potential source, it may be possible to inspire contempt, and the condescending carelessness that often accompanies contempt. A source who doesn't think the reporter will understand what is being said may be careless enough to answer all the reporter's questions merely to be done with the interview. Columbo, one of television's investigative wizards before he tripped on the Nielsen ratings, consistently employed this technique. The annoying, cross-eyed, confused look, which suggested he was paying more attention to his digestive system than to what his source was telling him, would probably have netted Peter Falk two or three investigative breaks a year had he switched from acting to reporting.

Playing dumb enabled one reporter to obtain some information that was probably unobtainable otherwise. Tax records in the reporter's county showed only that a parcel of land under investigation was owned by someone using a trust number, a legal method of hiding land ownership in that state. The reporter called the trustee-bank, identifying herself as the secretary of the suspected landowner. Trying to sound distraught, she told the bank official that she had to finish typing a letter before her boss returned from lunch, but for the life of her she could not read the third digit in the number on the note the boss had left her. The bank official, talking to a woman he assumed was a lowly employee of one of the bank's more influential customers, gave her the third digit and confirmed the rest of the number when she read that to him to "check the rest of the digits, too." Because the reporter had firmly identified herself as the landowner's secretary, the fact that the number was read to her over the telephone in response to her "boss's" name confirmed her suspicions about who owned the land.

In this instance the telephone was a handy tool. But it can be a positive hindrance when a reporter is attempting to interview somebody who would rather not discuss what the reporter wants to talk about. Gestures, facial expressions, and body contact are important in establishing relationships; physical presence is important in discouraging the premature termination of a conversation. As former reporter Louis Heldman, now a Knight-Ridder corporate executive, told us, "I've been hung up on countless times, but no one's ever told me to get out of his house or office or has walked away from me at a bar." In addition, those little details of scene and personality that can raise a story above the literary level of a laundry list can usually be gathered only in person.

One approach that often works well for reporters is to simply and offhandedly ask for the information they want, as if it were the most routine request in the world. The implication is that only a scoundrel or a crook would refuse the request. If the request is refused, their answer is "Really? You mean the state of Iowa is now refusing to let the public see its hiring records? How long has this been going on?" They whip out their notebooks and make the bureaucrat think that a refusal to answer will generate bigger headlines than Pearl Harbor. They make the potential embarrassment caused by the release of the information they seek pale by comparison. They paint a picture of a middle-level employee being mashed flat by a four-hundred-foot-tall printing press or TV camera, and they keep a straight face while doing so. If that doesn't work, they go over the bureaucrat's head. Eventually, they will get someone whose job depends on electoral popularity and will think twice before risking the anger of a television station, magazine, or newspaper. If, for example, a patrol officer won't honor a reasonable request, a reporter can trace the chain of command—to the mayor, if necessary. If that doesn't work, the reporter should file a freedom-of-information request (see chapter 5).

Some newspapers, magazines, and TV stations pay for information, but many editors believe that once word gets around that the publication or station is willing to pay, the flow of free information will dry up. Some publications, however, while refusing to pay directly for information, manage to have it both ways by dishing out small stringer fees to people who provide information in the guise of poorly written news stories. These publications also occasionally compensate people for providing information by putting them on a stringer list. Other papers sometimes pay when the information they seek concerns illegal activities, in which cash traveling from hand to hand is the usual mode of exchange, or when the source provides information that can be verified, without paying, elsewhere. Especially in the underworld, though, an artificial market creates its own artificial suppliers, and if large sums are paid, people will begin manufacturing information to attract those sums. On some occasions, an intimation that money is available may work as effectively as an actual transfer of funds.

Many sources can be successfully approached and interviewed if they are told that the information they provide will be used on an off-the-record or not-for-attribution basis. An off-the-record interview, meaning neither the remarks nor the name and title of the source can be used in the story, can provide valuable leads. Furthermore, such an interview allows a reporter to ask other sources the same questions on the record. The second time around, the questions will be more to the point because the reporter will already know a lot of the answers. And armed with that information, the reporter is in a much stronger position to dig for other answers.

Experienced reporters don't always assume that they should honor a source's request that a comment be considered as off-the-record. In the same way that actors loudly stage-whisper, sophisticated public officials sometimes talk off the record to add drama to their topic and thus generate more ink. In most instances, however, sources are serious about wanting their name not to be used. Often a source will go on and off the record, back and forth, a dozen times in a brief conversation, and it's hard for the reporter, let alone the source, to know what's mentionable and what's not. We've found that in most cases when a reporter wants to use something said off the record in such an interview, it is possible later to persuade the source to agree.

On some rare occasions, off-the-record agreements are simply ignored. If a person walks up to a reporter and says, "May I tell you something off the record?" the reporter is in a fix. By saying no, the journalist may miss a clue to a significant story that could later be independently documented. If the reporter says yes, the source may announce that he or she has just dumped a fifty-five-gallon drum of botulin (which causes botulism) into the water reservoir. By honoring the off-the-record agreement, that reporter is just as responsible for the ensuing deaths as the source. On the one hand, investigative reporters have to strive to maintain their profession's trustworthiness, but on the other hand, they also must recognize their obligations to their readers and to the general population. Newspapers have occasionally printed stories containing criminal or semicriminal off-the-record admissions, indicating in the same story that the conversation was conducted off the record.

Often when someone requests that certain remarks be considered as off-the-record, the reporter can suggest that if the source is worried about remaining anonymous, he or she might instead wish to designate the remarks as not-for-attribution, which allows use of the remarks, but not the source's name or title, in the story. Many laypeople confuse "off the record" with "not for attribution" and ask for the more restrictive off-the-record treatment by mistake. This is unfortunate, because the not-for-attribution device is the more useful of the two. Much more useful and reliable, of course, is accepting the source's remarks on an on-the-record basis, allowing you to quote the source by name and title. On-the-record quotes make the story more complete and allow its readers to evaluate for themselves any biases the source might bring to the subject.

If the subject can't be persuaded to go on the record, however, the problem arises of convincing the source that confidentiality will be maintained. Paul Branzburg, as a reporter for the *Louisville* (Ky.) *Courier-Journal,* wrote a number of stories about drug peddling based on interviews with drug dealers whose identities he promised to conceal. Later he was indicted for refusing to reveal his sources and fled Kentucky to avoid being prosecuted and naming his informants. He found sanctuary in Michigan, where the governor refused to cooperate with Kentucky's extradition efforts. At the *Detroit Free Press,* Branzburg, whose appeals to the U.S. Supreme Court were denied in the *Caldwell-Pappas-Branzburg* decision, told his own story to a number of potential sources to convince them that he would go to great lengths to honor his commitments to them.

Telling a nervous source something like "You will be astounded at the lengths I will go to to keep your name secret" or "I haven't lost a source yet" or "You won't even recognize yourself in the story" generally works well. The information a person may not tell a reporter outright can often be gleaned by asking "Would it be inaccurate to print a story saying . . . ?" Then all the source has to say is yes or no, and for some reason many people feel more comfortable saying yes or no than uttering complete sentences.

In their book *All the President's Men, Washington Post* reporters Bob Woodward and Carl Bernstein described a subtle and convincing method of demonstrating their commitment to confidentiality when they began interviewing employees of the Committee to Re-Elect the President (CREEP) to gather information for their Pulitzer Prize–winning exposé. In late-night appearances at the homes of CREEP employees, they would say, "A friend at the committee [CREEP] told us you were disturbed by some of the things you saw going on there, that you would be a good person to talk to . . . that you were absolutely straight and honest, and didn't know quite what to do." When the person they were seeking to interview asked which fellow employee had given the reporters the lead, Woodward and Bernstein politely but firmly refused to reveal the name of their source. They explained that their refusal was based on a commitment to the protection of confidential sources, thus giving an implicit assurance that the identity of the person they were talking to would be similarly protected. The other reason for not naming names, of course, was that the reporters were operating from an employee list smuggled out of CREEP headquarters: Their source was non-existent. Nevertheless, it was a great door opener.

U.S. Supreme Court decisions allowing reporters to be jailed for refusing to reveal their sources have had little perceptible impact on sources. Memory is short, and although several reporters were jailed soon after these decisions were handed down, to the accompaniment of much handwringing in the media, most sources were ignorant of the whole to-do even then. Because it is no longer front-page news, even more have forgotten about the controversy.

If a source refuses to reveal information for fear that colleagues may consider it an impropriety, the information may often be obtained off the record. Then the reporter can return later and persuade the source to allow the use of the information on a not-for-attribution basis. Perhaps newly discovered information or newfound relationships among sources and principals in the investigation will have changed what the source sees as his or her role in the matter.

Nothing prohibits a reporter from using several interviewing techniques at the same time or from switching from one technique to the other to extract information. Changing tactics is often the only course left. When a reporter has exhausted all the tactics, however, or realizes that further attempts will only appear ridiculous, a good final approach is to ask who else knows about the matter or which documents or reports might reveal more about it. Unless the source snaps back with "I don't have the slightest idea" and terminates the interview, the reporter will either get the name of another source or have an excuse to continue the questioning, or both. By suggesting a potential source, the person being interviewed is left open to more questions: How does the source know that the other person knows about the matter? What is their relationship in the context of this investigation? These are questions the reporter could not logically have asked if the interview had continued to focus belligerently on the source's direct knowledge of the matter.

A journalist can avoid the problems inherent in a one-to-one interview if the source can be heard in a noninterview context, such as a public meeting. Some public meetings are open to the public. Other "public" meetings are closed.

The 1976 federal Government in Sunshine law requires every federal agency and commission headed by two or more officials to conduct important business at public meetings, except for discussions of litigation, national security, or personnel. Similar laws were enacted by many states. However, critics have charged many federal and state agencies with transacting the substance of their work behind the scenes. In 1988, for instance, Peter Prichard, senior news editor of *USA Today,* said the law seems to have encouraged agencies "to conduct well-scripted meetings to fulfill the formalities of the law and to erect memorials to decisions that actually occurred outside the public view." Claudia Withers of the Women's Legal Defense Fund charged the federal Equal Employment Opportunity Commission with conducting its substantive business behind the scenes, canceling or rescheduling its public meetings with little notice, rewriting public-meeting agendas at the last moment, and never making available copies of documents discussed at the meetings.

Tips are often spun off by, and major scandals occasionally revealed at, closed-door "public" meetings. Such pseudopublic meetings are often entered by determined reporters. Many newspaper or broadcast lawyers can be persuaded to threaten legal action against bureaucrats who illegally close such meetings to the press and public.

If a reporter is unsuccessful in getting into an illegally closed meeting, it is standard procedure to begin a sort of ritualistic bobbing and weaving. The reporter may interview as many of the participants as possible, perhaps hinting to one person that others have already given their versions of what went on (suggesting that a possibly distorted story will result unless this person gives a straight account). Or the reporter may imply that others have already sketched an outline of the events in question and that only a few minor details are needed to fill in the gaps.

Some reporters attempt to find someone the source likes, make friends, and question the source through the friend. Suppose a reporter has heard a rumor that the grand jury has just voted to indict a local prosecutor, but the convening judge quashed the vote and ordered the jury to hear more witnesses. Suppose the reporter knows that the judge and the prosecutor are members of the same political organization and are friends but doesn't know any details, such as the charge or charges, who else may have been indicted, and even if the rumor is true.

The judge probably won't talk about it, nor will any of the special prosecutors, court reporters, or grand jurors. What the reporter needs is someone who can talk to someone else in a position to know what actually happened. A clever journalist will remember that many of the indicted prosecutor's assistants went to a certain law school. The reporter will then call some personal acquaintances who attended the same law school and ask if they know any of the assistant prosecutors. If they do, the reporter will repeat the rumor and explain that he or she wants to find out for certain what happened. If the reporter is lucky, the prosecutor threw a tantrum on hearing of the grand jury vote, and some of his assistants were aware of what happened and will tell their friends about it when they call. If the reporter is lucky, the friends will have all the details—how the jury voted, what the charges were, who the others indicted were, and who was named as an unindicted coconspirator.

CHAPTER 11

Short-term and recovery investigations

Not every investigative story is worth the weeks and months of effort that go into a major investigation. This is doubly true if the story has already appeared somewhere else and an investigator is assigned to write a new and updated version of that investigation for his or her own publication or station. This chapter deals with investigations of this sort — recovery investigations — and with original investigations that do not appear to be worth a substantial investment of time, which we call short-term investigations.

Short-term investigations

If a reporter believes that the human condition will improve only slightly as a result of a possible investigation, and that the time put into that story will drastically reduce the time available to pursue more worthwhile leads, there are three choices: Drop the story, perform a major investigation, or employ the techniques of the short-term investigation. What the editors think of a story, of course, will play a large role in helping a reporter choose from among these possibilities. If a reporter and the editors disagree on the worth of a proposed investigative story — assuming the disagreement is purely journalistic and not based on management's desire to protect the person or institution proposed for investigation — that reporter has little reason to put a lot of effort into the story. It will surely be buried on page 58, substantially reducing whatever impact it otherwise might have had. Unless there is good reason to believe that the story might develop into something the editors might appreciate, or unless there is some hope of free-lancing it to another publication, the reporter might as well go ahead with a quick once-over.

Out-of-town assignments — especially for a big-city reporter investi-

gating a small-town scandal — are often tailor-made for short-term investigations. The public records in a small town's archives are likely to be
somewhat less complicated, and a lot fewer in number, than those a
reporter would have to peruse for the same investigation in a large city.
(With luck, the town will also be the county seat, and therefore most or
all of the relevant public records will be in the same town as the story.)

Once the reporter has sifted whatever information he or she can
from the public records in the town, it will be possible to use that information more quickly and effectively in interviewing local officials and
other prominent persons than in a larger jurisdiction. Part of the reason
is that small-town officials are less bombarded by the media. They are
also less likely to be the targets of the public service law firms, political
groups, or aggressive neighborhood associations that bedevil public figures in larger cities.

(Small town or not, however, some stories force their own pace. A
story based on sources' memories will not be as solid as one buttressed
by public documents, but under some circumstances it will be a much
quicker story to research. Some such stories require a reporter to interview people so closely linked with one another that they must be interviewed almost simultaneously, to prevent them from contacting each
other and coordinating their versions of events. A long pause for research and contemplation between interviews could be disastrous in that
situation.)

Short-term investigations are grounded on reliable informants, the
rapid-fire collection of information through interviews, and bluffing. A
reporter should begin a short-term investigation by attempting to hy-
pothesize the shape and structure of the completed story on the basis of
what is already known, rather than attempting to draw a conclusion
from gathered facts. This process is similar to the one used by scientists
in attempting to explain various phenomena. First they create a hypothesis that would explain the circumstance, and then they draw a conclusion
from that hypothesis and test it.

This method was put to good use by a U.S. civil service investigator,
attorney Ben Joseph, while he was working on Chicago's Hatch Act
scandal. Joseph correctly reasoned that because so many political ap-
pointees were employed by the Cook County Democratic machine, some
mechanism must have existed to ensure that people who hadn't actually
worked precincts were not hired accidentally. When it came time for him
to cross-examine various personnel-department employees, Joseph stood
so that he could see into the manila folders the witnesses brought with
them to the stand. On the second day of questioning, his hand shot out
like a snake's tongue and withdrew a patronage hiring authorization

form signed by the mayor. Nobody had ever hinted to Joseph that these forms existed. He simply assumed they must to ensure that the machine made maximum use of the approximately forty thousand payroll jobs at its disposal.

Joseph, incidentally, was an absolute master at luring sources and investigative subjects into believing that he was the least competent person they had ever met. He sported baggy suits and raincoats that he appeared to have slept in. He would ask people three or four questions that proved beyond all their doubts that he had absolutely no idea what he was talking about. Then, without changing mannerisms in the least, he would fumble his way through a question to elicit an answer that would drop a judge's jaw open. A Philadelphia lawyer, Joseph penetrated further into the inner workings of the Cook County Democratic machine in the few weeks he was in Chicago than most Justice Department lawyers had in a lifetime.

Had the hiring authorization cards not been in those personnel files, Joseph would have lost nothing except the comfort of leaning against a court railing while questioning the witnesses. Although reporters are not afforded the luxury of compelling testimony in court, the same method works for them as well. What would the personnel man have said to a reporter who, in the midst of a rambling interview, asked to see the payroller's hiring authorization from the mayor's office? In nine out of ten tries, the official would have refused to show it. Perhaps he would have said something like, "That form is none of your business." The reporter would then know that such things existed just as surely as if he or she had seen one.

There's no reason why reporters on a short-term investigation shouldn't be influenced by their own journalistic assumptions, even if by assuming too much they risk losing the story. If the assumptions prove wrong, little is lost. And if the assumptions are correct, the bold hypothesis will have allowed a reporter to complete an investigation in a much shorter time.

By their nature, short-term investigations must rely heavily on successful confrontations. So it helps if the principal involved is someone who is not constantly in contact with reporters and thus is likely to tell the truth when interviewed. Public officials not used to dealing with the press sometimes fall into this category. For example, a reporter received a frantic telephone call one morning from the son of a dead Orthodox Jew. According to the son, the county medical examiner and his assistants, without excuse or explanation, had wrested his father's body from the hands of mourners who were in the midst of giving it a strict religious burial. Then, according to the son, the examiner performed an autopsy, although none was necessary, and did it on a Saturday, the Jewish Sabbath. Both actions violated Jewish religious law. The son also charged that the examiner had removed the father's brain from the body without medical justification and had allowed the body to be buried without a head, in glaring violation of Jewish law and modern custom.

The reporter found these charges difficult to believe, because even the most bigoted medical examiner should have sense enough to avoid antireligious activities, at the very least in the interest of staying in office. So, only half believing the charges, and not wanting to take the trouble to arrange all the interviews a major investigation would require, the reporter decided on the short-term approach: He would confront the medical examiner and watch his reaction.

At the interview, the reporter was astonished to hear the examiner not only admit to the son's charges but also deliver a lecture on the problems caused by dead Jews. While the reporter took copious notes, the doctor complained that the only way the county could satisfy Jewish burial requests would be to "bury dead Jews immediately and then dig them up again." He went on to say, "Jewish people present a unique problem. First you have to talk to the brother, then the wife, then later the rabbi. . . . How long is the Talmud anyway?" According to the medical examiner, burial policies in his county were "set up by Irish Roman Catholics" and "inflexible." He then admitted that he had had no real reason for performing an autopsy on the dead man nor for removing the brain.

With those admissions, all the reporter then needed to do was to check the hospital's diagnosis of the deceased's lengthy illness with the surgeon who had operated on him and confirm the son's interpretation of Jewish law with the area's chief rabbi. Because the medical examiner had already admitted to the son's charges, the reporter didn't need to interview the mourners and the examiner's aides for corroborating accounts.

The county commissioners reacted furiously to the story. They summoned the medical examiner, interrogated him until they were satisfied the story was accurate, and forced him to resign. Four hours of work had resulted in the unseating of the official and the end to some anti-Semitic burial practices.

The medical examiner's loquaciousness made him an easy target for a short-term effort. But even laconic officials can be successfully unseated with something less than a lifetime's work. One county commissioner met such a fate. Although the commissioner represented a low-income district, he lived in a luxury high rise in another part of the city—at least that's what his political enemies charged as election day approached. The reporter they told knew that election-time tips were generally untrustworthy, but the charge was serious. If rumors were true, the politician was violating a state law requiring commissioners to live in the districts they represented. So, overloaded with other assignments, the reporter decided on a short-term investigation.

His first step was to interview a few of the people who lived near the slum apartment the commissioner claimed he occupied. They said they rarely saw the man. The reporter then telephoned the commissioner's secretary from a handy pay phone, implied that he had to reach the commissioner at home on a political matter of the utmost urgency, and was given the commissioner's true home telephone number. He then called the telephone company's public relations man, who told him that, based on the digits, the number couldn't possible be located in the commissioner's district but might well be located in the luxury high rise. By calling the secretary of state's office, the reporter learned that the commissioner's driver's license bore his business address rather than the home address he claimed. That didn't prove he lived in the high rise, but it didn't prove he lived where he was supposed to either. Satisfied that his suspicions—although aroused by politically inspired rumors—were well founded, the reporter visited the high rise. When he knocked, the door was opened to reveal the beer-drinking politician, wearing a bathrobe and talking to a scantily clad woman. The reporter turned on his heel and returned to his office to write the story. After the story appeared, the county commissioner lost his bid for reelection. Total time on the story: two hours.

Reporters shouldn't let a few such short-term successes sour them on research, however. They may occasionally waste time on the rigorous and extensive background research that is a part of a full-scale investigation only to find that the principal in the story is ready to tell all to the first person who asks a leading question. But research is never wasted. Even if the principal spills everything before the reporter has had a chance to impress the subject with voluminous knowledge, the research will enable the reporter to understand the subject's admissions in depth. With that understanding, the reporter can recognize and pursue new leads revealed during the interview. Research will also protect the reporter against the possibility that the subject will squirm away to relative safety with a partial admission that a reporter with only partial knowledge would have no choice but to accept as the whole truth.

Recovery investigations

Recovery investigations usually begin when a reporter staggers into the newsroom one morning, stumbles over to the coffee machine, picks up a competing newspaper or magazine, and reads: MAYOR ADMITS TAKING $1.2 MILLION IN KICKBACKS. The first thing the editor will want to know is where the reporter was when the mayor confessed. That question will be asked with a straight face. Then the editor will say, "We ought to do something." That something is called a recovery.

Bad recoveries are easy: All the reporter does is rewrite the opposition's story, after making a call or two to see that it is true, and put a second-day lead on it. Bad recovery leads usually begin, "Authorities Tuesday are investigating charges that . . ." Good recoveries require considerably more effort and ingenuity. The reporter should set out either to add substantially to what the other paper has published or, finding its story false, knock it down. (A reporter shouldn't knock down a competing publication's story out of mere spite; any uncontrollable urge to do so should be treated with therapy.)

Almost every investigative story has holes in it, and those holes are what a reporter builds the recovery on. There is almost certainly some aspect the other reporter did not include—sources and officials who weren't interviewed, or even facts that were omitted because of a lack of space, news judgment, or nerve. A recovery reporter will generally have between six and eighteen hours—maybe a day, if the editor isn't hysterical—to gather those facts and reactions. The editor will probably assign the recovery to a reporter who already knows something about the topic or at least knows many of the public officials involved. If, however, no one on the staff has an obvious head start on the story, the reporter assigned to the recovery should count on skipping lunch.

First, the recovery reporter should read the initial story carefully. If the competition dug its story out of file cabinets, the reporter will have to get to those file cabinets right away, before some prosecutor or investigative agency subpoenas the information or otherwise ties it up. It is a good idea to find out which bureaucrats helped the other journalist gather information and persuade them to reveal whatever they showed the first reporter. The recovery reporter should do as much of the story as possible by telephone, because it's faster and will quickly uncover any errors the competition has made. (The person under investigation may be screaming foul by then.) Also, because the reporter will be under time pressure—perhaps trying to do in one day what another reporter took two months to do—there is good reason to politely, but frankly, cut people off if they begin to ramble.

Some reporters interviewing the subject of another investigation use the ruse that they think the allegations are untrue and indicate that they are trying to clear the person's name. For example, they say that they heard the same rumors a long time ago and decided then that they were untrue, or they confide that they think the other newspaper or broadcast station took a cheap shot. Some subjects approached in this fashion will reveal more to the second reporter than they did to the first.

Frequently, however, the subject of the investigation will be unavailable, on the advice of an attorney. Or if the recovery reporter does find the subject, the only comment may be "I'm afraid I can't comment because the whole thing may end up in court." The reporter might ask what's going to happen in court, and the subject might hint that he or she is considering suing the other newspaper or station (never that criminal charges might be brought against the subject), hoping that the threat of a lawsuit will scare the recovery reporter away. Unless the recovery lead will be "Dog Walk mayor E. M. Bezzlement refused comment Thursday on charges that he accepted a $1.2 million stock option from Wing-and-Prayer Airlines shortly after one of its 747s made a forced landing in the reactor core of the city's nuclear generating plant last November," the reporter should not settle for a "no comment."

Some reporters ask why there is no comment and whether the person isn't afraid that a "no comment" will cause readers to believe the other paper's or station's charges. If the person still has no comment, the reporters will badger the lawyer and ask what the defense will be. If the attorney claims not to know, they'll ask why the attorney thinks the client is innocent. If the lawyer hangs up, they'll call back.

Some reporters will call the subject's friends and political associates to solicit reactions. The reporters will ask those associates if they knew what was going on, and if they didn't, why didn't they. The reporters will call the local investigative agencies even if none were mentioned in the original story. If those agencies are working on the case, they may have cooperated with the original reporter. There's no reason why they shouldn't share their information with the recovery reporters as well. If they balk, reporters ought to get tough and tell them that official agencies shouldn't play favorites.

Some recovery reporters will even go so far as to call the original reporter, explain that they've been assigned the recovery, and congratulate their colleague on the story. It's sometimes wise to ask the original reporter for any recovery suggestions. Parts of the story, for example, may have been watered down, and the investigator might wish to see those selections printed in full somewhere. After all, once the story is out, the original investigator may regard the recovery reporter not so much as an enemy but as someone who can help expand the scope and impact of the original investigation. If, on the other hand, the recovery reporter is satisfied that the story is untrue—not just in minor details but substantially untrue—he or she may wish to find out if the account was deliberately falsified and why.

A good recovery, then, accomplishes four things. It verifies or shows to be false the original account, updates it, adds to it, and puts it in perspective. It retains the good parts of the original and improves on its weak points. It performs a tremendously useful social function, almost as useful as the original, by reinforcing the good investigation and serving as media criticism for the bad.

Writing a recovery is also useful for the recovery reporter, who will make a lot of new contacts and learn as much in a day or two about a new subject as would be possible in weeks of work by an original investigator. The recovery reporter may also find whole new fields to cultivate in the process. And writing a recovery may inspire the reporter to research and write initial investigative stories to such high standards that the opposition will be hard-pressed to improve on them. Although it is a goal rarely achieved, an experienced journalist gets a warm glow from reading or hearing a recovery that begins, "Authorities launched an investigation Tuesday into charges that . . ."

CHAPTER 12

Confronting the principal

Any reporter who spends more than two weeks on a story is likely to have accumulated a lot of seemingly disjointed information. It may be hard to tell whether the story involves three people or seventy-one, whether it's a corrupt-system story, a man's-inhumanity-to-man story, or something unique in journalism. But somewhere along the line, preferably before interviewing people and definitely before beginning to write, the reporter will have to organize the story. If the story is complicated, as most good stories are, it will need to be outlined (or at least a list of the high points will have to be made), and may even need a few charts and diagrams. Then there is no substitute for sitting back and looking for connections, explanations, relationships, and causes and effects that have been missed at first. Listing the various events in chronological order may help. Perhaps the reporter hadn't previously noticed that someone admitted knowing a certain parcel of land was for sale in May, although the land was not publicly listed until July. That knowledge would certainly give the buyer an edge over others interested in that parcel, and the reporter would then want to find out who told the buyer it was available and how that person found out.

At the outlining stage of an investigation, a number of important things must be accomplished. By completely and accurately analyzing all the information, the reporter should understand not only exactly what happened but also, as far as possible, the motives of everyone involved and the details of what was done. Everything done on a certain date may have been done purposely on that date. Why? The amounts of money involved were not determined randomly. Why so high or so low? Whose complicity was necessary? When the number of answers begins to approximate the number of questions, when the leftover questions begin boring everyone involved, or when the editor tells the reporter to produce or move on to something else, the reporter will have to quit asking questions of a mirror and prepare for the major interviews.

This heralds the confrontation. The reporter must approach the subjects of an investigation, outline the story, and elicit their reactions. It's only fair, after all, to hear and report their side of the story. If the reporter handles a confrontation correctly, it's possible not only to verify the information already in hand but also to expand it and thus round out the story. Some methods for accomplishing one or both of these ends are the subject of this chapter. In the ideal case, if the file cabinets and sources have been good to the reporter, there will be but one question for the principal: "What do you have to say for yourself?" It is more likely, however, that there will be a few missing details that only the subjects of the investigation can supply, and the reporter will have to worm those details out.

First, a word about timing. Suppose a source tells a reporter that the parks commissioner owns the company that sells swimming-pool chlorine to the city at inflated rates. The reporter picks up the phone, calls the commissioner, and screams, "I've got you now, buddy. I know all about the chlorine connection, and I'm going to set up a tent in your office and root through your file cabinets until I nail you. Why don't you save me the trouble and confess right now?" The commissioner is likely to say "I have no idea what you are talking about" and threaten to call a cop if the reporter doesn't stop being a nuisance. It's possible that the commissioner will then hang up calmly, dash to the files, rip up every chlorine contract, and type new ones that will be backdated, signed, stamped, photocopied, and left on a sunny windowsill for two days to age.

When the reporter calls back the next day, the commissioner will be out, as will everybody but the secretary, who will say it is impossible just to open the files, no matter how vividly the reporter describes the state's wonderful public-records act. When the reporter finally does contact the commissioner a week later, they will set up an appointment a week after that. Finally, when the request to go through the chlorine contracts is made, the commissioner will lean back, look businesslike, and say, "I'm fully aware of the public-records act, and I'll be glad to show you anything you'd like to see. However, I can't take the time to supervise you as you go through the whole filing system, and we must protect our records because they belong to the taxpayers. Nor can I put one of the secretaries on it, as they are all busy trying to actualize the summer swim program. If you have a specific document in mind and can either give me the invoice date or billing number, I'll be glad to comply with the law and show it to you. Oh, you don't have any billing dates or numbers in mind? Well, then, I'm afraid I can't help you." There now. The reporter must get a court order, spend a lot more time and money, or give up.

Instead, the reporter might have called the commissioner's chlorine company, expressed interest in buying a summer's supply of chlorine for a pool the size of those in the parks, and asked for a rough estimate of the cost. Suppose the answer was 25 cents a pound. Then, while the parks commissioner was out, the reporter could visit the commission office and tell the business manager about a discovery that a nearby town is paying 75 cents a pound for chlorine. The reporter might say that the records of two other towns showed that they are paying 30 to 45 cents a pound, and that just one more set of records is needed to verify that the 75-cents-a-pound town is being wasteful. Of course, such roundabout tactics must precede the confrontation to be effective.

In many ways, preparing to confront the subject of an investigation is similar to what a trial lawyer does in preparing to cross-examine a witness. It is said that good lawyers never ask a witness a question for which they don't already know the answer. Although that is a luxury rarely afforded investigative reporters (or lawyers), a reporter should be sufficiently prepared so that no answer is completely bewildering. A list of questions and their possible answers, plus questions based on those answers, should be drawn up before the confrontation interview. The only way to avoid being stumped by an answer is to anticipate the situation and be thoroughly prepared.

For example, suppose the president of the local police benevolent association says, "Sure, we have cops selling memberships. But they only do it when they're off duty, so there's nothing wrong with it." Even if the answer comes as a surprise, the reporter could respond that whether on or off duty, everybody knows that the people selling tickets are cops, so it's still a shakedown. Armed with a copy of the department's rules of conduct, however, the reporter could quote verbatim: "Police officers are not permitted to solicit money or valuable considerations for any purpose, in any manner, whether on or off duty." Then the association president might respond by saying either that the regulation is ridiculous or that the department doesn't enforce the rule, equally intriguing answers for story purposes.

A good way for a reporter to prepare for a confrontation is to ask a friendly prosecutor to take a look at the material before the final interview. In many cases a good attorney can point out laws of which the reporter was ignorant that were violated by the subject of the investigation. Although it is good to report that someone has acted unethically, it is better to prove that a person acted criminally. Moreover, it is always wise to avoid accusing someone of violating a repealed or otherwise inoperative law. Perhaps a court has recently declared the law unconstitutional or interpreted it so narrowly that it no longer applies. After talking to a lawyer, the reporter may end up with a story about how a company or union dove through a legal loophole to wallow in the public trough rather than a story about how so-and-so broke such and such law.

In preparing for an interview, the reporter should learn as much as possible about the subject's background. Knowing a person's past not only makes for a more useful interview but also can make the story much more interesting: "Twelve years ago, I. Will Steele ran for county tax collector on the promise of cleaning up scandalous Sewerville. Now he is . . ."

It's important to get some background from the subject if possible, even during the confrontation. Everybody writes about how the subject did it. Rarely do reporters exert sufficient effort to find out why the subject did it. To this day the conduct of former president Richard Nixon in the Watergate affair has been much better reported than his motives — whatever they were.

An experienced reporter reels off as many investigative findings as possible during the confrontation. Not only is that fair, because it gives a chance for rebuttal, but it also allows the principal to correct any errors the reporter may have made that, if left in the story, are likely to detract from its credibility. For example, if the reporter writes that a politician was given one hundred shares of preferred stock as a bribe, the politician, when interviewed, may point out that it was common stock or just a stock option. It is better to correct such mistakes before publication than after.

Sometimes investigative subjects will raise an argument or disclose some fact that effectively destroys a story, proving, for example, that nothing wrong was done, no laws were broken, and no one was hurt. Or, more commonly, they will argue that something wrong was done, but they aren't to blame. They may argue that they had a right to do it, that the whole thing is a coincidence, that there is nothing illegal or immoral about it, that everybody does it. Perhaps they will say that their staff did it, and they didn't know about it until the reporter mentioned it; that the end justifies the means; that they will sue if it is ever mentioned; or that the reporter will shortly discover that the story is untrue because the principal is a friend of the publisher.

Some of the arguments may be rational and effective. If any of them convince a reporter that the original concept of the story is wrong, then that concept should be revised. Going ahead with a story that has been robbed of its original justification will only make the reporter and the newspaper or station look silly. But the newspaper, the public, and the reporter should not lose a genuine story just because someone argues that everybody does it, that all companies operate like that, and that the whole world is corrupt anyway.

The argument that everyone does it should carry as much weight with the investigative reporter as it carries with a traffic cop or a parent. The reporter's obvious response is that exposing one person or institution may discourage others from acting similarly, an argument that supports the nation's entire judicial system. After all, it is said of many successful investigative reporters that their mere appearance in a government office means that thousands of dollars less will be stolen from the taxpayers that day. The argument that everything is relative is harder to refute. One writer vividly portrayed the persuasiveness of this line of reasoning in a *Harper's* wraparound article entitled "Corruption: Now You See It, Now You Don't":

> He (the subject of your story) will fatigue you with questions of degree. He will advocate small elasticities—pushing a boundary, stretching a point, bending a truth, extending a justification. At any given moment, he will assure you that outright transgression is at least three more fudges away. If you grow impatient, he will lecture you on the social machinery, arguing that it runs only because of the tolerance of slight accommodation. . . . He will maneuver you off the ground of principle and onto the ice of rules. While you slide around, he will calmly explain why certain rules don't apply or don't mean what they seem to. If you haven't lost your balance by then, he will hand you the pencil and ask you to draw the line. When you do, he will erase it. He will counsel you to reasonableness and ask you to draw it again. Again he will erase it, challenging your fitness to live in a relativistic universe.

When their conduct is challenged, even obliquely, most people will take whatever opportunity they are given to defend themselves as vigorously as possible. Few people do something they think is wrong. It may be wrong and they may call it wrong when someone else does it, but because they are the ones doing it, they convince themselves that it is okay. And some reporters find it difficult to remain unswayed when they confront a fellow human being who, in effect, begs for mercy. On the other hand, some investigative subjects will feel that they did what they had to do to advance their own personal best interests, and they would just as soon nobody else knew about it. Investigative subjects of this sort make a reporter's life easier by refusing to comment and by allowing the findings to stand uncluttered by denials or rationalizations. More often than not in these cases, the reporter will face the subject of a story only briefly, perhaps for as long as it takes the subject to say "No comment" or to gloss over the charges and refuse to discuss them further. Occasionally an investigative subject will threaten legal action if the story appears in the paper. Rather than flying off the handle, an experienced reporter will ask why the subject isn't as pleased as most people seem to be when told their names might soon appear in the paper. In other words, the reporter will use an attempt to end the interview as an excuse to prolong it.

A small percentage of journalists argue that investigators should not only confront their subjects but also show them the story written about them or their institution before it is printed. It has been counterargued, and we think effectively, that if a reporter with weak-kneed editors shows a story to the person who is featured in it, only trouble will result. The subject of the story is likely to call on the editors and the publisher. If they haven't closely followed the course of the investigation, the subject may be able to convince them that the reporter is all wet. Particularly if the principal and the publisher belong to the same country club, the reporter is better off letting the publisher read the story when it appears in the paper. Then the publisher will be defending a fait accompli when the subject of the story calls — as well as trying to stave off a libel suit — and will be more likely to take a hard line in the reporter's defense.

Different interviewing techniques must be used with different subjects, depending on how much they know the reporter knows (and on how much the reporter knows they know he or she knows) about their involvement in the matter under investigation. Some reporters find it helpful to scatter significant questions among a number of insignificant ones to mask the purpose of the interview and perhaps avoid a quick brush-off or panicky denial until the interview is well advanced. (For different reasons, this same tactic is employed by psychologists who make up personality tests. Sprinkled among such questions as "What street do you live on?" and "Where were you born?" are questions like "Do you hate black people?" and "Should children be beaten?") Stories about intricate financial dealings are most adaptable to this scattered-question technique. When financial dealings become complicated and interlinked with applicable laws and regulations, it is relatively easy to conceal the trend of many of the questions — especially when a reporter seems to be an admiring financial writer doing a success story.

A related distraction technique is to touch on issues that have emotional meaning but are unrelated to the investigation. An example might be the person's divorces or romantic attachments. By referring to these matters as if intending to write about them, the reporter can distract the principal while probing for answers to the important questions.

Sometimes camouflage questions will even turn up leads to new stories a reporter might never have discovered otherwise. Two reporters once conducted a confrontation interview with a state representative who was campaigning for an elective judgeship. The reporters were questioning the candidate about a story, already confirmed through documents and sources, that he had been seeking the early release from state prison of two mobsters, even though he was not their attorney and had had no previous legitimate contact with them. The implication was that he owed the mobsters a favor for something illicit they had done for him in the past. The reporters scattered their questions concerning the mobster-related activities in among a number of other questions on what they thought were noncontroversial aspects of the candidate's life. For instance, the candidate, who was divorced, was said to be friendly with a divorced woman, hardly a sensitive matter, one would have thought. But when the reporters asked the candidate about her, to divert attention from what they considered more important questions, he leapt to his feet and shouted, "Who I [sleep with] is none of your goddamn business!" — ending the interview. (His outburst also ended, for several moments, all other conversation in the exclusive restaurant where the interview was being held.) When the reporters told their editors of the representative's reaction to a mention of his girlfriend, a third reporter was assigned to look into the matter. The upshot was an exposé of Glenda McGuire, the woman on William Milliken's payroll, discussed in chapter 6.

Investigators should not be embarrassed about using such camouflage questions, no matter how transparent they may seem. After all, without knowing what the reporter is really after, the principal won't know which questions are serious and which are not. Even if an investigative subject begins to grasp what the reporter is doing, there's no need to stop. Perhaps the person fears the exposure of a multitude of sins and will still have to guess which area is under scrutiny.

Pressure of a different sort can be brought to bear by having two reporters present at the confrontation interview. One reporter can pepper the principal with sharp, accusatory questions while a colleague, cautioning "Take it easy — be objective," asks softer but still relevant questions. (The police frequently use this good guy–bad guy technique to extract confessions.) If the principal is anything but a computer, he or she may blurt out honest or at least accommodating answers to the friendly questioner as a protection from the nasty one. The principal may even see cooperation as a way to influence the outcome of what seems to be a competition between the reporter who likes him and the reporter who is out to get him.

Some reporters even choose to augment this two-on-one technique by seating themselves far apart, forcing the principal to keep snapping his or her head back and forth. This will contribute to the principal's impression of being alone and defenseless and greatly increases the chance that the truth will be blurted out. The state representative who reacted so violently when his girlfriend's name was mentioned, incidentally, recognized this ploy immediately. When the two reporters initially sat down, almost facing each other, the representative motioned angrily straight ahead and told them they had better sit together — "so I can look at both of you boys at once" — or he would end the interview. Experienced investigators don't make it so obvious.

If a reporter decides against taking another reporter to a confrontation interview, the reporter may discover that the principal has not been so foolhardy and has asked a cohort to sit in on the session. In this situation the reporter is at a tremendous disadvantage. Not only must answers and comments from two people be dealt with and kept separate in the notes, but it is also likely that the reporter's preparation won't have been sufficient. (Thinking up new questions while taking notes is an exhausting and usually unprofitable procedure; when two reporters are present, one can be assigned to perform each function.) About all a reporter can do in this situation is to delay. By asking a few more questions that will produce answers the reporter already knows or doesn't care about, it is possible to catch up on note taking or question preparation.

A reporter lucky enough to have a cooperative friend in a government investigative agency may be able to persuade the friend to come along on a confrontation interview and lend the implied weight of the agency to the questioning. If an organized-crime investigator or an FBI or IRS agent is sitting next to a reporter during the interview, the principal may make the erroneous but tongue-loosening assumption that one of those agencies is asking the questions, not a lone reporter.

Few government agents are likely to agree to this procedure. But if a reporter is working in the same general field or on the same specific investigation as a government agency, friendly agents might be willing to ask questions or obtain documents during their own interviews that are more relevant to the reporter's story than to their investigation and to pass the information on. Cooperation, however, works both ways. Journalists should beware of a government agent who wants information on someone the journalist thinks isn't doing any wrong or is performing some good. It is sometimes easy to feel pressured to turn over information because the agent has helped out on a few confrontation interviews in the past.

Experienced investigators find that a friend also comes in handy when two people who should not be allowed to coordinate their answers must be interviewed. Sometimes a reporter is able to do this by telephone, if a call to the second person can beat the warning call from the first. It is possible to win this speed-dialing competition with a push-button phone if the first person is still using a dial model or if the reporter dials the second person on another phone before hanging up on the first. But as we discussed earlier, a reporter can't see the subject's reactions or use physical presence to keep the interview going over the telephone. (Of course, the other person can't see the reporter's nervous tics either.)

The obvious solution to this dilemma, but one that is often ignored because reporters think they must do all the work on their own stories themselves, is to brief a colleague and then conduct the interviews simultaneously. Reporters not connected with the investigation can often be counted on to solicit better answers anyway. For instance, if the subject of the investigation is at all well known, it is likely that another reporter once wrote a favorable article about the subject and could be persuaded to visit again and ask the nasty questions that need to be answered. The subject will be more likely to respond to a reporter responsible for a puff piece than to a reporter who may be preparing something uncomplimentary.

Nothing, however, should prevent a reporter from being as kind as possible to the subject of an investigation. It is possible to indicate that, in the reporter's opinion, there is nothing wrong with what the subject did, although the story as eventually written may take the opposite point of view. For instance, if a reporter has just asked a politician about a secret interest in a business firm, and the politician seems reluctant to respond, the reporter can interject, "You know, it doesn't matter to me. If people didn't invest in business, nothing would ever be manufactured." Or if the reporter has asked an official about taking a bribe, one approach might be to say, "Don't worry about it. If I did stories on all the people I know who have taken small gratuities, I'd write nothing but penny-ante stories all the time. I'm after much bigger stuff, stuff you can help me with."

A reporter can attempt to mitigate the implied accusations of a confrontation interview by reserving the hard questions for the part of the person's conduct that is under investigation and praising other aspects of the person's work. This may sound a bit forced, but rarely does the average reporter ask all the important questions during a confrontation interview. Generally, after studying the principal's answers, the reporter will think of more questions. By being pleasant and complimentary to the subject during the confrontation interview, the reporter may be able to call back, ask those additional questions, and have them answered. But if the reporter was insulting during the interview, it will be rough going to get the subject to answer any more questions. (If an investigation is running as a series, the wise reporter will solicit all the needed answers before the first installment appears and alienates the subject forever.)

Some reporters go so far as to tell the subject of a story that they believe the subject's own version of events and that the only reason they are doing the interview is to substantiate their belief in the person's honesty. Rone Tempest, formerly an investigative reporter in Oklahoma City and now a reporter for the *Los Angeles Times,* used this technique to gain admission to the mansion belonging to the man responsible for the scandal-ridden Four Seasons nursing home empire. Tempest used the interview to gather colorful details about the mansion and its luxurious furnishing, which he used to good effect in his story.

Another ploy reporters find useful is to tell the subject of the story that they think the person was wrong but suspect that other forces were at work, perhaps sinister people higher up or tragic circumstances, such as debts, alcoholism, or family problems. The reporters sympathize, list their own troubles, say they know what it means to protect a job and that is why they have gone through all the trouble to investigate — so that other people don't get so hassled. If it turns out the subject of an investigation was just following orders, so much the better. It means the possibility of an even deeper, more incisive story about who gave the orders.

If an investigator can manage to don a feature writer's smile, he or she can sometimes get even more information. If, for instance, the subject violated all but 2 of the 805 articles of the city building code in constructing a housing project, a clever reporter may be able to imply that the subject of a Sunday supplement feature the reporter is preparing will be one of the rare men who can profitably turn urban-renewal rubble into gleaming new houses for the poor.

Other ruses are often difficult to pull off but can vastly improve the quality of a story. Without knowing everything, a reporter can drop a couple of hints about the investigation and then tell the subject, "Well, I've got a job to do and have to go ahead with it. I'm sorry about it because I've always liked and admired you. What I'm really interested in, though, is a sidebar to run along with the investigative piece that would tell our readers what you feel about being caught, your regrets perhaps." Approached in this way, the principal may cooperate, thinking the story will be told in any case. With luck, the subject will try to recoup as much ground as possible by coming clean. A reporter may even say that he or she is there only to hear and record the principal's side because all the investigative work on the story was done by another reporter.

During an interview, an experienced reporter does not always insist on directing the conversation. The more the principal talks without the reporter's direction, the more likely it is that important new topics will be uncovered. A reporter once began an interview simply by telling the general counsel for a large railroad company that he was about to write a story about how the railroad was selling land it wasn't legally allowed to sell. (The land had been granted by the state to the railroad for railroad purposes only.) The lawyer could hardly dismiss the reporter with a "no comment," for fear that would enrage certain politicians who would summarily snatch the land back. Instead, he set out to convince the reporter that the project was good for the city. Before he had finished, he had also admitted that neither the railroad nor those who were buying its land were paying property taxes. Had the reporter belligerently insisted on directing the conversation, the subject of taxes might never have been broached.

Despite the efficacy of these approaches, reporters need not always treat their investigative subjects with great deference or conceal their natural antagonism toward someone who may have been, for example, forcing low-paid city employees to finance an expensive reelection campaign. Arrogance is sometimes an effective technique. Some reporters advise telling the principal that a lot of the reporter's time will be saved by talking at this stage of the inquiry, implying that cooperation will make things easier on the person. Some reporters say that others involved in the scandal have talked and that the reporter can't understand why the subject is the only one who isn't cooperating. Does the person have more to hide? Does the person want to be the only one mentioned in the story who refuses comment? If others have admitted their roles, it may be possible to persuade the remaining holdout to cooperate by spelling out a few details from their statements.

Even more blatant techniques sometimes work, especially with less sophisticated investigative subjects. If someone has committed a possibly criminal offense, a reporter might want to drop subtle hints that somehow the prosecutor is involved in the investigation. If the prosecutor is, so much the better. There's no law against talking to the prosecutor and detailing an ongoing investigation. It might help in producing follow-up stories, anyway, if the prosecutor launches a public investigation.

Once a reporter becomes fairly well known as an investigator, however, people may be reluctant to talk, no matter what approach is used. A reporter in this bind may want to ask another reporter to take over questioning the subject of the story.

It would be a mistake, incidentally, for a reporter to assume that questions must always be straightforward. Reporters should do what lawyers do: ask leading questions. A certain fact or relationship can be confirmed by asking a question that presumes it is so. For example, suppose a reporter wants to find out if A knows B. A person-to-person call placed to B at A's number may provide the answer. Or the reporter might call B, say that A's number doesn't answer, and ask for a confirmation that the number is correct. Of course, as investigative devices grow more and more complex, there is always the possibility that the subject of an investigation will see through one of them. Some subjects may even have read this chapter.

Any reporter worried about looking foolish in pursuit of a story, however, should remember the case of the Illinois secretary of state Paul Powell, whose every deed, and many of whose words, conveyed the same message to the media: "Sure, I'm a crook. Just try to catch me." No one ever did. And when Powell died, $400,000 in cash was found in his closet. It's too bad somebody wasn't a bit more curious about the secretary of state's office while Powell was alive and running it.

CHAPTER 13

An introduction to investigative reporting with a computer

Computers have been used to analyze and report such varied investigative subjects as fat cats making illegal campaign contributions to politicians, students in small rural high schools falling behind academically (see example 3 in the appendix), state officials giving out low-interest-rate mortgages to the politically well connected, dangerous criminals being allowed out on work-release programs, and unusually high death rates at certain hospitals around the country.

The computer has brought a whole new world of records into the investigator's purview: Most stories done with computers in a few weeks would have taken several years if done with pad and pencil. In the deadline-ridden world of American journalism, that means they wouldn't have been done at all.

Many of these stories have been of vital importance. In 1985 the Providence (R.I.) Journal *used its computers to compare the names of those holding bus driver's licenses with the names of traffic violators and convicted felons. The comparison revealed that some bus drivers had been ticketed as many as twenty times in three years and that several had been convicted of felonies such as drug trafficking and racketeering. Although the* Journal *is way ahead of most American newspapers in its use of computers for investigative reporting, other papers, such as the* Philadelphia Inquirer, *are also prominent in this field, and still others are playing catch-up with some success.*

In the following chapter, DAVID WALONICK, *owner of Walonick Associates and the primary author of StatPac Gold, one of the best-selling statistical analysis programs in the U.S., writes about the purchase and use of computer hardware and software for investigations.*

133

Every seasoned reporter knows how dramatically his job has changed since the advent of the word processor. The very foundation of the way we write has been altered. Finished documents can be organized, written, reorganized, and rewritten in a fraction of the time it used to take. The word processor was the eighties tool for writing.

Not surprisingly, it's only part of an evolutionary process. History demonstrates that the tools we use continue to improve. The word processor, as good as it is, will soon become obsolete, giving way to the talking-writer. Later in the nineties you'll be dictating your stories into the talking-writer, which will produce perfectly typed manuscripts complete with punctuation. The word processor will be used for touch-up work. This is not a fantasy. Working prototypes are already being tested.

Many people think that the word processor is an electronic box designed to do word processing. Actually, the word processor is a computer designed to act like a word processor.

At the heart of every word processor is a general-purpose (and extraordinarily dumb) computer. The computer itself has no brains at all. It doesn't know how to monitor the keyboard, let alone do any kind of sophisticated word processing. Without instructions, the computer is nothing more than an expensive paperweight.

A computer program is a set of instructions. When a word processing program is loaded, the computer will act like a word processor. If another program is loaded, the computer will follow the instructions of that program. The same computer can perform a variety of functions by running a variety of programs.

There are many different types of programs that the investigator will find of benefit. These include programs for telecommunications, data base management, and statistical analysis. Many large newspapers already own communications and data-base-management software, and some own statistical analysis programs. Sometimes the software has been chosen by computer professionals, sometimes by other reporters. But often when starting a project involving a great deal of data or statistics, you will either have to acquire the software to handle the data or have to buy upgrades to replace obsolete software.

Choosing the best software program can be somewhat like buying a new car. You'll probably like some features of one car and some of another. The situation becomes even more confusing when the car salesman tells you about the new ultratronic widgomatic feature and you have no idea what it does. The final choice is usually a compromise among many factors.

This is exactly the kind of situation you'll face when you choose computer software, except you will have even more choices. Hundreds of programs are available for any application you want.

The best way to find out what programs are available is probably to ask your friends and colleagues what programs they use. Their experience with a particular software program will tell you more than a vendor's sales literature. Also, they may be able to help you if you run into difficulties later. We cannot overemphasize this point. In any case where the software is reasonably close to what you want, get what your friends or colleagues have.

The alternative is usually hours spent poring through terribly written manuals to perform even the simplest tasks. The same is true of hardware. If most of your friends are using, for example, IBM compatible PC-DOS or MS-DOS computers, it might not be wise to buy a machine that runs on a different standard and uses different software.

"DOS" refers to "disk operating system" and is a basic program relating the computer to its monitor, keyboard, and higher-level software. At present it seems most accounting and scientific operations are using PC-DOS/MS-DOS IBM clones. We would also suggest using the fastest central processing unit (CPU) available. Many large spreadsheets can take ten minutes or more to appear on the screen of an older 8088-based computer. At the time of this writing, it is unclear whether the relatively new microchannel system being offered by IBM will catch on and become a new desktop standard.

Computer user groups are also a good source of information about programs, as are some computer stores. Directories of computer software can be found in most bookstores. In addition, a quick look through any of the more than two hundred popular computer magazines will reveal many ads for the kinds of software you're looking for.

The object is to choose the best program for your needs (now and in the future). The two most important criteria for selecting a program are its capabilities and ease of use. A program must be capable of doing what you require, and it must be easy for you to use. Like buying a new car, choosing the best program involves finding a balance. One program may be easy to use but have limited capabilities. Another program may be more difficult to use but have more extensive capabilities.

The capabilities of a program are usually referred to as the power of the software. Generally, the more powerful the software, the more difficult it will be to learn, but the additional time spent learning will give you added capabilities. Don't choose the most powerful software just because it's the most powerful. Try to pick software that provides a comfortable balance between power and ease of use.

Support is another essential feature of any software. When you have a problem, you must have a way to get help. Generally, software vendors have a technical-support phone line. The quality of support varies dramatically from vendor to vendor. In most cases you pay for the call, and with some vendors you can anticipate long waits while you're put on hold. That is when it pays to have a friend or colleague who uses the software and can advise you on the quality of the vendor's technical-support program. More important, your friend can help you directly, particularly during evening hours when most software companies are not open. If you purchase the software through a local computer store, the salesman will often be familiar with a vendor and be able to offer intelligent comments on a firm's technical support.

"Compatibility" has become a key word in the computer software industry. With the increasing number of computer programs, it has become increasingly important for programs to be able to share information with each other. For example, if you enter information into a data base manager and then decide to do a statistical analysis, the statistical analysis program must be able to read the data from the data base manager. Because each program has its own way of storing data, this can be a problem.

A good software package will be able to convert its format to several other formats (export) and vice versa (import). The "universal" format is called ASCII (pronounced "ass-key"). If a software program can read and write ASCII data files, it is compatible with most other software.

The cost of a software package should have a low priority in the selection process. The amount of time you will spend learning any software package is substantial and far outweighs the cost of the package itself. You'll be spending hundreds of hours using the software, and the initial cost is trivial by comparison.

Reviews in computer magazines are among the least helpful of all sources for evaluating software. In the best of all worlds, reviews would be honest and impartial. On the contrary, many excellent products are never reviewed because they do not advertise in the magazines. Because magazines depend so heavily on advertising revenue, they are under considerable pressure to produce good reviews for their advertisers. The situation is worthy of some investigative journalism. We are told that one of the most common word processors used in the newspaper industry is never reviewed in a major PC magazine because the company that manufactures it doesn't advertise.

Comparison charts can be especially deceptive. How good or poor a software package looks in a comparison chart depends entirely on the items chosen for the chart headings. Any software package can be made to look strong or weak, depending on the criteria chosen for comparison.

The most important way to determine the ease of using a software package is to actually try it. Every responsible software company will offer a low or no-cost evaluation copy of its package. But if the evaluation copy looks like a slide show, forget it. Many software companies use the "demo" as a computerized brochure. This is completely worthless in helping you make an intelligent decision about how a program will work for you. Such a computerized brochure almost always gives a false impression of the capabilities of the package. The question to ask the vendor before you order an evaluation copy is, Can I use my own data to test the evaluation copy? If the answer is no, don't consider the software.

Nearly all evaluation software will have some limitation when compared with the full package. Usually the amount of data and/or the number of times the evaluation copy can be used before it will stop working are limited.

Communications

Another aspect of desktop or microcomputers having a significant impact on investigative reporting—and likely to have a major impact in years to come—is data transmittal by telephone. A telecommunications program (often called a terminal program or communications software) will allow you to communicate with another computer by telephone. More and more information is accessible by telephone.

A wealth of information is available if you know how to find it. Large data bases exist for virtually any subject, and you can tap into them to extract the information you need. The process of transferring information from another computer into yours is called downloading.

Because a computer can't do anything without a program, you will need a program to tell your computer how to send and receive information over the phone line. Information is transferred over the phone line by quickly pulsed tones. Each character sent over the phone line is converted to tones, and the receiving computer converts them back to a character. The device that sends and receives the tones is called a modem. Most modems are on a circuit board installed in one of the computer's expansion slots; this board contains a modular plug that can be connected to a phone or phone jack. Other modems sit on a desk near the computer. Each arrangement has its advantage. The internal versions generally cost less and save desk space. The external versions have blinking lights that make it easier for you to figure out what's going on, and they leave your expansion slots for other uses.

Telecommunications programs are somewhat difficult to use. Generally it will take a little practice to get comfortable with a modem and its software. The first thing the program will do is dial the number of the computer you want to call (called the host computer). When the host computer answers, some kind of log-on procedure will ask you to verify that you are an authorized user of the host computer.

After that, you'll issue commands to the host computer to retrieve the information you want. When the host computer sends the information to your computer, the terminal program will capture the information and save it for future use by other programs. Although this may sound difficult, it is in reality quite easy.

A wide selection of telecommunications programs is available. They all have similar capabilities. Choose the one that seems easiest to operate. Unless you plan to spend a lot of time downloading information, stay away from programs with a large number of bells and whistles, because they tend to complicate a relatively easy procedure.

Data base management

Investigative reporting is not just the uncovering of information deliberately hidden from the public. More and more, it involves the organization and explanation of information that is available but is too complex for the public to analyze. For example, you could collect facts and figures on a state's economy and demographics. But the averages, means, medians, and totals could mask wide differences between various regions.

In a growing number of states, officials keep detailed records on a city-by-city and county-by-county basis. In Minnesota the state auditor's office collects annual data on about fifty variables in all 87 counties and the state's 750 largest cities—including population, number of houses, number of businesses, taxes collected, police budget, park budget, number of families on welfare, and so on. Although such information is or should be readily available, it is certainly too complex to be meaningful and too voluminous to be read. It is more and more the job of the reporter to examine the data in ways that allow meaningful patterns to emerge.

Computers are good at the organization of large quantities of data (data base management). A data base manager is a computer program that tells the computer how to act like a sophisticated filing cabinet. When you run a data-base-management program, the computer will be able to store and retrieve information.

Records and fields are two important concepts for understanding data base management. A field is the smallest unit of information in a data base. It represents an individual item of information. Each of the fifty variables mentioned above would be called a field. A record is an aggregate of fields. All of the fifty variables (fields) for a specific county make up a record. The sum of all the records is the data base.

All data-base-management programs have three major functions: sorting, selecting, and reporting data. The ability to sort allows you to reorder the information by one or more variables. For example, it would allow a reporter to rank the counties for each of the fifty variables, and it allows massive calculations. With a data-base-management program, you could create for each county a field of the percentage of families on welfare and then sort all the county records to get a list running from those counties with the highest percentage of families on welfare to those with the lowest. Or you could create a field of sales tax collected per capita in all 750 cities, then sort the cities by their distance from a major urban area. It may sound dull, but it's an art that can benefit by as much imagination as you can bring to it.

A data-base-management program's ability to select allows you to examine selectively the information that meets a specified criterion. Libraries have been using computerized searches for many years. A subject search produces a bibliography and abstract from only selected articles out of the incredible volume of published data. Or in the example above, you could have the computer and software select the twenty cities that had the fastest-growing welfare percentage and focus in on them.

When choosing a data base manager, look for the one that seems easiest to use. Modern data base managers have become very sophisticated, and that translates into more time learning to use them. To avoid frustration, find a package you can learn to use with a minimum of effort. Pay particular attention to the software tutorial and the owner's manual. They will tell you much about the complexity of the software and the interest the vendor had in making it understandable to you.

Statistical software

Statistics are the way we make summary statements about the content of a data base. Unfortunately, most data-base-management programs have minimal, if any, statistical-reporting capabilities. A statistical analysis program is a necessity for a detailed investigation of a data base. It would seem that because the two functions are so closely related, data base managers would contain statistical analysis capabilities, but this is usually not the case. On the other hand, many statistical analysis packages have some data-base-management capabilities. Depending on your needs, a good statistical analysis package may be able to double as your data base manager.

Compatibility, as we mentioned earlier, is an important feature to look for. You must choose a statistics package that is compatible with your data base manager (the data base manager can export data to the statistics package, or, stated another way, the statistics package can import data from the data base manager). Ease of use is the other important feature to look for. Statistics can often be confusing, and a difficult-to-use package will only compound the situation. A good measure of the ease of use is to ask the software vendor what your learning time will be.

At a minimum, you will need a statistics package that performs frequencies, crosstabs, averages, t-tests, correlations, and regressions (including significance and probability). There are, of course, many more sophisticated types of analyses, but these six will handle nearly all your applications.

The most elementary statistics are frequencies (counts and percentages). They can be easily interpreted and are understood by almost everyone. The simplicity of counts and percentages does not make them less powerful than other statistics. On the contrary, it is their simplicity that makes them so meaningful. "Five out of ten (or 50 percent of all) fatal driving accidents involve alcohol" is a strong statement. There is no confusion about what the statement means. If you can make your statement with counts and percentages, it will be the most effective method of presentation for the general public.

Do not be deceived by the simplicity of counts and percentages. They can distort the truth as much as any other statistic. The investigator must be ready to evaluate the real meaning of a statistic critically. As an example, airport noise was a well-publicized issue in one major metropolitan area where the airport was near the inner city. The airport commission had been given the task of deciding if a new airport should be constructed farther away from the city or if the existing noise could be reduced to a tolerable level. They reported that because of the use of newer, quieter airplanes, the average noise level in the metropolitan area had been reduced by 12 percent, even though the number of takeoffs and landings had increased by 5 percent.

A reporter could accept these "simple" statistics as evidence that the airport is not harmful to the community and that the airport commission is doing a good job. Or the reporter can examine what the statistics really mean.

Several unanswered questions make it impossible to interpret these statistics without additional information. How is the "average noise level" measured? Can a person notice a 12 percent decrease in noise? Because takeoffs and landings are more numerous, the public is exposed to longer durations of jet noise than before. Does the public notice the increased duration? What times of day and what days of the weeks are the new takeoffs and landings? Where were the noise monitors located? When these questions are answered, then and only then will the statistics have meaning.

As it turns out, in this case the noise level was measured in decibels, and a 12 percent drop in decibel level is barely noticeable by the human ear. What the commission really stated was that it had increased the amount of time that the public was exposed to jet noise, but the public was unable to detect a significant decrease in the intensity.

Because of their simplicity, however, counts and percentages will always remain the most popular statistics. If you have a choice between a simple statistic and a more complex statistic, use the simple one. It will be more likely to be understood by your reader.

Crosstabs are a method of comparing two variables, such as race and sex, to see how they relate to each other.

"Average" is the most abused statistical term. It generally tells little about what exists in the world. A reporter in one area studying how quickly the police responded to emergency calls stated that the average response time in January was nine minutes. He had added up all the response times and divided by the number of calls. Had he been more acute, he would have discovered that more than 90 percent of the calls from the south side (affluent area) of the city had a response time of less than three minutes, but almost all the calls from the north side (ghetto) had response times of more than eleven minutes. In other words, the average by itself presented a distorted picture of reality.

To make matters more confusing, there are three entirely different ways to calculate or measure central tendencies — what are often generically referred to as averages.

The mean average is the sum of the values divided by the number of values. It can present a distorted view of the data when there are a few very high or low data points. Mean averages may be calculated only for continuous data. ("Continuous data" means that a response can take on any value; it doesn't have to be a discrete unit. For example, a person can answer the question "What is your age?" with the response "31,"

"32," "31½," "31¾," or whatever. Categorical data require that each response be discrete, separate from all other responses. For example, a person can answer the question "What is your sex?" only with the response "female" or "male.")

The mean average may be of value to the investigator in situations when the data can be represented by a normal (bell-shaped) curve. When the data are skewed (lopsided) in either direction, the mean will present a distorted view. For example, the mean would not be a good way to describe the average income of all city employees. Most employees' incomes are clustered in a small-salary range, but a few city employees make an extraordinarily large salary relative to the rest. The mean will imply that most employees earn more than they actually do.

The median average is a better way to describe data that contain a few very high or low values. It is simply the middle value. That is, half the data values fall above the median and half fall below. To find the median, the data are first sorted, and the value in the middle is called the median. Always use the median instead of the mean whenever the data could be skewed because of a few very high or low values. As a general rule, both the mean and the median averages should be calculated because the difference between the two can provide valuable information.

For example, a reporter was investigating how well small-community volunteer fire departments performed relative to larger-community salaried fire departments. He was able to gather response-time data on several departments. The volunteer fire departments had a mean response time of 12 minutes and a median of 8 minutes. The salaried fire departments had a mean of 7 minutes and a median of 7.5 minutes. Had the reporter looked only at the means, he would have concluded that salaried departments respond more quickly than volunteer departments. But because the mean and the median for the volunteer departments were so different, the reporter began to look for an explanation.

He discovered that the volunteer fire departments did nearly as well as the salaried departments when the fires occurred within the city limits. However, when the fire occurred on a farm some distance from the city limits, volunteer fire departments had to travel farther and consequently the mean average was distorted. The long distances were usually much farther than the salaried fire departments ever had to travel. With distance information factored in, the investigator found no major differences in response times between the two types of departments.

The third sort of average is the mode—the most common value or response. If you looked at a list of individual test scores and found the one that occurred most frequently, that would be the mode. In a normal distribution—a traditional, bell-shaped curve—the mean, the median, and the mode all have the same value.

A key concept in statistics is significance. Is a response time of 7.5 minutes significantly different from a response time of 8 minutes? Is 20 percent significantly different from 25 percent? Unfortunately, there is no simple answer. Significance deals with the realm of mathematics called probability and is an essential part of any statistical analysis.

Two numbers can be very different without being significantly different. A statistic called the t-test (or t-statistic) is used to determine if a significant difference exists between two numbers or two percentages. The t-statistic in and of itself has little meaning. Its value arises when the probability of the t-statistic is calculated. The probability for a t-statistic is the probability that the difference between the two numbers occurred by chance. A probability near zero (.05 or less) indicates that there really is a significant difference between the two numbers; that is, the difference is probably not due to chance. A high probability (.06 or higher) indicates no significant difference between the two numbers; that is, the difference is probably due to chance.

The significance level, or probability, of a t-statistic depends upon the amount of data analyzed. For example, a pollster asks two people from the ghetto and two people from the other side of the tracks if they are satisfied with the police service. Both people from the ghetto say no, and the other two people say yes. Is there really a difference of opinion between people in the two areas? What if the pollster asks two more people from each group and gets the same answers? The reporter will be more confident that the difference is significant, but there's still much room for doubt. What if one hundred people from each group give the same answers? Is there a significant difference now?

As you can see, the confidence we have in a statistic depends upon how many people were interviewed. If the number is small, we will have minimal confidence in the results. That is, the probability that the difference occurred by chance is high. If the number is higher, we have increasingly higher confidence that the difference is significant; that is, the probability that the difference occurred by chance is small.

Reporting an insignificant difference as if it were significant is a serious statistical mistake called a Type I error. The question becomes, How many is enough? Fortunately, many statistics program packages will allow you to estimate the sample size required to discover a significant difference if it exists. As a general rule, the more data you collect, the more likely you are to find any significant differences that exist.

The study of relationships is one of the most useful and most misused statistical techniques. Correlation and regression are the two methods most often used to examine relationships between variables.

One of the most valuable statistics is the correlation coefficient, which can vary from -1 to 1. A negative correlation means that as one variable is going up, the other is going down. A positive correlation means that as one variable is going up, the other variable is also going up. A correlation near zero implies that no relationship exists between the variables.

Correlations are often incorrectly used to imply causality. For example, an investigator studying a local educational system found a high positive correlation between the budget of a school system and the achievement of students on college-entrance exam scores. The only correct conclusion is that students from well-financed school systems do better on college-entrance exams than students from less affluent school systems. Even though it might appear to be obvious that more money causes students to do better on test scores, it is wrong to make that statement based on just the simple correlation.

The two variables are certainly related, and the correlation coefficient reveals the relationship, but it doesn't prove that one causes the other. Affluent school systems probably produce better-educated students for a number of reasons, including better teachers, more-modern classroom materials, better-educated parents, and more learning opportunities away from school. These factors probably contribute to higher achievement levels. We would most likely find a strong correlation between them and achievement scores as well, but again the correlation coefficient only reveals the existence of a relationship. It does not prove causality.

There are two basic types of correlation coefficients: Pearson's product-moment coefficient and Spearman's rank-order coefficient. Both are interpreted identically. The difference between them depends on the kind of data examined. For continuous data, the correlation coefficient is calculated using Pearson's method, and for categorical data, Spearman's method is used. A statistics program will not automatically use the correct method. You must tell it which method to use.

An investigator studying capital punishment was interested in finding out who agreed with capital punishment and who disagreed with it. He developed a survey that contained a variety of factors (education, income, political party affiliation, and so on) he thought might be related to a person's beliefs about capital punishment. People filling out the questionnaire had to rank various statements of opinion in one of five categories: strongly agree, moderately agree, neutral, moderately disagree, or strongly disagree. In other words, the investigator was gathering categorical data, so he chose Spearman's method to examine the relationships.

If correlation does not prove causality, the question then becomes, How can we statistically prove that a change in one variable causes another variable to change? From a statistical standpoint, this is extremely difficult. One method, known as causal modeling, involves sophisticated techniques and is beyond the knowledge of most statisticians. Regression analysis has a bearing on the causality issue because it allows us to predict the value of a variable when one or more other variables are known. Like the correlation coefficient, it doesn't prove causality, but it goes a step further because it has prediction capabilities.

For example, the National Weather Service keeps extensive historical records on rainfall, and the Department of Agriculture has historical information on crop harvests. Obviously, a correlation exists between precipitation and harvest levels, but the correlation coefficient just tells us that a relationship exists. Regression analysis enables us to predict harvest levels when the amount of rainfall is known.

A word of caution: Unless you have a great deal of confidence in your ability to handle statistics, and your confidence is well placed, you should always take the time and trouble to have your methods and conclusions reviewed by at least one person with recognized credentials in the field. But we would also caution you that simply turning over your data to computer or statistical experts employed by your newspaper, magazine, or station is also risky:

You are most likely to be the one who is familiar enough with the issues involved to spot something of interest in the data.

You will ask more intelligent questions and seek more interesting correlations if you are intimately familiar with the data.

You will have to be able to recognize a mistake in the data once it is delivered.

In summary, the investigative reporter will find the computer an increasingly useful tool. We wouldn't go so far as to say the computer is your friend, but it can be lots more entertaining than a typewriter and a hand-held calculator.

CHAPTER 14

Dropping the investigation

Reporters who give up on difficult stories after checking two or three sources and finding nothing useful quit too soon to pierce the facade of anything well concealed. On the other hand, reporters who continue pursuing fruitless leads for weeks after it has become apparent that the story they're seeking doesn't exist or is unprovable waste time and discourage their editors from spending money on future investigative reporting.

A reporter who has decided to embark on a particular investigation must be prepared for numerous discouragements. Many investigations will not result in stories: There are just too many rumors, jealousies, and fabrications in the world. And while the reporter is trying to find out whether a story is going to be one of the many failures or one of the few successes, colleagues and readers alike will ask questions like "Do you still work for the paper?" or "Say, are you an editor now?" or "I haven't seen you on the air lately. Something wrong?" Many investigations move so slowly that an average of only one publishable, relevant fact may turn up per day, and that fact may be only a small piece of the puzzle. There will be many days when the reporter will find nothing or will discover that a trail leads nowhere.

An investigation should be dropped when a reporter becomes convinced that the original information was inaccurate; that the subject's actions were not immoral, illegal, or novel; or that no matter how much effort is expended, the reporter will not be able to nail down the story. The difficulty comes in deciding when any of these is true. Far too many journalists decide which stories should or shouldn't see print or be broadcast on the grounds of "what's good for the public" — an indication of the amount of ego involved in journalism.

Unreliable information is part of a normal day's work for most investigators. Nine out of ten tips that apparently point toward investigative stories point nowhere except the wastebasket. An inspiration for

146

much unreliable information is attorneys who charge outrageous fees, explaining to their clients that someone had to be paid off. The lawyer then wins the case either on its merits or on a legal technicality, but the client thinks it was won because the fix was in. Consider the case of a drunk driver who pays a lawyer $5,000 to bribe the judge. The lawyer has the case continued five times, telling the client the judge is holding out for an extra $3,000. Eventually the harried arresting officer doesn't show up, and the case is dismissed. At first the client is glad it took only $5,000 instead of $8,000, but a few months later he or she decides it's time to get even with the judge by calling an investigative reporter. After talking to two or three such persons, the reporter may become convinced that the judges are on the take, even though they are not. What may prompt the journalist to investigate is the sources' sincerity; after all, they were sure the judges were taking bribes.

On some occasions, a reporter will drop a story without knowing whether it's true or false. It may be that even if the story is true, it is of such minor importance that it would not be worth the time required to do it. The reporter may have tried a preliminary confrontation with the principal and failed to elicit any encouraging information or admissions, or perhaps the relevant documents and witnesses are spread out over such a large geographical area that the story would cost more money to complete than it would be worth.

Sometimes journalists report their findings to officialdom rather than to their readers and then write a story about the beloved officials' having corrected the situation. This can happen quite by accident if an investigation into some situation begging for reform comes to the attention of the responsible officials, who hurriedly make the necessary changes and then call a press conference to herald their good work before the reporter can write the story.

A reporter may ask a mayor why one of the staff was allowed to commit some awful deed, and a half hour later the mayor may fire the aide. This is probably not a bad happenstance as far as public policy is concerned, but a reporter should never take the results of an investigation to a public official with the understanding that if the official speedily rectifies the situation, the story will not be printed. That makes the reporter an accomplice in whatever malfeasance was committed and deprives the public of knowing if the government is doing its job properly.

Some investigators drop stories when they learn that a competing publication or station is on to the story and is far ahead of them. A strong case can be made for that decision. If they are reasonably sure the competition is competent and will report the scandal as thoroughly as they could, they might as well work on another story. That way at least two stories will be written instead of one. If, in a white heat to beat a rival to the punch, a hurriedly inadequate story is produced, the reporter does little but blunt the impact of the findings and perhaps make it easier for the subject of the investigation to squirm out of danger. Of course, a reporter can take up an investigation where another reporter leaves off. There may be sources the first reporter either doesn't know or doesn't know well enough, and a fresh approach can produce a recovery story that is even better than the original. (See chapter 11.)

A reporter should never drop an investigation so completely that notes are discarded, sources are forgotten, and the whole idea is lost. One never knows when the information gathered during a partial investigation will suddenly become useful. Weeks or months later the roadblock that stymied earlier efforts may disappear. Or perhaps some official agency will later investigate the same area, and the reporter can use the partial information in writing an analysis or as background for a straight news story. When dropping an investigation, some reporters make it a habit to write up their notes and file them in the newspaper's library among the relevant clips so someone else can find them while preparing another investigation of the topic.

Before filing away notes and putting the story on a back burner, a reporter should take at least one last look. Perhaps there is a good feature, analysis, or hard news story in what has been found. Even if a reporter's material doesn't lend itself to this kind of treatment, he or she ought to look closely at what has been discovered to see if it contains the germ of a story requiring investigation in a different direction. In any one of a number of American cities, for example, a belt of "bombed-out" urban-renewal land may spark a journalist's curiosity, prompting a suspicion that city officials owned that land and condemned it to get high prices for their own properties. An investigation may show this is not the case. But what may have been uncovered is the story of how racist officials — or officials representing racist constituents — discouraged black families from moving into white areas by creating an urban-renewal no-man's-land between white and black neighborhoods.

Suppose a reporter hears that certain city contracts are being awarded without bids. By finding out which people are being awarded the contracts and what their relationships are with the contract-awarding officials, the reporter may hope to find a brother-in-law or two in the pot. Instead, it may be that in some areas certain sorts of contracts — such as contracts for professional services — are awarded quite legally without the submission of any bids. The reporter may end up not with a story about illegal contract awards or officials awarding contracts to their friends and relatives but with a perhaps even more significant story about lazy bureaucrats awarding contracts to the same old firms again and again, without searching out the best contractual bargains for tax-payers' funds.

Another example of how a search for one investigative story can lead to another was provided by a reporter whose sources told him that the local driver's license examiners were taking bribes. Attempting to check out the story, the reporter took a driver's license test himself and purposely did badly on the driving portion of the test. The examiner, instead of asking for a bribe, passed him without any illegal payment, in spite of the reporter's shoddy driving performance. So the reporter did a story on how he tried to fail the test and couldn't—not the story he had in mind but a good story nevertheless.

Almost every investigator wonders at one time or another whether any story worth writing is hidden in that pile of notes. Whenever such doubts set in, it's often wise to bounce the story off a neutral observer or two. Sometimes a reporter can become so enmeshed in the intricacies of a story or in one side's point of view that it's hard to see what the facts will suggest to a reader who hasn't been immersed in researching the story. When a reporter is delving into a technical field, in which a gener-alist's knowledge alone does not suffice, a point may come in the investi-gation when both sides seem to make equal sense, especially if the story involves a lot of numbers. Or after spending so much time talking to those who seemed to be the perpetrators of a scandal and finding them to be pleasant, likable people, the reporter may begin to wonder who's really who. Many reporters give up at that point. It's easy to give up. All the reporter has to do is tell the editors that if continued, the investiga-tion will yield only a confusing, soporific article detailing charges and countercharges.

Rather than abandon the story, however, and waste all that effort, a reporter's best course is to enlist the aid of a third party, preferably a knowledgeable neutral. A situation ripe for this approach occurred a couple of years ago in one American city when some citizens began to complain that the new houses going up in vacant lots among their own houses were rickety "cracker boxes" that would bring local property values down. The reporter assigned to the story talked to one of the neighbors, an old-time construction man, who denounced what he called scandalous inadequacies in the construction of the new houses. The re-porter then consulted a city housing inspector, who admitted that the houses weren't well built but insisted that most modern construction was equally shoddy. At this point, the reporter should have consulted with experienced people from other construction firms (not firms in direct competition with the company putting up the cracker boxes), housing inspectors from nearby cities, or architects to obtain an informed, neutral assessment of the work in progress. But he didn't, and the houses were built, for good or for ill.

Another story suited to this approach dealt with a refusal by federal officials to approve an allegedly less costly redesign for a new federal building. The story implied that officials rejected the proposed new design because they were being pressured by a U.S. senator in the state involved, who was running for reelection, to stage a ground-breaking ceremony before the election. The ground-breaking ceremony could not be held unless building plans had been approved. The story dealt sensitively with what appeared to be evenly balanced arguments on both sides. The federal officials argued plausibly that with inflation, the time spent on writing the new design into the construction plans would offset whatever savings were inherent in the plan itself. The story also pointed out that proponents of the redesign included contractors who would profit from its adoption. Although politics was obviously a factor in the rejection of a plan, what the article badly needed was the testimony of a neutral, out-of-town architect to provide the paper's readers with a nonpolitical view of the merits of the competing arguments.

If outside neutral testimony will not help a story, and dropping the story becomes the foremost thought, the reporter should take a minute to consider what dropping it would do to relationships with sources and potential sources. If a reporter drops a story out of laziness, and it is rumored that the story was dropped because of political pressure or other professionally dubious reasons, the reporter's flow of tips may come to a complete halt.

The best thing to do with a good investigation that is temporarily in bad straits is not to drop it but to think more about it and work harder on it. Call more people, read more documents, talk to more sources, discuss the story with fellow reporters, get more ideas on how to keep it alive, and keep the faith.

CHAPTER 15

Writing investigative stories

Writing styles for investigative exposés range from the quasi-legalistic to the new journalistic. Further, some of the articles are so short that readers are given the impression the topic is of only marginal importance, and others are so long-winded that they are read in their entirety only by the paper's copy editors. Between these extremes is some good, clear, lively writing. For a variety of reasons, however, the stories that derive from investigative reporting are usually not as well written as most other newspaper and magazine articles.

Perhaps investigators become so totally absorbed in their projects and find them so fascinating that they believe the reader will share their interest and hang on to every word, ill chosen or not. Sometimes investigators put so much of their mental energy into the investigation that none is left over for the word processor. Often, we fear, they are so relieved of tension when the threads of their yarn are finally knit together that they merely go through the motions of writing, in the belief that the story has somehow written itself.

Some of the quasi-legal briefs that pass for investigative stories are probably written by reporters anxious to impress their colleagues, or anyone else possessing a high boredom threshold, with technical jargon and legalese. Some are attempts to dazzle with footwork: "Look, Ma, at all the uncovered facts!" What it all comes down to, we think, is that too many reporters are willing to spend four hundred hours investigating something but then write up their findings in four hours so they can get on to their next exposé. All too often, the stories are practically incomprehensible to readers who are not already experts in the areas covered by the investigation.

It may be difficult to accept, but most readers cannot name their two U.S. senators, have no idea who their state representatives are, and think zoning is something that happens on football fields. Some Chicago reporters refer to their hometown as "no-shit city" because they believe that newspaper readers see a scandal on page 1, read the first paragraph, say "No shit," and turn to the advice columns or the sports page. Journalists say that readers display this attitude because there have been so many scandals for so many years that the stories have become repetitive. What is unexplained by this theory is that the advice columns and sports pages are equally repetitive. Perhaps the reason so few people bother to read about many investigations is that those investigations are often so poorly presented.

In this spirit, we suggest some fairly simple rules for investigative writing. First, it is important to write to the length warranted by the importance of the material and by likely reader interest in it. Sometimes editors will want a river of verbiage stretching on for days or weeks to justify the amount of time invested in digging up the story. Or perhaps the editor wants to keep the story short because it is scheduled for publication the same week that a comely suburban heiress goes on trial for the ax murder of her milkman-boyfriend. In this case, the reporter should certainly ask to have the piece delayed until the woman is acquitted or elopes with a bailiff.

Experienced reporters do not overestimate their readers' education or knowledge about an esoteric field. They explain in clear, simple language why a particular example of conflict of interest is against the law, how property taxes are determined, what effect a future land-use plan has, or the rationale for spot zoning. On the other hand, it is important not to underestimate the reader's intelligence, either. The average IQ in this country is a little over 100, among newspaper readers it's probably around 110, and among those likely to read investigative stories it's probably even higher. You need not insult readers by informing them, for example, that a lot of people like money.

When possible, a story should be related to its effects on the readers. Comparisons and analogies are particularly useful to illustrate just how the wrongdoing is costing them tax money or how it relates to the destruction of their neighborhoods. If, for example, the city designated thirty acres of some hapless neighborhood as an urban-renewal area and then delayed rebuilding it, the reporter can point out that the loss in property taxes, building-permit fees, and payroll taxes would have hired ten more cops and twenty more schoolteachers. Or the reporter can explain that if the local judges worked a forty-hour week like everyone else, the county prosecutor could have tried another one thousand felony cases instead of plea-bargaining them, which would have had the effect of getting perhaps another three hundred muggers, burglars, and rapists off the streets. Not every story, of course, needs to be linked so concretely with the reader's life. Stories dealing with sex, glamor, or immense wealth are gobbled up voraciously by newspaper readers even if their lives are not affected at all.

Writing an investigative story is not like preaching a sermon. There is no reason to assume that the audience is on your side or that it even wants to be in better moments. Every allegation should be supported with as many facts as possible; every instance in which the subject of the investigation has violated either the law or accepted practice should be pointed out. Even when this is done, reporters will find that many readers display a surprisingly high level of tolerance for corruption. It's a reporter's job to show why and how the corruption that has been exposed is bad for them, for a significant number of other people, or for an individual they can relate to.

Reporters who have spent week after week trying to corner the subjects of their stories for confrontation interviews or to locate public documents hidden by obstructionist bureaucrats are often angry at the principal of their investigation even if the investigation uncovered little. But in most cases readers are not interested in the trouble and frustrations a reporter suffered. They're interested in the story itself. Unsupported allegations or gratuitous insults directed at the subject of an investigation will always work against the reporter. Readers will not be interested in those opinions unless the reporter is overwhelmingly famous or respected. They're interested in the facts the reporter has uncovered, and insults thrown at the subject of the story will only get in the readers' way.

But the reporter need not cram every single uncovered fact into the story. It is a news story, not a legal brief. If a lawyer were to describe the nature of proof generally accepted by newspapers, magazines, and broadcast stations, the "preponderance of evidence" cliché would probably be cited. It's not necessarily enough to convict anyone of anything, but it is enough to reveal the substantial truth to the mass of readers or listeners. So unless every bit of evidence gathered is independently sexy or necessary to the story, the reporter should be discriminating.

Excluding extraneous information from an investigative story is important because most investigative stories are too long. No one reads many of them except specialists in the field, the close friends or bitter enemies of the subject of the story, and the subject himself. For example, *Newsday*'s famous investigative team once produced a fascinating series on President Richard Nixon's pal Bebe Rebozo, his finances, and his land dealings that was at least thirty newspaper pages long. The number of Long Island newspaper subscribers who were willing to read thirty pages about Bebe Rebozo's bank accounts while their children ran through the living room and their television sets broadcast prime-time football could have danced on the head of an editor. In any case, the massive investigation didn't seem to hurt Rebozo any. Perhaps its length reduced its impact.

It is possible, however, to write at great length and still interest many readers. New journalists like Tom Wolfe have shown one way. Wolfe's nonfiction magazine articles read like novels. He tells us what the subject of the piece was thinking when she did such and such, and what she was wearing while alone in her study. Some of this sort of information can be deduced from what is generally known about a person; the rest comes from asking him or her. Investigative journalists would be wise to try the same approach. Even the dreariest financial scandals are perpetrated by real people, often by colorful, charismatic spellbinders. Their personalities are as much a part of their corrupt schemes as the stocks in their portfolios. People like to read about people, and the more human a reporter can make the subject of an investigation, the more reader interest the investigation will generate.

So let's assume a reporter has packed the story with colorful details, supported every assertion with enough but not too many facts, eliminated egregious criticisms, and crossed out the sermons. The article may still be ruined by poor layout and display. Nothing is as discouraging to the average newspaper or magazine reader as a mass of gray type. When two hundred hours were spent researching and writing an investigative story, simple common sense would surely dictate spending ten hours to lighten it with art, cleverly lay it out, or break it into readable parts so it can be run as a series.

Television has demonstrated its own creativity in presenting complex investigative and analytical reports to viewers. (See chapter 19.)

Printing a newspaper or magazine investigative report as a series breaks up its bulk, allows the use of more creative page makeup, leaves room for more imaginative art, and allows multiple repetition of the main themes of the story. Not the least of the advantages of a series is that it allows the use of such end-of-installment questions as "What happened to the payoff money?" and "Did the police pursue this lead?" Corny, yes, but useful. When the various parts of a series are given unequal play by the news desk on different days, however, the readers may miss a crucial point if the fourth installment is buried on page 63. Also, the longer a series runs, the more likely it is that a major news event will come along and drive the story deeper inside.

Readers who might not want to tackle a massive, one-shot investigation may well be tempted by the creative use of sidebars. These might detail past scandals the individuals were involved in, similar scandals elsewhere, other scandals involving the same project or institution, or possible legal remedies for what has taken place, all spiced up with graphics.

Because most newspapers and broadcast stations are committed primarily to daily news coverage rather than long-range investigative coverage, an investigative reporter can almost never lose by taking advantage of some current event as a news peg for an investigative story. Some investigative reporters have been lucky enough to dream up an idea for a story, work long and hard at it, and then have it ready just as some disaster makes the story topical. They are then able to impress their colleagues by producing "overnight" a major investigative report related to an occurrence everyone learned about just the day before. A Detroit reporter was lucky enough to have finished an investigative story on the misuse of city-owned artworks on the same day that a vandal in Cambridge, England, defaced Rubens's *Adoration of the Magi*. The reporter's paper may have been the only one in the world that day to run an investigative story on possible damage to local artworks concurrently with the story about the damage to the Rubens.

Some investigators argue that making investigative stories too appealing tends to cheapen them and that a story should be aimed exclusively at those expert enough to understand the issues involved and influential enough to end the illicit practices the story reveals. But the powerful are more likely to do something about a scandal if they are convinced the masses are about to storm the palace. If the stories are dull, readers will ignore them, and so will experts and responsible officials.

CHAPTER 16

Objectivity

$\mathbf{I}$n squabbling over whether a story is fair or objective, too many journalists have lost sight of the more important criterion—accuracy. Does the story mirror the events? Do readers come away with the same information they would have if they had covered the event at the reporter's side? In researching the story, has the reporter asked the same or even more pointed questions than readers would have asked had they been there? Has the reporter taken every precaution to ensure that the event was reported the way it actually occurred?

Mature, allegedly experienced journalists go round after round debating whether a story is objective, whether the language is suitably neutral, and whether it is fair to the subjects of the story. Such debates are most entertaining when everybody involved is using a different definition of "objective." To the great distress of journalists and to the even greater confusion of readers, the definition of "objectivity" varies widely from publication to publication, from station to station, and from city to city. What is considered fair at the *Manchester* (N.H.) *Union Leader* is not necessarily considered fair at the *Boston Globe*.

At any rate, nobody who has thought about it for more than ten or twenty seconds believes that perfect objectivity is attainable. It is not expected on the sports, society, real estate, or fashion pages. It is not attained by scientists or IQ tests, and it should not be expected from investigative reporters. We do not mean to suggest, however, that on second reference the person under investigation be called "the crook" or "that snake." Relevant, clearly stated, and well-ordered facts can speak for themselves with little help.

The very nature of an exposé presumes a subjective, not objective, viewpoint, that is, that whatever is exposed is wrong, either morally or legally. It also presumes that what is exposed is important enough to be exposed. Not everyone will agree, for example, that all corruption is bad. Many political theorists, and even muckraker Lincoln Steffens in his later years, have argued that a certain amount of bribery, back scratching, and thievery is necessary to oil the machinery of society. Exposés of such activities imply that something is wrong, that the activity should cease.

Objectivity, nonetheless, is not without its uses. The reporter who goes into an investigation with rigid preconceptions about what will be discovered is not only likely to fulfill those preconceptions (even if they are false) but also liable to overlook evidence of other activities that may be more reprehensible. Objectivity builds credibility, making it easier to get investigations past nervous editors and to attract more (and more-accurate) sources. Furthermore, any biases a reporter may have will be apparent to readers. If a reporter investigates only liberal politicians or institutions, for example, or if the stories are written much more dramatically than the findings justify, a knowledgeable reader will realize it, and the reporter's work will accomplish little beyond impressing his or her relatives.

Striking a balance between listing seemingly unrelated facts and writing a story that reads like propaganda is one of the most difficult things an investigator tries to do. The closer a reporter is to a story and the longer it is researched, the more difficult that feat becomes. Rarely will a reporter uncover a story so clear that its undisputed facts can be simply stated without background, interpretation, or analysis. Most investigative stories are too complicated for the average reader to understand unless they are written in precise, simple language that details what happened, what it means, why it happened, what effects it has on the readers, and whether any laws were broken.

Take the classic example of a politician who rezones land he secretly owns (or land that is owned by people who give heavily to his campaigns). Most readers will be able to understand that the politician used his office to make himself or his friends a lot of money. But many will not connect the zoning practices with the poor planning of most cities: Factories adjoin once-peaceful neighborhoods, busy shopping centers are located across the street from grade schools, and the main thoroughfares of most suburbs have become ugly neon forests. A reporter who goes too far, however, in tone or choice of language will lose everything — including, possibly, a libel suit. Employing loaded language and shrill tones and drawing conclusions in such a way that the careful reader is led to believe that the conclusion came first and the supporting facts were found later will blunt the impact of an investigative story.

Investigative reporters also have to be careful to maintain their objectivity when under pressure to reach a certain conclusion. Perhaps the source is a personal friend, or perhaps the newspaper's management has indicated in advance what conclusions it would like to read. This is sometimes referred to as the hired-gun mentality. Some publishers send their investigators out to do hatchet jobs on their enemies. Typically the reporter is casually told, "I think So-and-so is a crook. Why don't you take a few weeks and look into it?" The hired gun then goes out and comes back with a story that says So-and-so is a nefarious crook, philanderer, and child molester. The publisher pats the reporter on the head and gives him or her a three-day weekend and maybe a small raise.

In other cases reporters find themselves under pressure to conclude that both sides are wrong. For example, if a story is being prepared showing that one candidate is a crook, editors will often ask for a similar story on the opponent. Then some small indiscretion committed twenty years ago is dragged out and given equal play with the first story. Often such pressure is so subtle that a reporter doesn't even notice it. It is a good idea, therefore, to develop a reflex habit of pulling back from a story every so often to see just what the facts are and if they warrant a major, clear-a-space-on-the-trophy-shelf treatment.

Once an objective and thorough investigation has led a reporter to conclude that a major political or social change is necessary, there is no need to become overwrought if the story reads like it is advocating that change. If a reporter writes a story about slum kids' being eaten alive by rats because landlords only have to pay a $25 fine for each death, anyone reading the story will conclude that the fine should be increased. Many editors, in fact, prefer that a story that points out problems should also suggest solutions to those problems. Although the reporter can baldly state suggested solutions, it might go down better with readers if sources with obvious qualifications in the field under discussion are quoted as advocating such solutions rather than the reporter.

To advocate dispassionate investigative writing is, obviously, easier than actually to write that way. After a reporter has been on a certain story more than a few days, some conclusions about the direction in which the story is going are inevitable, and sometimes they either are inaccurate or oversimplify the actual situation. In these situations, some reporters find it helpful to talk over what they are doing with outside experts or to ask a friend to play devil's advocate with them. They then attempt to close the loopholes, double-check the facts, and perhaps quiz additional sources. If too many holes have been punched in the story, it should be either changed or dropped.

A factually accurate story, however, should never be killed simply because it is unfair in the sense that all contrary assertions are not published along with the damaging facts. The stories published about the space program, for example, were true even though they didn't contain rebuttals from the Flat Earth Society. Conversely, a sloppily researched story is not made more thorough and accurate simply because it tells both sides. Nothing makes a story look sillier than an obvious and unnecessary attempt to do so:

> DOG WALK, MASS.—A Wing-and-Prayer Airlines 747 crashed into a nuclear generating plant near here Tuesday killing 348 passengers and seven crew members, while 12 other Wing-and-Prayer flights landed successfully at their destination.

The public relations people at Wing-and-Prayer may love it, but then none of them live in Dog Walk.

CHAPTER 17

Getting the story published

Ⅰt is only a slight exaggeration to say that, in all but a handful of newspapers, magazines, and broadcast stations in this country, persuading the editors to print or broadcast an investigative story is often more draining and time-consuming than reporting and writing the story. Yet many publications and broadcast stations pride themselves on their hard-hitting investigations. What they often mean is that they will joyously investigate prostitutes, dope dealers, cops on the beat, minor politicians, and anyone else without great power who is not one of their advertisers. The crunch comes when reporters investigate corruption involving large corporations, powerful local politicians, police administrators, charities, churches, and other newspapers or broadcast stations.

It is rare for an editor to tell a reporter that a story will not be published because it will offend an advertiser or bring more heat than the publication or station is willing to handle, although we do know of a few such cases. Generally, the story will be attacked on its merits or because of judgments implicit in it.

For example, one big-city newspaper once had a story in hand about two city council members who voted to sell two alleys to a real estate speculator for about a tenth of their market value the same month the council members came into a large number of shares of stock in a bank run by the speculator. The council members paid about half what the stock was worth. A conflict of interest, you say? Not so, said the editor. He said that because the alleys were sold to the banker, not the bank, the case was not solid enough to warrant a story. Two years later, when both the editor and the reporter were working for other newspapers, the editor mentioned that he had known that it was a bona fide story, but the publisher had chanced across it in the back shop and ordered it killed. The editor told the reporter he had questioned the merits of the story rather than admit the real reason for dropping it and risk the reporter's quitting the paper.

Managements may have different reasons for killing good stories. In the previous case, the newspaper earned substantial revenues from the city government in the form of legal-notice advertising, and the council members involved had sufficient clout to curtail that advertising had the story been published. In other cases, editors will kill a story for fear of losing a libel suit. Others, even those who believe a story is not libelous, will still spike it to escape incurring the cost of defending themselves against even the most futile of libel claims. Stories will also be spiked for reasons of political kinship or personal friendships between the subject of the story and management. These abuses occur most frequently in small cities, particularly those with a single newspaper.

But the reason most stories are killed, we think, is that editors and publishers are simply unwilling to take the heat that a controversial story generates: charges and countercharges, enemies, outraged readers, anger among advertisers, denials, explanations, perhaps even lawsuits. The editor who publishes a controversial story knows that it will have to be defended on its merits to his or her superiors, some of whom may not share the same sense of moral outrage. To ask an editor to run a story he or she thinks may precipitate a confrontation with the publisher means, in too many cases, asking the editor to jeopardize chances for further advancement.

Attitudes toward publishing controversial stories vary widely from newspaper to newspaper and from reign to reign within each newspaper. A lot can hinge on the reaction to the paper's last foray into investigative reporting, and even on such things as the level of tension between editors and reporters due to labor-management negotiations or union-organizing drives. Consequently, there is no single best way to handle such confrontations. What would be a convincing argument at one newspaper or broadcast station would be considered nonsense at others.

In most cases, however, we think the best way to persuade management to publish a controversial story is to act as if it is as innocuous as the most routine obituary. The least bit of apprehension will certainly be transmitted to others handling the story. The reporter should merely send the story to the proper queue and wander off to the coffee machine. The same advice applies to asking for the time necessary to do a difficult investigation. The reporter should merely tell the editor what the tip is, what the preliminary research shows, and that a few days will be needed to work on it. The reporter should leave it to the editor to explain why it's more important to do a cute feature story.

Suppose the editor reads the piece, ponders it two-tenths of a second, and screams, "What! Are you crazy? We're not about to print a story attacking all the banks in the city just because they won't make home loans in certain neighborhoods." Or, more likely, suppose the story is set aside and two days later the reporter learns it has been spiked. That should not be the end of it. After conniving, digging in files, making endless phone calls, and having showdowns with heavyset security guards, one more such encounter should not discourage the true investigator. What probably happened is that a bunch of editors discussed the story, and either one faction convinced the other that the story shouldn't run, or one of the higher-ups overruled one of the lower-downs. That's why it took two days. The problem with letting the decision stand is that whoever was arguing in favor of publication obviously doesn't know as much about the story as the reporter does and probably didn't argue for the story as well as the reporter could have. The reporter should find out who wanted the story killed and then talk to that person.

In order to get the story published, the reporter must permit some face-saving. Consequently, it is wise to stay calm and relaxed and discuss the story rationally. The first step is for the reporter to say that it's a good story, not that it will prevent teen pregnancy or halt creeping socialism or the readers will like it or the publisher will like it — just that it's good. The reporter should let the editor supply a definition of "good" and argue that the story doesn't measure up. That way the reporter will get an inkling of what the editor doesn't like about it or its likely effects and will be better able to find a way to get the story published. Perhaps the editor will say the story needs more work — more research or another rewriting. The reporter should ask for suggestions and politely but carefully find out just what facts the editor wants or what the lead should say. It is important to be alert to any suggestion of a new lead or some particular wording. By using the editor's key phrases, the reporter may still be able to keep the story intact. If the reporter doesn't pin the editor down closely, however, the editor can say later on, "Something is still missing. Maybe we ought to let it sit awhile." Then the story is dead.

Often investigative stories are the result of many compromises between reporter and editor, reporter and libel attorney, and editor and editor. How far a reporter should go in compromising a story is a matter of judgment and circumstances. In some instances, the journalist will be doing a greater public service by getting at least part of a story in the paper or on the air, where it may be picked up by other investigators. In other cases, the proposed solution may either distort the facts of the story or compromise the reporter's integrity. If no compromise seems acceptable, the reporter could remind the editor that dozens of people have been interviewed and that by now everyone in the statehouse undoubtedly knows about the story. By killing the story, the paper or station may seriously jeopardize its own credibility and reputation in important circles. In convincing the editor, a reporter may also find it handy to be conversant in libel law. The landmark *New York Times* v. *Sullivan* libel decision by the U.S. Supreme Court is continually undergoing modification, and reporters should keep up with these cases. But in general, a plaintiff who is a public figure cannot win a libel suit even if some of what was written about him or her was inaccurate, unless the plaintiff can show that the reporter deliberately falsified facts or acted in reckless disregard of the facts.

Furthermore, those who are truly criminal tend not to sue for libel. That's because if they sue, the newspaper or broadcast station involved will have a right to what is commonly called discovery: the access to many private records. For example, if the subject of the story has been caught rezoning his or her own land in one part of town and secretly owns and has rezoned land in another neighborhood, the reporter will have a good chance of discovering that during the suit. In most cases the subject of the story would rather not risk broadening the charges or giving the local prosecutor something extra to hand a grand jury by suing for libel.

If management absolutely refuses to run a story for fear of a libel suit, and the reporter involved absolutely refuses to have it kept secret from the public, some perfectly ethical alternatives exist. A reporter can ask about selling the story to another publication. The question may incite an editor to genteel riot, but it will also make the editor think again about the story and the treatment it deserves. A reporter who is told that the story can't be sold is being misled. The story cannot be sold as written for the newspaper, magazine, or station, but the information can be used to write another article: No media outlet has sole control over any set of facts. The reporter's superiors can put the reporter on the night police beat or even fire him or her, but they'll lose any lawsuits that claim they are the sole legal outlet for stories about, say, corruption in their circulation area. They may even lose the suit for wrongful dismissal that the reporter files against them.

While discussing whether or not an investigative story should be published, the reporter must decide how important his or her job is and how difficult it would be to get a comparable job elsewhere. We would suggest that quitting is not a good solution. It doesn't result in the publication or broadcast of the story, it won't change a publication's or station's attitude toward controversial stories, and it won't aid in informing the citizenry. A wiser course for the journalist would be to persuade someone else—a prosecutor, a public service law firm, the local Public Interest Research Group—to make the charges. Then a straight news story reporting on the charges can follow. Extreme measures are rarely necessary. Knowing that most editors have retained at least a soft spot for journalism, a smart reporter avoids fireworks and probes calmly until that spot can be found.

CHAPTER 18

Keeping the heat on

Perhaps the rudest awakening for the novice investigator is catching a person doing something outlandish in secret, writing about it in phrases that will live forever, and then watching with dismay when nothing happens. Pulpits do not ring with scorn at the water commissioner's nakedness nor is the commissioner spat upon in the streets. In fact, he or she will remain at a desk drawing a salary. By midafternoon the reporter may have the distinct feeling that if anyone gets tarred and feathered, it will be the reporter. To get a reaction—the firing, disbarment, indictment, or official investigation of someone—the reporter will have to write follow-up stories. On many occasions people in official positions will take a reporter's charges seriously only when they read them in the paper the third or fourth time. The masses will not rise up after the publication or broadcast of a single story. In fact, a lot of them will not have read it. They were on vacation, new in town, trying to earn a buck, fighting with their spouses, bowling, reading *Scientific American,* or doing drugs the day the story ran.

As is the case with any other news story, a follow-up story has to have a reason for being. It is not enough to write: "Yesterday this newspaper exposed the water commissioner. For all you folks who missed it, here is that story reprinted." The reporter will have to find a news peg for the story, generally a reaction to it by some prominent person. The most immediate reaction is likely to come from the people most embarrassed by the story. They will say any of a number of things, usually one of the following:

"The charges are false. My lawyers are preparing . . ."
"The charges are false. They are part of a plot by . . ."
"The charges are false. I stand on my record of . . ."
"The charges are false. The reporter who wrote this story is a . . ."
"The charges are false. You can't believe everything you . . ."
"The charges are false. I broke no law, and besides everybody . . ."

Rarely will the principals admit the charges. If they do, they'll often assert that the charges are insignificant. Sometimes, corrupt politicians are even revered as heroes and reelected after they are convicted. Cornelius Gallagher, a former New Jersey representative, was treated to a get-out-of-jail party attended by more than two thousand of his constituents after he had served seventeen months for income tax evasion. One time Jersey City boss Frank Hague managed to blunt a number of investigations aimed at him by depicting the charges as being aimed at all the residents of Hudson County. Hague's successor, John Kenny, won reelection to a second term after he admitted lying to a waterfront commission during an investigation of racketeering.

Public officials charged with doing something unethical may defend themselves by saying they did nothing illegal. Those charged with breaking a law may say they are innocent until proven guilty. Those found guilty may say the case is under appeal.

The most savvy politicians, businesspeople, or other public figures embarrassed by an exposé will go after an investigative reporter with all the tenacity and skill with which the reporter went after them or their agencies. They will hire competent and articulate lawyers. They will attempt to convince editors and publishers that the story was nonsense, that the reporter made it up, was duped by their political enemies, or simply didn't understand certain processes of law. This is another reason for a reporter to develop an extensive background on the subject under investigation. If the reporter is unaware of any single related fact, whether it is relevant to the charge or not, a sophisticated lawyer can use that lack of knowledge to convince a publisher or an editor that the reporter can't even spell the subject's name correctly, much less write an accurate story.

If this technique doesn't work, it is not unusual for the embarrassed parties to use threats, withdraw advertising, or file a libel suit. At least one public official implied to a newspaper's owners that the tax assessments on the newspaper's warehouse would be raised if any more stories resembling the first were printed. This is the second rudest awakening an investigative reporter often comes to: learning just how rough the professionals play.

Counterattacks can be flamboyantly newsworthy, sometimes even more so than the original story. For example, the report that valuable art objects lent out by the Detroit city museum were being misused by various officials prompted Mayor Coleman Young to publicly denounce the reporter who wrote the story and bar him from the mayor's office without a police escort. The mayor was particularly piqued by a photograph of a valued statue sitting on a file cabinet in a mayor's office hallway surrounded by dirty coffee percolators and coffee cups. Weeks later, on a TV talk show, the mayor said the reporter was barred from his offices not to prevent such photographs but because, the mayor said, the reporter set the coffee cups there himself and because on another occasion a secretary had caught him reading the mail of a mayoral aide. The aide, however, knew nothing about it when asked, and the reporter denied reading anybody's mail. A slightly more subdued response is exemplified by Chicago mayor Richard Daley's reaction to the charge that he transferred city insurance business to one of his sons. Daley told a news conference, "Any father that wouldn't help his children in a legitimate, legal way isn't much of a father."

Obviously, a reporter needs to write more than one story to make the charges stick. One way of doing so is to make maximum use of the glorious democratic system of government that has kept America strong and free and its sons and daughters virtuous and high-minded and that always makes it possible for a lazy reporter to dig up one politician willing to denounce another. Almost anyone a reporter writes about—especially an elected public official—has an enemy somewhere who will be only too willing to call for an investigation as a result of the story. Such a follow-up, based on a relatively uninformed denunciation, is a cheap shot. But if a reporter believes in the findings of an investigation, it is important to keep the story alive so the findings will have some effect.

Even if no denunciation is forthcoming, the same democratic system that enables a reporter to write a story about an elected official and then seek denunciation without fear, enables a reporter to sit back and wait for voter reaction at the polls. Numerous officials who were justly pilloried by investigators have been defeated in subsequent elections. This has led some newspapers to delay publication of some stories, investigative or not, until election eve in order to inflict maximum damage on their targets. This practice, however, is not only unfair to the candidate but may actually backfire because many voters will think it unfair.

If, however, there is no newsworthy reaction to a reporter's story and the subject of the investigation is an appointed official, the reporter should not hesitate to ask the people responsible for the appointment what they plan to do about it. They may denounce the man or take the more cautious, official approach and order an investigation of the charges. When calling for the investigation, they may find themselves pressed to say why they think an investigation is necessary, thereby providing quotes for a follow-up lead.

The announcement of an investigation, however, should not be welcomed with unmitigated glee. In fact, an official investigation is often an easy way for a politician to get rid of some messy allegations—for the time being or forever. In many cases an official will be glad to announce an investigation, bask briefly in the resulting favorable publicity, and then retire to a smoke-filled room while both the public and, unfortunately, the media forget the whole affair. Reporters have perhaps shorter attention spans than others, even in these situations. Someone once compared the average reporter to the family pet that plays with a rubber duck for a while, then drops it and charges into the living room to chase a plastic mouse.

The alert reporter, realizing that the announcement of an investigation is different from its consummation and from the disclosure of its findings, should prepare several fallback positions in case the matter is quietly forgotten. The reporter could point out that the investigation announced with so much fanfare six months ago never got under way, was just a smoke screen to begin with, or never resulted in official findings. If the official investigation was stalled by pressure from the original subject of the journalistic investigation, it is almost imperative to do a second investigative piece. A diligent search should be made for any conflicts of interest or collusionary links between the original subject and the people directing the official investigation.

The article could be coupled with or written as an analysis of the reasons the official investigation was stalled. Often the same editors who demanded facts and only facts in the publication of a reporter's original investigative piece will allow the reporter to use the news analysis form—with its greater latitude for editorializing—after the reporter's original investigative piece has stood a short test of time. Columnist Murray Kempton once wrote, "Editorial writers are people who ride down out of the hills after the battle and shoot the wounded." Nevertheless, it is no disgrace for a reporter to ask for an editorial in support of an investigation.

If an investigation has pointed out enough possible illegalities, any member of a grand jury may read the story in the paper or see it on TV and take up the cause without alerting the reporter involved. The reporter may get an inkling of what's going on only when the county prosecutor calls to ask for help in locating a witness to appear before a grand jury. If warrants are sought and the principals in a reporter's stories are arrested, charged, and tried, the follow-up opportunities are obvious.

Prosecutors and grand juries, however, are not always in action, and sometimes even an editorial and a news offensive causes no forward movement. Nevertheless, the determined investigative reporter doesn't give up easily. If the statute of limitations will allow a pause until after the next election, a whole new set of officials may then be in office, people who have no stake in the conditions that led to the original investigation and who have something to gain from painting the previous officials as incompetent or crooked. If the reporter is lucky, the new officials will be the same politicians who denounced the old guard when the stories were first published and are now eager for immediate, favorable press coverage such as: "Only two weeks after taking office, Prosecutor Mary Smith moved today to investigate the campaign-financing scandal that her predecessor in the prosecutor's office refused to touch. . . ."

Even if such favorable electoral circumstances do not develop and the situation originally uncovered continues to exist, nothing prevents a reporter from waiting six months, a year, or even two years and then writing another story on the original theme. The story might say that the original subject of the investigation is still being permitted to do business as usual despite antics brought to the attention of the appropriate officials many months ago. If the malfeasance described peaks at definite periods — tax sales, court hearings, or the like — the reporter has natural news pegs on which to hang other similar stories. Stories detailing election fraud fall easily into this category. If no action has been taken on a scandal revealed during the previous election, the reporter is free to write such leads as this: "On election day next week, those 600 dead bodies who voted in last year's municipal race will have a chance to vote once again. They're still registered."

Other possibilities remain if all else fails. Perhaps the original stories will attract new sources with new information. Maybe something unfortunate will occur as a result of the unchecked continuance of the scandal and will bring the story to a head. Or perhaps the original subject of the investigation will do something else both evil and newsworthy, and the reporter will be off and running once again.

CHAPTER 19

Investigative reporting for television

Television reporters have become increasingly prominent as investigative reporters in recent years. In the following chapter, DON SHELBY, a prize-winning investigator for WCCO-TV in Minneapolis and one of the researcher-investigators for example 5 in the appendix, writes about the art and science of investigative reporting for television.

There is no question that television reporters have produced important pieces of investigative journalism. But can every story that comes an investigative reporter's way be turned into a television report? People who say no argue that the attention span of the TV audience is too short to follow complex investigations. They also argue that television cannot afford to spend the time it takes to tell complex stories even if the viewer's attention span could accommodate the information.

The fact is, TV investigations must be not only journalistically sound and well written but also visually appealing to sustain viewer attention. Even critics of broadcast news say television reports can be most compelling when reporters focus their cameras on the actual wrongdoing. Print reporters confess that magazines and newspapers cannot compete with the drama of that sort of caught-in-the-act documentation. Those same critics, however, question whether television reporters can carry off a good paper-trail investigation involving mountains of numbers and slow-moving detail. They have a point.

Slow, laborious, nonvisual, highly detailed, and complex stories are difficult for television. They can be written and broadcast successfully, but they require additional skills, tools, and time and some very creative storytelling.

For the most part the techniques taught so far in this book apply to all forms of investigative reporting—electronic and print. However, this chapter will attempt to define the sharp distinctions between the demands of print and TV. Throughout this chapter, incidentally, it will be assumed that television reporters' skills and training are equal to their counterparts in print. Although arguments are made from time to time that television reporters are less concerned with fact and detail and more concerned with flash and bang, those arguments will have to be waged elsewhere. In this chapter everyone is presumed equal.

In the following pages we will focus on six specific areas: storytelling, presenting documents, visualizing the investigation, catching wrongdoers in the act, using graphics, and confronting the principal. Each category has a print parallel. But this discussion will demonstrate the sharp distinctions and additional demands on TV reporters who wish to delve into investigative journalism.

Storytelling

Although there are dozens of different ways of telling investigative stories, some lend themselves to television better than others. Two of the most successful have been adopted from sources outside television. The first is the prosecutorial style. When lawyers talk about prosecuting a case, they are referring to the orderly and systematic presentation of evidence, both testimonial and material, to a judge or jury. The way the evidence is prosecuted bears heavily on how the jury will decide the case. A prosecutorial approach in television reporting is designed to convince the audience of the reporter's findings and assertions.

Keep in mind that a prosecutorial approach does not call for a reporter to behave like Hamilton Burger in the old "Perry Mason" shows. It merely means the reporter presents the evidence gathered during the course of the investigation in a logical, orderly, and convincing manner. If you have ever watched a criminal or civil trial unfold, you may recall prosecutors or plaintiff's attorneys beginning their case with opening remarks that outline what they hope to prove with the evidence. Following that, the prosecutors call witnesses who provide information to support the claims. Each new witness builds upon the foundation laid by the preceding one. In other words, each witness introduces the audience or the jury to the next level of information in logical sequence. And wherever possible, material evidence and documents are used to support the witnesses' statements. The documents give the witnesses credibility and vice versa.

The prosecutorial approach to investigative reporting on television breaks with its legal model in the application of balance and fairness to the report. In criminal proceedings the prosecutors don't call defense witnesses, nor do they give the defendants a free chance to clear themselves. But the reporter must and will.

The reporter using the prosecutorial method will introduce, or allow the principal of the investigation to introduce, information that may tend to refute the allegations. If the refuting statements cannot be rebutted or refuted by the facts at the reporter's disposal, the reporter hasn't completed the investigation or had better start looking for a new one.

By using this method of storytelling, the reporter builds layer upon layer of information needed to make the allegations believable and understandable. Despite the discomfort some people may have with the terms used to describe this approach, an investigation does resemble a trial proceeding in many ways. But investigative reports are journalism, not a court of law. So although the terms used to describe this method have legal connotations, the reporter is wise to remember that the story is simply providing information to the public and not seeking justice. It is helpful to keep that in mind throughout a career.

The prosecutorial storytelling method is a handy way of covering complex stories that may require several separate reports. Each layer of information should conclude with a summation and a preview of the ground the reporter intends to cover in the next report. Each succeeding segment should begin with a brief recap of the information presented so far and then continue into the next layer of fact. The entire report concludes with the customary summation.

This method also gives the reporter the opportunity to check at various stages of the story whether the points are being clearly made, whether the information is being presented logically, and whether the audience is keeping pace. It provides the reporters' editor an easy method of checking whether each segment has the proper impact and whether more evidence needs to be introduced to make the reports complete.

Although the prosecutorial approach is a good method of delivering facts, it often has a tendency to appear, and sometimes is, heavy-handed. The prosecutorial approach often suffers from a "Just the facts, ma'am" style. This style doesn't provide much room for the often compelling individual stories of the real victims of wrongdoing. Victims are best presented in another style of storytelling known as the vignette.

The vignette style of reporting has grown popular among writers who are fond of the *Wall Street Journal*. Editors and writers at the *Journal* often make hard-to-understand economic and business stories more digestible by focusing the effects of these big issues on the lives of individuals or families. In the same way, hard-core investigations can be made more understandable and compelling if victims of a larger wrong are given the opportunity to tell their personal stories. The reporter then weaves the factual matter into the broadcast through the lives of the victims. This sort of talking-head television can often be the best sort of television.

A number of variables determine whether a vignette style will work for a given investigation. The first is whether the victims are themselves compelling. Do they tell their own stories well and convincingly? In the prosecutorial method the witnesses and documents are the skeleton that the reporter fleshes out with a story line. In the vignette style the reporter builds the skeleton of facts, and victims provide the flesh and blood and emotion.

These two storytelling styles are similar to methods used in print, but the greatest difference between the media's use of the styles centers on the tools used to record the words of those witnesses and victims. It is one thing to persuade a victim, witness, or principal to talk to an inquiring reporter armed only with a pad and a pencil. It is quite another thing to persuade a person to say those things into a TV camera. Although Andy Warhol prophesied a world in which everyone would be a television star for fifteen minutes, it is still difficult to persuade people to spill their private stories into a television lens. It is harder yet to persuade a witness to make an accusation for the television record. This is the real difference between print and broadcast investigations.

A print reporter is asked in most cases to grab only the facts in the process of investigating a case, but the television reporter is asked to grab not only those same facts but also pictures of facts, sounds of facts, and spoken words and images of all the participants. Every word written by a television reporter must be accompanied by a sensible picture supporting it. Reporters seeking to tell investigative stories on television must learn to visualize their copy and obtain those visuals once they are conceived. It is a huge obstacle in the process of gathering the facts to support an allegation, but often those images make the most compelling journalism we have today.

Presenting documents

The best investigations, whether print or broadcast, require documentation. Two types of documents are used in TV reporting. The first is the document that provides background and understanding and is primarily for the in-house use of the reporter. The second is the paper trail itself—documents that serve as evidence of wrongdoing. Documents that implicate or inculpate must be seen to be believed, so they must be videotaped as part of the reporter's production file. Although print reporters simply gather the documents, the television reporter must tape the paperwork, display it logically, and use special effects to highlight specific areas for the audience, such as signatures, dates, contract language, and figures.

Sometimes it is necessary to videotape reporters as they conduct portions of the document search. Videotape of that process will be used in reports to cover copy dealing with the search for information. ("Cover" is the television term for placing pictures and words together. The pictures that accompany the spoken copy must match or else the audience becomes confused.) So if the reporter is talking about the searched-for documents, it is appropriate to see the reporter conducting the search. A print reporter can toss a few lines into a story about filing a Freedom of Information Act request, but the same copy in a television report would require videotape of the reporter's filling out the request and perhaps of the Justice Department building in Washington, D.C.

Print reporters often take issue with what they see as gratuitous and unnecessary reporter involvement in TV investigative reports. What they are seeing often is simply the video record of the investigation, what they might find themselves doing if a TV camera followed them in the course of an investigation. A video record of the investigation does add the appearance of greater personal reporter involvement in the story, but videotape of portions of the investigation is still worthwhile and functional in other ways. It will often provide useful cover visuals and be helpful in explaining, visually, the steps taken to uncover the facts.

Wherever possible documents should be copied or returned to the studio, where they can be photographed clearly for later inclusion in the reports. If copies are unavailable, the reporter and photographer should videotape several views of the documents at the scene.

A print writer can report having seen the books of a local union and finding several strange entries. The television reporter can say the same thing in one of two ways: by looking into the camera and making the allegation or by showing the books to the audience. Given the two choices, the most compelling and most believable is presenting the books on the screen. So when planning an investigative report for television, think from the beginning in terms of words and pictures.

Visualizing the investigation

When a reporter has completed an investigation, it is too late to begin thinking about how to produce it into a fitting television story. The most difficult thing for print reporters who have crossed over to television to learn is how to think in terms of pictures from the beginning of the investigation.

A skillful television reporter thinks of pictures and words simultaneously. A reporter who comes up with an important fact without a corresponding picture to support and explain it has done only half the job. Once having learned to think of facts and pictures together, the reporter is over the biggest hurdle in adapting investigative journalism to television.

The next step is seeing those visual images flow together in a logical sequence. Old hands in television argue that a good investigative report could air with the sound off because the visuals alone would tell a compelling story. Here's a suggestion for the person just learning the techniques of this craft: overshoot. If you think you have taken enough videotape, shoot some more. You'll need plenty of pictures of all the players in the probe, important locations, houses, buildings, cars, documents, signs, and logos, and if you are lucky while you are shooting, you may end up with one of those priceless caught-in-the-act pieces of videotape upon which careers have been made. But don't count on it.

Catching wrongdoers in the act

One of the most dramatic uses of video in television investigations is the documentation of the wrongdoing as it happens. The technique has been called many things, from surveillance to entrapment. Despite criticism it has been widely and successfully used at local and network levels and remains, against any argument, the best evidence of the behavior complained of.

The effort to document the wrongdoing requires additional planning in the early stages of the investigation. Some investigators have placed cameras inside the homes of cooperative citizens and taped illicit sales pitches from behind two-way mirrors. Some investigators have hidden cameras in bars and taped public officials as they demanded bribes and payoffs. Some reporters have put cameras in vans and cars and followed public employees for weeks to document chronic laziness and illegal time off. Nothing is so convincing as seeing the substance of the allegation played out on the screen. And it saves the reporter a great deal of writing. Instead of long paragraphs detailing the complexities of the

176   Techniques

behavior, the reporter simply says, "Watch this."

A warning about this technique: Privacy laws of the state in which hidden cameras and microphones are used may proscribe the behavior. In some states the technique is a criminal violation. All states have some laws governing when and where hidden cameras and microphones can be used. Before planning a surreptitious video or sound taping, make sure you know the law. It's a good idea to talk with an attorney familiar with this area of law. And keep in mind that in most cases, you will be dealing with two distinct elements of law: the surreptitious recording of pictures and the surreptitious recording of voices. Different laws, rules, and regulations govern the two. A distinction is made, generally, between what we regard as eavesdropping and what is sometimes called eyedropping.

Using graphics

The most recent advances in broadcast technology have gone a long way toward making the life and work of the television investigative reporter and producer easier. Complicated stories involving interlocking directorates or a difficult-to-follow chain of evidence are made easier to produce and understand with the use of electronic graphics. Even the smallest station has electronic graphic capabilities, and reporters and producers should learn how to use them.

With today's technology, graphics can be animated, and charts can be made to flow on command. One of the most difficult stories to tell on television involves the tracing of money through a system of blinds or laundering scams. No amount of caught-in-the-act video will make this kind of story easier to understand. This is a story requiring graphics.

Today's broadcast technology allows multiple images to be stored and brought to the screen. The images can be frozen, miniaturized, moved around on the screen, and blown up full-screen. Creative producers have told complex tales about money-laundering schemes by placing a number of small photographs at the corners of the screen, each photo representing one of the players in the conspiracy. As the reporter's voice details the movement of money from one to another, a miniaturized stack of money snakes across the screen from one person to the next.

The surest way to tell whether your investigation requires graphic support is if you have to reach for a pencil and paper and draw a picture in order to make your editor understand the complexities of your story.

Confronting the principal

No chapter on TV investigative reporting would be complete without a discussion of how TV reporters confront the principals of their investigations. It is tough even for print reporters to go face-to-face with the subjects of their stories. Often the print reporter uses the telephone to conclude this sensitive and important part of the probe. Although telephones may sometimes be enough for the TV reporter, every effort must be made to get the principal to respond to the allegations on camera. If it is tough for print reporters to get on-the-record responses in the quiet of a paper-and-pencil interview, imagine the difficulty for the TV reporter who must attempt the same thing while a full crew sets up lights and the camera lens focuses on the principal's unhappy brow.

In the past, TV has used a run-and-gun style of confronting principals. It has also been called ambush journalism. We've all seen it: The principal steps from a car, and the reporter pounces upon him, thrusting a huge microphone into his face. "How do you respond to our charges?" shouts the reporter, and the principal ducks off, pulling his coat over his head. It used to be great TV.

When TV investigative reporters began to be criticized more roundly for their reporting style than the subject was for a wrongdoing, it was time for television to change, and it did to a degree. No longer is it customary for TV reporters to barge into offices with cameras whirring and lights blazing, demanding to hear the truth. The techniques have grown more civilized only in part because TV has grown more civilized. The techniques are out of favor now because they began to get in the way of the stories.

Many subjects of investigations have simply learned to avoid the cameras. And though it is proper to respect those wishes to a certain extent, it is also incumbent upon the reporter to provide that principal with an opportunity to respond to the allegations. If the reporter is unable to get ahold of the principal, or if the principal continues to refuse comment, that must be documented. The audience must be convinced that the reporter used every effort to give the principal the opportunity for rebuttal.

In most cases the reporter's efforts to reach the principal, like other parts of the investigation, should be documented by videotaping the undertaking. If the reporter has tried several times by phone to reach the principal, the videotape should clearly demonstrate that. If the reporter has gone to the principal's home, that too should be videotaped. Sometimes, while such attempts are being documented, the principal has a change of heart, and the photographer captures whatever happens next.

Of course, if the principal wishes to respond and rebut, the interview is conducted in the customary fashion.

Conclusion

Television reporters have long been considered a lower form of life by their print brothers and sisters. Some of the animosity is earned, but most is petty. Print reporters who have ventured into television will readily admit that they were ill prepared to face the additional obstacles and burdens that television places on the investigative reporter. What the print reporter may do with a phone call, the TV reporter must do with a full crew of technicians, lights, cameras, and sound. Although a print reporter can make that quick call to the governor's office for a comment, the TV reporter must go to the state capital, schedule interview time, ship the equipment and crew, and commit the governor to tape. And though print reporters become anonymous and blend into the crowd, the TV reporter stands out like a billboard.

Some print reporters who have tried to make the transition have failed under the weight of the additional demands. But it is the ability to see and hear stories as they will unfold, as difficult as the process may be, that makes for some of the best journalism in the United States. The additional burdens are in many ways blessings. The trick is to see the additional work, obstacles, and techniques as opportunities to tell a story more vividly, with flesh-and-blood players and with the capacity to portray a wrong on the screen as it is described. The television camera is simply another tool the committed journalist uses to document facts that others would keep out of public sight.

Investigative Examples

EXAMPLE 1

Public official
profits from rezoning

The *Miami Herald*'s stories about Dade County manager Sergio Pereira, printed on January 27 and February 11, 1988 and reprinted here with permission, illuminate the apparent ease with which holders of public office in this country can make money on the buying, selling, and rezoning of land within their jurisdiction.

The *Herald* story is distinguished by its calm and measured tone, which, perhaps inadvertently, causes the various intemperate comments of the principals to stand out in sharp relief from the rest of the story. The story's calm tone also makes it easier for readers to follow the complex chronology of the deal. Such reader effort is aided by the illustrated chronology of events on page 12A of the January 27 issue (see Fig. A.1a).

A.1a. The *Miami Herald* January 27, 1988, story about Dade County manager Sergio Pereira.

181

Pereira failed to disclose land deal

PEREIRA/from 1A

secret land transaction were obtained by The Herald.

They show that Pereira's interest in the transaction was held in trust on his behalf by Camilo Padreda, a developer who is one of his closest friends and the godfather of his oldest daughter. Padreda is also an officer of a corporation that runs a county-owned gun range. Pereira supervises that contract.

When first questioned, Pereira denied ever having been in business with Padreda.

'A little insulting'

"I find that a little insulting, to be honest with you," Pereira said. "My reaction is if I had a business relationship with any of these folks, somebody's been gypping me, because I'm not getting nothing."

Later, when shown copies of the documents, Pereira stared at them for about 20 seconds. He then confirmed his role in the land transaction, but said he remembered few details.

Pereira's attorney later said Padreda, who had paid a down payment for the land, held Pereira's 25 percent interest for him.

Pereira joined a group of investors who agreed in early 1985 to buy the land from Lopez-Castro. Pereira was an assistant county manager then.

The investor group found a potential buyer who wanted to build a shopping center. The group filed for rezoning with Dade County in February 1985. Pereira left the county to become Miami city manager that March. The rezoning was formally approved by the Metro-Dade Commission in June 1985.

A sworn disclosure form filed by the attorney who handled the zoning case failed to reveal the existence of the investor group that stood to profit from the rezoning. It failed to list the names of Pereira and other investors. The form listed only the Panamanian corporation as having a financial interest in the transaction.

Pereira and his fellow investors never took title to the land. Instead, the group purchased what Pereira described as an "option" to the property. Acting through a trust, they waited until the land was rezoned, then bought the land from Lopez-Castro and simultaneously sold it to the shopping-center developer, who paid them a large profit.

That procedure meant their names never appeared in the public record.

Interviews and documents gathered over the past month reveal many details of the Pereira land transaction.

The 4½ acres, on the northwest corner of West Flagler Street and 114th Avenue, had been vacant for decades when two Miami families bought it together in the 1970s. One investor was Clyde Mabry, an aging millionaire who has since left Miami and lives most of the year in Macon, Ga.

Mabry and his fellow investors got the land rezoned for residences, but never built any. In 1981, they were approached by Lopez-Castro, a lawyer with an office at 1640 Coral Way.

Mabry said it was clear Lopez-Castro was acting on behalf of others.

"It was a Panama outfit," Mabry said. "I think they covered their tracks pretty good."

The two families agreed to sell for $500,000, taking back an eight-year, $375,000 mortgage.

Later that year, public records show that Lopez-Castro transferred the property to a Panamanian company that he controlled called Highland Park Development Corp.

Federal authorities do not know if Lopez-Castro used drug money to buy the land.

A federal investigation later showed that he was receiving wire transfers of thousands of dollars in drug profits from Panama for investment in Dade County at around the time the purchase occurred.

Lopez-Castro went to the county building in 1982 seeking business zoning on the land. The two county departments that review

Study: Aspirin cuts risk of a first heart attack

STUDY/from 1A

attack.

The finding has broad implications because an estimated 1.5 million Americans suffer first heart attacks each year and a third of them die as a result.

In the 57-month study, whose participants were all male physicians, 104 of the 11,034 who took aspirin had heart attacks, compared with 189 heart attacks in the 11,037 who took only a sugar pill, or placebo. Statistically, the numbers mean that ordinary aspirin reduced the heart attack risk for healthy individuals by as much as 47 percent.

Previous studies have shown that daily aspirin use by heart attack victims could reduce the number of second heart attacks. But the new study is the first to show that aspirin can reduce the risk of first heart attacks.

Despite that finding, however, physicians were not ready to recommend that everyone take aspirin, because it has many side effects.

For one thing, the incidence of stroke was about 15 percent higher in the aspirin group, with 80 strokes, compared with 70 in the placebo group.

But the increase in strokes was so small that "it may be only by chance," said cardiologist George B. Hutchison of Harvard Medical School.

Conditions that would bar the use of aspirin include history of liver disease, peptic ulcer, gastrointestinal or other bleeding problems and a history of certain types of stroke.

Further, there is virtually no evidence that aspirin would confer a similar protection to women, although "there is no reason to believe women will respond differently," said Hutchison. Women were not included because their risk of heart attack is only about 25 percent of men's risk.

zoning issues fought it.

"Commercial use of this property would be detrimental," said the Planning Department.

"Unacceptable," echoed the Building and Zoning Department.

Lopez-Castro was turned down by a 3-0 vote of the County Commission.

He held onto the land through the first half of 1983. By then, Lopez-Castro had been indicted by the U.S. attorney's office for laundering drug money from smuggler Jose Antonio Fernandez.

A detailed account of the indictment appeared on the front page of The Herald on Dec. 13, 1984.

Days later, a longtime friend of Sergio Pereira's, real-estate broker Michael Vazquez, learned that Lopez-Castro, free on bond, had some land to sell.

Vazquez said in a recent interview that he brought together the group of potential investors, including Camilo Padreda, who set up a cash down payment. He could not recall the amount.

Vazquez offered sketchy details of the transaction and promised to search for documents. He later failed to return a dozen telephone calls and one telegram seeking elaboration.

The group sealed its deal with Lopez-Castro on Jan. 4, 1985. One of the investors — Bergigoo Arnau, listed on documents as a "foreigner" — signed the contract as trustee for purchase of the land. He agreed to pay $925,000.

He also signed a document, called a declaration of trust, stating that he was really acting on behalf of himself and nine others: Padreda, Michael Vazquez, Michael Vazquez Jr., Rose B. Vazquez, Jose E. Caro, Arnaldo Iglesias, Osvaldo Iglesias, Ileana Iglesias and Enrique Trans.

The declaration of trust shows that most of the nine were minor investors, with Padreda controlling 20 percent of the land trust.

Vazquez said Padreda realized soon after the deal was signed that he could not afford a 50 percent interest.

Vazquez gave this reason: There was some chance the investors would not succeed in finding a new buyer for the land before they were required under their contract to buy it from Lopez-Castro. In theory, Vazquez said, Padreda could have been forced to come up with half the purchase price out of his pocket — or the group could have lost its deposit.

So Padreda signed a new document two days later, an addendum to the declaration of trust.

It said: "Camilo Padreda hereby declares that he holds the interest for the benefit of Sergio Pereira in the amount of 35 percent and the remainder 25 percent will be for the benefit of Camilo Padreda himself."

Risk rewarded

Pereira's lawyer, Hank Adorno, said Pereira never made any down payment. But he said Pereira was taking the risk that he might have to come up with a quarter of the purchase price. The profits Pereira ultimately received were his reward for that risk, Adorno said.

The investor group soon found a potential buyer, Emilio Cruz, who wanted to build a shopping center called Flagler Square.

Padreda asked a zoning lawyer, Alberto Cardenas, to represent the investor group in seeking to get the land rezoned. Cardenas said in a recent interview that he never knew Pereira was part of the investor group.

He applied on Feb. 7, 1985, for the sales business zoning that county commissioners had refused to grant on the property three years earlier.

Cardenas filled out the disclosure form required by county rules to reveal everybody who stood to benefit from the rezoning.

The document did not include the names of Padreda, Pereira or any of the other investors who would profit. The document listed only the Panamanian corporation.

Cardenas said this week he would retrieve his file from a warehouse to try to figure out why he omitted their names, but that will take several days.

"That's certainly a valid question," Cardenas said.

Pereira was an assistant county

from Pereira, already running the city but still a well-known and highly regarded figure at county hall.

"That sort of thing never happens," said Jerry Proctor, head of zoning control. "If it had, I would remember it like a bell."

Pereira said he never contacted anyone in the Building and Zoning Department or on the County Commission about the zoning case.

The Planning Department, as it had three years earlier, recommended against the business zoning.

When the two departments come to the County Commission divided over a zoning issue, the commission frequently votes for whatever department favors the developer. That happened in this case, after Commissioner Clara Oesterle emphasized that the Building Department recommended approval of business zoning.

The vote was 7-0 in favor of the developer, with Mayor Steve Clark and Commissioner Harvey Ruvin absent.

Several commissioners who voted for the business zoning say they don't remember the case, but were not lobbied by Pereira or his friends.

"I would definitely remember that," said Commissioner Beverly Phillips.

The zoning was approved on June 20, 1985. The Pereira group closed the deal a month later, simultaneously buying the property from the Panamanian corporation for $925,000 and selling it to developer Cruz at a higher, undisclosed price without taking title.

Each member of the Pereira group received a share of the profits by check.

Pereira refuses to discuss how much he got.

"That's none of your business," Pereira said. "I got to draw the line with you guys somewhere."

The only available figure on the profits from the land transaction comes from developer Padreda, the most forthcoming of all participants in the land transaction. He owned the same interest in the transaction as Pereira, 35 percent.

'A substantial amount'

Padreda said he checked his income-tax return Monday evening. He could not remember the precise profit Tuesday, but said it was definitely between $70,000 and $75,000.

"It was a substantial amount of money," Padreda said.

Cruz, the shopping-center developer, failed to return repeated telephone calls seeking details of his role in the transaction. A Cruz associate, Jose Bravo, said he was unfamiliar with the deal.

Lopez-Castro, the drug lawyer,

No interference

Those high-level officials say they do not remember much about the zoning case now. But they are certain of one thing: There was never political interference from the county manager's office or

manager at the time the zoning application was filed, though he was not in charge of zoning. He left at the end of March to become city manager of Miami for about eight months.

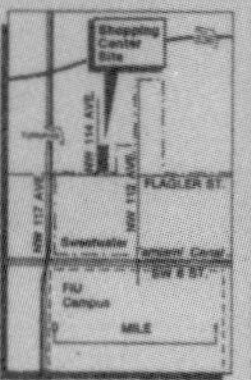

Documents show that two level county staff members continued to fight business zoning on the property, just as they had in 1982.

Zoning reviewer Frank Richmond reviewed the property on June 4, 1985, filling out a standard work sheet.

Compatibility with surrounding land uses: "Incompatible."

Use of site: "Inadequate."

Location of buildings: "Inadequate."

Landscaping: "Inadequate."

Richmond wrote a recommendation. It is now missing from county files, though it apparently urged that the business zoning be turned down.

High-level officials of the building department apparently overruled his recommendation on June 13, reversing the department's stance of three years earlier.

could not be reached for comment on his role, either.

He was convicted in the Sunglass State Bank case on Oct. 7, 1985, less than three months after the property deal was completed. He got 27 years.

He was let out on bond to take care of personal business. He

A.1a. *(continued)*

The sidebars help as well, especially the piece in the February 11 issue headed PRIVATELY, HE HAD A HEART: PUBLIC RARELY SAW HUMANIST SIDE OF PEREIRA (see Fig. A.1b). By showing Pereira's other side, this sidebar allows the *Herald* to appear more evenhanded than it would if it ran only negative stories concerning him. This sidebar and the accompanying boxes also answer several other often-repeated criticisms of investigative stories: that they tend to be more about public records and dry facts than about people; that they don't show the main figure in the story as a colorful human being, which the person often is; and that they seem to indicate, by the prominence they give the transgression of the main actor in the story, that the person has never done anything else at all. This story, we believe, successfully avoids all those pitfalls.

Reprinting Pereira's letter of resignation in full also avoids another charge thrown at some investigative stories: that they extract, and reprint out of context, the subject's rebuttal, while leaving the reporter and editor free to write what they want.

Pereira's initial defenses against the *Herald*'s accusations in the January 27 story are both spirited and dismissive. Pereira first says he finds "insulting" the charge that he is in business with any of the people the *Herald* says he has been dealing with. Then, after being shown the incriminating documents, he caves in. This demonstrates how far a reporter can get with interviewing, especially with interviewing accompanied by documents. It also shows how deeply one should believe even the most indignant denials.

Pereira goes on to say he simply "forgot" to disclose his financial interest in the 1985 land sale, as required by Florida ethics laws. He also argues that the fact that he reported the gains on his income tax return shows he didn't mean to hide them from the public. In spite of this bold bluster, when shortly thereafter the *Herald* asks him about a sale of two houses that he didn't report on his 1985 income tax form, he resigns before the paper even publishes the story. (The story about his resignation and the story about his failure to report the sale of the houses both appear in the February 11 issue of the paper.) "He was so weakened by the first story that he was like a piece of fruit ready to fall off the tree," said one observer.

Some might criticize this story, as investigative stories are often criticized, because it doesn't show the quid pro quo. That is, it shows what the others in the land-buying group gave Pereira but never shows exactly what he gave them (although his presumed influence in the zoning procedure might certainly appear valuable to the other members). It also could be criticized, as other investigative stories have been, because all Pereira was doing was trying to get rich, as many other red-blooded Americans are.

FINAL EDITION

VARIABLE CLOUDINESS. HIGHS IN MID-70s. LOWS NEAR 60. DETAILS, 2A.

EASTERN SUES PILOTS TO DEFEND SALE OF SHUTTLE, 8C

COOL CRITIQUE: RATING THE DEEP-FREEZE DINNERS, 1E

TRAFFIC JAM: ACCIDENT TIES UP PALMETTO FOR 20 MILES, 1C

The Miami Herald

140 PAGES   THURSDAY, FEBRUARY 11, 1988   Contents Copyright 1988 The Miami Herald   25 CENTS

Dade manager Pereira resigns

Martinez proposes record budget

Reaction in Dade / 1C

By PAUL ANDERSON
Herald Capital Bureau

TALLAHASSEE — Gov. Bob Martinez proposed Wednesday a $20.3 billion state budget for 1988-89 stressing a leaner payroll, improved health care, school drug-use prevention, new roads and prisons, and protection of natural resources.

"We believe it's a good, balanced budget with major initiatives for major needs — and without any general tax increase," Martinez said, previewing the sales pitch he'll use on taxpayers and legislators.

Critics of his priorities responded quickly.

"He's got some worthy new things in there," said Senate President John Vogt, "but with the state growing at the rate we've been growing, it's definitely going to be tough to meet all the needs in the programs already in place."

What could be the largest-ever state spending plan — to keep pace with a $1.2 billion, or 10.5 percent, from this year — is stoked by nearly $1.2 billion from the sixth penny of sales tax that took effect Feb. 1. $192 million from increased property taxes for schools, and a bundle of fee increases.

Martinez wants to charge higher tuition at community colleges and universities; hike the freshwater fishing license fee and start charging for saltwater fishing; increase fees for septic tank permits, health clinic screenings and $50 to existing drunk driving fines.

Each higher fee would be linked to an improvement in a related service. For example, the saltwater fishing license — expected to net $24.4 million — would hire 150 new Marine Patrol officers and otherwise "enhance marine resources." The extra fine on drunk drivers — producing an estimated $2.5 million — would expand crime labs.

Martinez, elected in 1986 on a pledge to cut waste, insisted that he'd use both the new money and recurring resources wisely.

Please turn to BUDGET / 26A

County leader quits with swipe at news media

By CELIA W. DUGGER
Herald Staff Writer

A composed and somber Sergio Pereira announced his resignation Wednesday night, signaling the end of his tempestuous two years as Dade County manager. He said he will stay on until Feb. 20 to ensure a smooth transition.

His decision to leave came as The Miami Herald prepared to publish a story that said he did not report his sale of two houses in Hialeah on his 1985 income tax return.

Pereira's support from his bosses on the Metro Commission had eroded in the last two weeks after revelations in The Herald that he did not disclose his role in an unrelated West Dade land transaction that brought him $137,978 with no investment on his part.

After a day of speculation that he would quit, Pereira went live before television cameras at 11 p.m. to announce his resignation.

"It is clear that the unrelenting and unethical actions of some members of the media have contributed to a serious and unhealthy situation for our community and county government," said Pereira, 43.

"I am proud of my record as

Please turn to RESIGN / 22A

INSIDE

IF PEREIRA'S flaws seemed bigger than life, so did his heart / 22A.

THE MANAGER'S accomplishments and problems / 22A.

DEWEY KNIGHT is likely to be named acting county manager today / 1C.

county manager and I believe I have accomplished a great deal," he said.

The Dade state attorney's office is investigating Pereira's part in the West Dade deal, as well as his use of county helicopters. And his role in the controversial Salt Cane has not yet been resolved. A grand jury indicted him in October for buying allegedly stolen nails from a Miami duplex, but the charges were dropped on a technicality.

Wednesday evening, two dozen of Pereira's friends and co-workers from Metro-Dade huddled with him in the Coconut Grove

Please turn to BUDGET / 26A   Sergio Pereira leaves lawyer's office after announcing his resignation.
JON KRAL / Miami Herald Staff

Pereira's tax return omitted house sales

By LISA GETTER
And JUSTIN GILLIS
Herald Staff Writers

Dade County Manager Sergio Pereira did not report on his 1985 income tax return the sale of two houses he built in a controversial Hialeah development.

Pereira resigned Wednesday night, a day after Miami Herald reporters first questioned him about the Hialeah land transaction. He refused to comment on the sale of the houses.

Earlier Wednesday, Pereira's attorney, Hank Adorno, said the sales were not reported to the Internal Revenue Service because Pereira's accountant determined there was no profit.

Adorno said Pereira and his former wife actually put a small amount of money in the 1985

transactions, but he would not release records documenting any loss.

A detailed review of public records at the county courthouse and Hialeah City Hall indicates that the Pereiras sold the houses for $48,350 more than the listed price of the land and the construction costs estimated on the building permits. There is nothing in the public records to show what, if any, other costs Pereira might have had.

James Richardson, public affairs specialist for the IRS, said a taxpayer who developed property and sold it would be obligated to report the transaction even if there was no profit.

The individuals would still

Please turn to PEREIRA / 23A

Army ban on homosexuals unconstitutional, court says

SAN FRANCISCO — (AP) — The Army's ban on homosexuals was ruled unconstitutional Wednesday by a federal appeals court that said homosexuals are entitled to the same protection against discrimination as racial minorities.

The discrimination faced by homosexuals is not merely a prejudice. is plainly no less pernicious or intense than the discrimination faced by other groups" afforded

protection from discrimination, said the Ninth U.S. Circuit Court of Appeals.

The ruling was the first by a federal appeals court to grant strict constitutional protection to homosexuals and to prohibit a branch of the armed services from excluding people on the basis of sexual orientation.

It affects all military branches because

Please turn to ARMY / 10A

Pilot Floyd Carlton testifies Wednesday with head covered by black hood.
Associated Press

Bank card snafu linked to slime eel

SAN FRANCISCO — (UPI) — The ugly hagfish, also known as the slime eel, has been accused of causing jumbled codes on automatic teller machine cards.

John McCosker, director of the Steinhart Aquarium and a leading ichthyologist, said he discovered that the foot-long hagfish was the probable culprit after a bank official asked him to join an investigation of "eel skin" handbags and wallets.

McCosker said this week that the hagfish hide is sold as eel skin and it may be demagnetizing and scrambling the electronic codes on ATM and credit cards.

The eel skin wallet problem has become so serious that such banking giants as Bank of America, Wells Fargo and Great Western are warning card holders.

McCosker suspects the trouble is caused by a metallic residue left over from the tanning process.

Or, he said, the problem might be from the "colloidal goo that comes out of the slime glands of those awful things."

Franchising terror

Drug-dealing 'Miami Boys' hit South

By FRED GRIMM
Herald Staff Writer

ATLANTA — In the meanest housing projects, in the poorest, most dangerous neighborhoods of the South, the very mention of "Miami Boys" evokes a peculiar sort of recognition, as if it were a ghetto version of a familiar business trade name.

But the Miami Boys owe their rapidly growing reputation to three factors: high-quality, inexpensive drugs; a business arsenal of automatic weapons; and a propensity for violence new to the streets of Atlanta, Charleston, Savannah, Augusta.

"It's like opening a franchise," said John Turner, an Atlanta assistant district attorney. "They come into a housing project calling themselves Miami Boys, people

know what it means."

Police across the South say groups of young black men from South Florida, calling themselves Miami Boys, have pushed into public housing projects, taken over the illegal drug trade by underselling local cocaine dealers and intimidated competitors with automatic weapons.

They sport Miami T-shirts and jackets to underscore their origins. One coke dealer was arrested last month with M-1-A-M-I spelled out in diamonds on his gold-capped teeth.

The Florida gangs are thought to have only a minimal association with one another, sharing a name, perhaps a common

Please turn to ATLANTA / 15A

Ex-aide: Noriega OKd contras' use of bases

By ANDRES OPPENHEIMER
Herald Staff Writer

WASHINGTON — Panamanian military leader Gen. Manuel Antonio Noriega let U.S.-backed Nicaraguan rebels use two army bases in his country for training three years ago, a former Noriega aide told a Senate subcommittee Wednesday.

The testimony by Jose Blandon, fired by Noriega last month as Panama's consul general in New York, prompted charges by some legislators that the Reagan administration turned a blind eye to

widespread reports of Noriega's involvement in drug trafficking because the Panamanian leader was helping the contras.

In other testimony before the subcommittee Wednesday, Panamanian pilot Floyd Carlton, his features hidden by a black hood, said Noriega contracted in 1982 with Colombia's Medellin cocaine cartel to protect cocaine shipments flown into Panama en route to the United States. Noriega was indicted last week

Please turn to PANAMA / 4A

Jose Blandon, Says Noriega, met aboard yacht

County manager Pereira resigns, criticizes media

RESIGN / from 1A

offices of his attorney Hank Adorno.

First to arrive was a tight-knit group of secretaries who have worked for the manager since he first took office in January 1986. The women, who looked stricken, crowded into the elevator. One of them, Cirie Campos, sobbed.

Deputy County Manager Dewey Knight, whom Pereira recommended to commissioners as interim manager, as well as several of Pereira's closest assistants, joined him later.

The commissioners were at the Sheraton Bal Harbour for a dinner in honor of Commissioner Sherman Winn. They watched a stage show that featured men in skintight bikinis and a live alligator, but they were thinking about the Pereira controversy.

"I think he's been a good manager," said Metro Mayor Steve Clark. "No one has ever knocked his ability to manage. Other things may have happened of a personal nature. I have no knowledge of that."

Commissioner Clara Oesterle, who had asked Pereira to step aside while the investigations involving him were completed, said she was unhappy that Pereira had not provided the commission with the full real estate records disclosure it requested.

"I was very disappointed to see the things he turned in to us were not complete. In fact, it was an abortion," she said.

Commissioner Barbara Carey said she was sad his career with Metro had to end this way.

"It's a disappointment for any ethnic group to have someone rise to that level, and then have to go out this way," she said. "His continuing to be there was polarizing the community along ethnic lines."

Pereira, the first Cuban-born county manager, has depicted the critical news coverage of his tenure as ethnically motivated. Spanish-language radio stations had continually defended him.

> Throughout the evening and night, television and radio stations interrupted their programming to announce the inevitability of Sergio Pereira's resignation.

Herald reporters first questioned Pereira and Adorno about the Hialeah land deal Tuesday, and submitted questions in writing Wednesday morning. Adorno sent a response to the newspaper at noon Wednesday and sent copies to the commission.

By late afternoon, rumors swept through the Metro administration building that Pereira would resign. Throughout the evening and night, television and radio stations interrupted their programming to announce the inevitability of Pereira's resignation. Each cut-in was brief and followed by regular programming — except on Spanish-language WQBA-AM.

WQBA, which has vigorously defended the county manager in recent weeks, aired a special call-in program for listeners to express their outrage. Calls were taken by news director Tomas Regalado, who said Miami was "very upset" by Pereira's departure.

The Metro Commission is expected to meet soon to designate an interim manager. Several commissioners said they hope Deputy County Manager Knight will step in as he has in the past when other managers departed.

Metro Commissioner Jorge Valdes, who has been one of Pereira's staunchest defenders, said he wants the manager's successor to be recruited from within Dade County.

"I'm not going to vote for any county manager that would come from outside," he said.

But Oesterle said she would probably favor a nationwide search, though she would want to find out first the wishes of the other commissioners.

"We have some very good assistant county managers. If one of them can do the work and do it well, we should look to them," she said.

The commissioners' questions about Pereira's finances will probably go unanswered. They will not be provided with more records they requested from Pereira, said Metro spokesman Bill Johnson.

Said Johnson: "Those were records he said he would turn over to keep a job he no longer wants."

Herald staff writers Christine Evans, Lourdes Fernandez, Dave Von Drehle and Luis Feldstein Soto also contributed to this report.

Privately, he had a heart

Public rarely saw humanist side of Pereira

By JUSTIN GILLIS
Herald Staff Writer

The man and his coterie of loyal aides always said he was misunderstood.

Publicly, Sergio Pereira was a back-slapping, cigar-chomping, glad-handing boss who seemed to run Dade County government as if it were his kingdom, ordering expensive furniture, hopping around in county helicopters, dressing in heavy jewelry and expensive Italian suits.

El caudillo, one of his critics called him. The big man.

Privately, he was a humanist. If his flaws always seemed bigger than life, so did his heart.

"I am not going to appoint someone because he is or is not a green, gay Filipino," Pereira once said, explaining his refusal to promote Hispanics as rapidly as some critics wanted. "I'm hung up on talent. I'm not hung up on color or nationality. I am sorry, but I'll just die that way."

It was a side of him that county commissioners, reporters and his closest aides noticed often, one the public almost never saw. He came across publicly as arrogant. But he was really a friendly man with a ready laugh, a quick wit and a sense that the world was a little mad.

While he labored unnoticed over county budgets, fretted over public housing, struggled to reform a bloated transit agency with the painful step of chopping 200 jobs, he managed to land in a series of bizarre controversies — unrelated to job performance — that ultimately cost him his career.

When he joined the county, he submitted a resume that can charitably be described as misleading. He was ultimately caught.

When he became county manager, he ordered a custom marble desk and conference table that set the taxpayers back $10,000. He took flying lessons in county helicopters at public expense. He bought fine suits of uncertain origin from a dubious retailer.

He was finally undone by the disclosure that he was wheeling and dealing in real estate while holding public office.

Pereira plowed away at his job, trying hard not to take the controversies seriously.

In many ways he was a perfect leader for a troubled town. He was the first Cuban-born manager of the city of Miami, the first Cuban-born manager of Dade County. He was a focus of pride for many Hispanics. He dealt easily with blacks and with the white male power structure of downtown Miami.

Miami Commissioner Miller Dawkins once said Pereira would be a perfect city manager because "he's Cuban, he acts black and he looks white."

He survived in the topsy-turvy world of Miami city politics, and he thrived as manager of Metropolitan Dade County. He gradually converted the 5-4 majority that chose him county manager in late 1985 into unanimous support.

Pereira thrived in part with the help of Charles Scurr, a loyal, precise, urbane executive assistant who counseled the manager often on how to avoid controversy and do the right thing. Despite such advice, Pereira's personal life — Scurr once called it a "mess" — ultimately caught up with him.

Pereira leaves a dual legacy, warm-hearted patriarch to those who knew him and insufferable dandy to those who didn't.

Under his silk shirts, Pereira sometimes wore a gold chain with two charms. Dangling side by side from his neck were a Playboy bunny and the Virgin of Guadalupe.

PEREIRA'S ACCOMPLISHMENTS

Last week, Sergio Pereira distributed to the media a list of what he considered his major accomplishments as Dade County manager, including:

REORGANIZING Little HUD, the county department that oversees public housing projects.

RESTRUCTURING the transportation department to provide more efficient service to the public.

SAVING more than $4 million with personnel cuts in 1986.

INTRODUCING countywide drug testing and counseling for employees.

COORDINATING Pope John Paul II's visit to Dade County last September.

ADDING more than 216 buses to the county fleet.

NEGOTIATING a 15-year contract for the operation of the Solid Waste Resources Recovery Plant.

RESTRUCTURING the county's long-term bond debt to take advantage of lower interest rates.

HELPING Dade County become the first local government in the United States to raise $1 million for the United Way.

PEREIRA'S PROBLEMS

FEBRUARY 1985 — While applying for Miami city manager's job, Pereira's academic credentials are questioned by Korn/Ferry, a search firm hired to recommend candidates. Korn/Ferry's managing vice president, Norman Roberts, said Pereira told him he received an undergraduate degree from Montclair State College in New Jersey in 1967 and a master's degree from the University of Utah in 1969. The check revealed he didn't graduate from either school. The city hires him anyway.

JANUARY 1986 — County commissioners are surprised to learn that Pereira had spent $31,513 on new office furniture. He bought a $9,400 aqua-green marble desk and two tables, a $9,950 custom-built bleached oak credenza and an $6,900 custom-built, cream-colored leather sofa.

SEPTEMBER 1987 — The Dade County state attorney's office investigates Pereira for learning to fly Metro-Dade Police helicopters at public expense. During the first six months of the year, he logged 29.4 hours in the air. The investigation is still pending.

OCTOBER 1987 — The Dade County grand jury indicts Pereira for buying stolen designer suits from a cut-rate haberdasher who peddled clothing from a rented Miami duplex. He is charged with three third-degree felonies for buying seven stolen suits at the duplex, where suits worth up to $900 went for as little as $150 without tax. Pereira said he didn't know the suits were hot. The Metro Commission suspends him with pay, but reinstates him a month later when Dade Circuit Judge David Gersten dismisses the indictment on a technicality.

JANUARY 1988 — A Miami Herald story reveals that Pereira failed to report a $127,878 profit in a secret land deal in 1985. Pereira was one of a group of investors who acquired a contract to purchase a 4½-acre parcel in West Dade from a Miami lawyer who is now a federal fugitive convicted of laundering drug money through land deals. Pereira claimed the profit on his income tax return, but did not include it on his financial disclosure form for the county. The Metro Commission later gives him a vote of confidence.

THE LETTER OF RESIGNATION

This is the text of the letter County Manager Pereira sent to Metro commissioners Wednesday night. At a press conference, he read virtually the same statement.

Dear Mayor and Commissioners:

It is with the deepest regret that I tender to you my resignation as your county manager effective Feb. 29, 1988.

I have dedicated the last 15 years of my life to serving the people of our great community. Public service has been more than a job for me, it has been my life. I have served to the best of my ability and with distinction and integrity. I am proud of my record as county manager, and with your support we have achieved a great many accomplishments.

I have consulted with the leaders of our Hispanic, black and Anglo communities as well as with my friends, colleagues, supporters and especially with my family. It is clear that the unrelentless and unethical actions of some members of the media have contributed to a serious and unhealthy situation for our community and county government. I have always had the best interests of our community at heart. I now sincerely believe that it is in the best interest of the community for me to step down as county manager.

I am recommending that Deputy County Manager Dewey Knight be designated as interim manager. If you concur, I will immediately begin the transition process with Mr. Knight and anticipate that very shortly we will be able to effectuate a smooth and complete transfer. I want to reassure our citizens that all county services will continue to be provided with the same level of excellence and commitment that has been our trademark. I personally plan to spend some time with my family, put this experience in perspective, and evaluate the opportunities before me.

I want to thank you, Mr. Mayor, and each member of the commission for your continuing friendship, support and counsel. I want to thank the many hard-working and dedicated professional men and women of Dade County who make our government work so well. I also want to thank my staff and my many friends, colleagues and supporters in the community, for without them, none of our achievements would have been possible. Finally, and above all, I want to thank my family.

Sincerely,
Sergio Pereira

M UST HAVES . . .
from our Precious
Jewels Collection.

Neiman-Marcus has gathered a special collection of Precious Jewels from all 22 N-M stores and we are presenting them as a special treat to you. This remarkable selection is priced from 500.00 to 25,000.00. With each collection purchase you will receive double InCircle' points (as well as special financial arrangements for items over 2,000.00). Exclusively at Neiman-Marcus Bal Harbour and Ft. Lauderdale stores. Precious Jewels.

Neiman-Marcus

In addition to the Neiman-Marcus charge card, we welcome the American Express® Card.

Do you wear one of these patches?

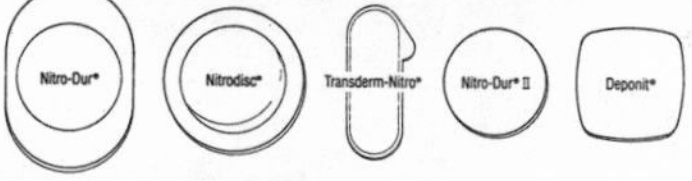
Nitro-Dur®
Nitrodisc®
Transderm-Nitro®
Nitro-Dur® II
Deponit®

Nitroglycerin patch wearers across the country are participating in a survey on what they like and don't like about patches.

We'd like you to participate.

To get your survey questionnaire, simply fill out and return the coupon below or call **1-800-338-5252.**

Yes, I would like to participate in the survey.

Name ____________________

Address ____________________

City ____________ State ______ Zip ______

Mail coupon to: **Protocol Studies, Inc.**
11 East 26th Street
New York, NY 10010
6th floor

RK NT-1105 a

Nitro-Dur is a registered trademark of Key Pharmaceuticals; Nitrodisc, of Searle Pharmaceuticals; Transderm-Nitro, of CIBA Pharmaceutical Company; Deponit, of Wyeth Laboratories.

A.1b. *(continued)*

Pereira didn't report sale to IRS

Transaction lost money, attorney says

PEREIRA / from 1A

need to show that on their return,"
Richardson said.

"If there is a problem, it's a problem the Internal Revenue Service can raise with us, not The Miami Herald," Adorno said. "It's none of your business. It's a private matter."

Pereira's 1985 tax return would normally be private, but he disclosed the entire return recently to quell a controversy over an unrelated 1985 land transaction, involving land in unincorporated Dade County near Sweetwater.

In that transaction, Pereira earned $127,978 — more than his public salary that year — with no investment of money on his part. Pereira did not list that transaction, as required by law, on a state financial disclosure form filled out 10 weeks after he reported the profits on his tax return.

Pereira said the fact that he reported that land transaction on his tax return proved that he simply forgot it when filling out the public disclosure form.

Pereira reported his ownership of the Hialeah property, located in a subdivision called Mango Hill, on a 1984 state disclosure form. Deeds show that he and his wife, who held the property in their own names, sold the two houses the next year.

"He did what he was supposed to do, report it on his state ethics form," Adorno said.

Portions withheld

When Pereira first released his 1985 tax return last week, he withheld some portions, and it was not clear whether he had reported the Mango Hill property sale to the IRS.

Under continued pressure from county commissioners, Pereira this week released the withheld portions of his 1985 return and his entire return from 1986.

The Mango Hill transaction does not appear on either return.

"If for some reason the accountant was wrong, he'll report it and show whatever fee he had," Adorno said. "If the accountant is wrong, it's not Sergio's fault." The accountant, Felix Caceres, said he could not discuss Pereira's tax return without permission.

Mango Hill has been under investigation by the U.S. attorney's office since 1985, when it was the subject of a report in The Miami Herald entitled *Hialeah: Zoned for Profit.*

That report quoted two developers of Mango Hill who complained that public officials in Hialeah had pressured the developers into selling lots to them at low prices. At the time, those same officials were reviewing plans for the development at City Hall.

The developers said the public officials sought low lots for quick profits, gave some to their friends and developed others.

No charges

Philip Spiegelman, an official of Mango Hill's developer, Del-Form Inc., said at the time. "Everyone got greedy." No charges have been filed as a result of the Mango Hill investigation.

Adorno, Pereira's attorney, said Wednesday in a letter to The Herald that neither Pereira nor his wife "had anything to do with the zoning of the Mango Hill lots, nor did they request or receive any assistance from any public official with respect to the purchase, development and sale of these two lots."

Developer Spiegelman said he did not remember Pereira's purchase of the lots.

Spiegelman, who has been questioned extensively by the FBI on Mango Hill transactions, now heads his own Broward development firm. He declined extensive comment.

"Whatever is in the public record, God bless you," Spiegelman said.

Courthouse records indicate that Pereira and his former wife, Esther Perez Pereira, bought Lots 3 and 4 of Block 8 of Mango Hill on May 31, 1984, from Del-Form for $40,000.

In June 1984 contractors working for Pereira took out various construction permits on the two lots. The contractors estimated on building permits that they would construct identical three-bedroom, two-bath houses on the property for $30,000 apiece.

Contractors are required to give a written estimate of the cost of construction when they take out building permits. The law requires that the estimate be fairly accurate, since the fee to take out the permit is based on the estimated construction cost.

An architect and another developer who worked in that part of

Mango Hill said the estimate of $26,000 per house in construction costs sounded about right. "It's not an expensive market, but it's a good market," said architect Oscar J. Gonzalez. "Whatever you build there gets sold."

On July 23, 1984, the Pereiras took out a loan of $61,200 from Consolidated Bank in Hialeah, pledging the land as collateral. The loan was apparently intended, at least in part, to pay for construction of the houses.

It is not clear who built Pereira's houses.

Adorno, Pereira's attorney, said he believed Vicente Leal, who owned numerous parcels in Mango Hill and was a member of the city's planning and zoning board at the time, built the houses for Pereira.

Leal's name appears on architectural plans for the two houses. Leal is a leading figure in Hialeah land transactions. He has never publicly discussed his role in Mango Hill. His attorney, Frank Holden, did not return telephone calls.

The general contractor listed on plans filed at Hialeah City Hall for the Pereira houses was G&M Construction. The owner listed in state records for that firm, Mario E. Garcia, also did not return telephone calls.

City Hall records show that construction proceeded on the two houses — at 1148 and 1158 W. 40th Pl. — through the latter part of 1984. Construction was finally completed and the houses certified for occupancy on Dec. 17, 1984.

Pereira did not sell the houses until well into the next year.

The first house, at 1148 W. 40th Pl., was sold on Aug. 16, 1985, to Francisco T. Gonzalez and his wife, Estrella, for $68,400.

Estrella Gonzalez described Pereira as "the best person in the world."

"He behaved very well with us," she said. "He didn't trick us or anything."

The second house, at 1158 W. 40th Pl., was sold on Sept. 16, 1985, to Oscar Martinez and his

wife Guillermina for $69,000. They refused to comment.

The sale prices of the houses, as reported to public records, were in line with others in the neighborhood.

The public records indicate that Pereira and his wife paid $40,000 to buy the land. The estimates filed by the contractors put the cost to build the houses at about $52,000. That put the Pereiras' estimated costs reported in public records at $92,000. They sold the properties for $138,300. The difference is $46,300.

Adorno said the total costs exceeded the sale prices, but he refused to make public the documents that would prove a loss.

"Did you ever hear of cost overruns, architectural fees, professional fees, change orders?" Adorno said. "Write whatever you guys want, but you guys are buying a lawsuit. There's no way you guys are going to be right."

Herald staff writer Tina Mondal-so contributed to this report.

CHUCK FADELY / Miami Herald Staff
The houses, at 1148 and 1158 W. 40th Pl., were built in 1984 and sold in 1985.

But the facts of the story mitigate against any such criticisms: Pereira, unlike many other struggling would-be millionaires, invested nothing to earn himself $128,000. That immediately separates him from most other American investors who don't happen to hold public office.

Pereira failed to disclose land deal
County manager: 'Oversight' reason for not revealing transaction

By Justin Gillis
Herald Staff Writer

Dade County Manager Sergio Pereira failed to publicly disclose a 1985 land sale that earned him an estimated $70,000 with no investment of money on his part.

The sale of the 4½-acre parcel in West Dade came after Metro-Dade commissioners rezoned it to permit construction of a shopping center.

Pereira said his failure to disclose his financial interest, as required by Florida ethics laws, was "an oversight." He filed an amended financial disclosure form with county clerks and the Metro-Dade commission Tuesday evening, following inquiries by The Miami Herald.

He told commissioners in a memorandum: 'I simply forgot to list that source of income, for which I apologize.'

Pereira was an assistant Dade County manager at the time he got involved in the land transaction. He said he played no role in the rezoning that increased the value of the land.

Pereira was one of the group of investors who secretly acquired a contract to purchase the land in early 1985 from a Miami lawyer who is now a federal fugitive convicted of laun-

dering drug money through land deals.

"Jesus," Pereira said Tuesday. "I'm a passive investor in this thing. I had no idea who these people were."

Pereira's attorney said he paid nothing to acquire his 25 percent interest in the transaction.

Though Pereira refused to disclose his profit, one of his partners in the transaction said it would have been $70,000 to $75,000.

Pereira's fellow investors made arrangements to buy the land from a Panamanian corporation controlled by Miami lawyer Manuel Lopez-Castro. The investor group signed the first set of documents in the deal 4 days after Lopez-Castro was indicted by a federal grand jury on charges of using Panamanian corporations to launder drug money.

"I'm not trying to hide anything," Pereira said. "I reported the damn thing on my income tax."

Pereira said he forgot to put the land transaction on his financial disclosure form, which he said he filled out 13 months after the land was sold.

The Florida Ethics Commission investigates possible violations of financial disclosure laws when a formal complaint is made. Penalties range from public censure and fines to removal from office.

The stories in example 1 are reprinted with permission of *The Miami Herald*.

Documents revealing Pereira's role in the secret land transaction were obtained by The Herald.

They show that Pereira's interest in the transaction was held in trust on his behalf by Camilo Padreda, a developer who is one of his closest friends and the godfather of his oldest daughter. Padreda is also an officer of a corporation that runs a county-owned gun range. Pereira supervises that contract.

When first questioned, Pereira denied ever having been in business with Padreda.

'A little insulting'

"I find that a little insulting, to be honest with you," Pereira said. "My reaction is if I had a business relationship with any of these folks, somebody's been gypping me, because I'm not getting nothing."

Later, when shown copies of the documents, Pereira stared at them for about 20 seconds. He then confirmed his role in the land transaction, but said he remembered few details.

Pereira's attorney later said Padreda, who had paid a down payment for the land, held Pereira's 25 percent interest for him.

Pereira joined a group of investors who agreed in early 1985 to buy land from Lopez-Castro. Pereira was an assistant county manager then.

The investor group found a potential buyer who wanted to build a shopping center. The group filed for rezoning with Dade County in February 1985. Pereira left the county to become Miami city manager that March. The rezoning was formally approved by the Metro-Dade Commission in June 1985.

A sworn disclosure form filed by the attorney who handled the zoning case failed to reveal the existence of the investor group that stood to profit from the rezoning. It failed to list the names of Pereira and other investors. The form listed only the Panamanian corporation as having a financial interest in the transaction.

Pereira and his fellow investors never took title to the land.

Instead, the group purchased what Pereira described as an "option" on the property. Acting through a trust, they waited until the land was rezoned, then bought the land from Lopez-Castro and simultaneously sold it to the shopping-center developer, who paid them a large profit.

That procedure meant their names never appeared in the public record.

Interviews and documents gathered over the past month reveal many details of the Pereira land transaction:

The 4½ acres, on the northeast corner of West Flagler Street and 114th Avenue, had been vacant for decades when two Miami families bought it together in the 1970s. One investor was Clyde Mabry, an aging millionaire who has since left Miami and lives most of the year in Macon, Ga.

Mabry and his fellow investors got the land rezoned for residences, but never built any. In 1981, they were approached by Lopez-Castro, a lawyer with an office at 1840 Coral Way.

Mabry said it was clear Lopez-Castro was acting on behalf of others.

"It was a Panama outfit," Mabry said. "I think they covered their tracks pretty good."

The two families agreed to sell for $500,000, taking back an eight-year, $375,000 mortgage.

Later that year, public records show that Lopez-Castro transferred the property to a Panamanian company that he controlled called Highland Park Development Corp.

Federal authorities do not know if

Lopez-Castro used drug money to buy the land.

A federal investigation later showed that he was receiving wire transfers of thousands of dollars in drug profits from Panama for investment in Dade County at around the time the purchase occurred.

Lopez-Castro went to the county building in 1982 seeking business zoning on the land. The two county departments that review zoning issues fought it.

"Commercial use of this property would be detrimental," said the Planning Department.

"Unacceptable," echoed the Building and Zoning Department.

Lopez-Castro was turned down by a 5–0 vote of the County Commission.

He held onto the land through the first half of 1985. Lopez-Castro had been indicted by the U.S. attorney's office for laundering drug money from smuggler Jose Antonio Fernandez.

A detailed account of the indictment appeared on the front page of The Herald on Dec. 13, 1984.

Days later, a longtime friend of Sergio Pereira's, real-estate broker Michael Vazquez, learned that Lopez-Castro, free on bond, had some land to sell.

Vazquez said in a recent interview that he brought together the group of potential investors, including Camilo Padreda, who put up a cash down payment. He could not recall the amount.

Vazquez offered sketchy details of the transaction and promised to search for documents. He later failed to return a dozen telephone calls and one telegram seeking elaboration.

The group sealed its deal with Lopez-Castro on Jan. 4, 1985. One of the investors—Benigno Armas, listed on documents as a "foreigner"—signed the contract as trustee for purchase of the land. He agreed to pay $925,000.

He also signed a document, called a declaration of trust, stating that he was really acting on behalf of himself and nine others: Padreda, Michael Vazquez, Michael Vazquez Jr., Rosa B. Vazquez, Jose E. Carro, Arnaldo Iglesias, Osvaldo Iglesias, Ileana Iglesias and Enrique Yanes.

The declaration of trust shows that most of the nine were minor investors, with Padreda controlling 50 percent of the land trust.

Vazquez said Padreda realized soon after the deal was signed that he could not afford a 50 percent interest.

Vazquez gave this reason: There was some chance the investors would not succeed in finding a new buyer for the land before they were required under their contract to buy it from Lopez-Castro. In theory, Vazquez said, Padreda could have been forced to come up with half the purchase price out of his pocket—or the group could have lost its deposit.

So Padreda signed a new document two days later, an addendum to the declaration of trust.

It said: "Camilo Padreda hereby declares that he holds the interest for the benefit of Sergio Pereira in the amount of 25 percent and the remainder 25 percent will be for the benefit of Camilo Padreda himself."

Risk rewarded

Pereira's lawyer, Hank Adorno, said Pereira never made any down payment. But he said Pereira was taking the risk that he might have to come up with a quarter of the purchase price. The profits Pereira ultimately received were his reward for that risk, Adorno said.

The investor group soon found a potential buyer, Emilio Cruz, who wanted to build a shopping center called Flagler Square.

Padreda asked a zoning lawyer, Alberto Cardenas, to represent the investor group in seeking to get the land rezoned. Cardenas said in a recent interview that he never knew Pereira was part of the investor group.

He applied on Feb. 7, 1985, for the same business zoning that county commissioners had refused to grant on the property three years earlier.

Cardenas filled out the disclosure form required by county rules to reveal everybody who stood to benefit from the rezoning.

The document did not include the names of Padreda, Pereira or any of the other investors who would profit. The document listed only the Panamanian corporation.

Cardenas said this week he would retrieve his file from a warehouse to try to figure out why he omitted their names, but that will take several days.

"That's certainly a valid question," Cardenas said.

Pereira was an assistant county manager at the time the zoning application was filed, though he was not in charge of zoning. He left at the end of March to become city manager of Miami for about eight months.

Documents show that low-level county staff members continued to fight business zoning on the property, just as they had in 1982.

Zoning reviewer Frank Richmond reviewed the property on June 4, 1985, filling out a standard work sheet.

Compatibility with surrounding land uses: "Incompatible."

Use of site: "Inadequate."

Location of buildings: "Inadequate."

Landscaping: "Inadequate."

Richmond wrote a recommendation. It is now missing from county files, though it apparently urged that the business zoning be turned down.

High-level officials of the building department apparently overruled his recommendation on June 13, reversing the department's stance of three years earlier.

No interference

Those high-level officials say they do not remember much about the zoning case now. But they are certain of one thing: There was never political interference from the county manager's office or from Pereira, already running the city but still a well-known and highly regarded figure at county hall.

"That sort of thing never happens," said Jerry Proctor, head of zoning control. "If it had, I would remember it like a bell."

Pereira said he never contacted anyone in the Building and Zoning Department or on the county commission about the zoning case.

The Planning Department, as it had three years earlier, recommended against the business zoning.

When the two departments come to the county commission divided over a zoning issue, the commission frequently votes for whatever department favors the developer. That happened in this case, after Commissioner Clara Oesterle emphasized that the Building Department recommended approval of business zoning.

The vote was 7–0 in favor of the developer, with Mayor Steve Clark and Commissioner Harvey Ruvin absent.

Several commissioners who voted for the business zoning say they don't remember the case, but were not lobbied by Pereira or his friends.

"I would definitely remember that," said Commissioner Beverly Phillips.

The zoning was approved on June 20, 1985. The Pereira group closed its deal a month later, simultaneously buying the property from the Panamanian corporation for $925,000 and selling it to developer Cruz at a higher, undisclosed price without taking title.

Each member of the Pereira group received a share of the profits by check.

Pereira refuses to discuss how much he got.

"That's none of your business," Pereira said. "I got to draw the line with you guys somewhere."

The only available figure on the profits from the land transaction comes from developer Padreda, the most forthcoming of all participants in the land transaction. He owned the same interest in the transaction as Pereira, 25 percent.

'A substantial amount'

Padreda said he checked his income-tax return Monday evening. He could not remember the precise profit Tuesday, but said it was definitely between $70,000 and $75,000.

"It was a substantial amount of money," Padreda said.

Cruz, the shopping-center developer, failed to return repeated telephone calls seeking details of his role in the transaction. A Cruz associate, Joel Benes, said he was unfamiliar with the deal.

Lopez-Castro, the drug lawyer, could not be reached for comment on his role, either.

He was convicted in the Sunshine State Bank case on Oct. 7, 1985, less than three months after the property deal was completed. He got 27 years.

He was let out on bond to take care of personal business. He disappeared.

Cruz, the shopping-center developer, completed Flagler Square late in 1987. A sign went up not long ago. 'Now Leasing.'

Herald staff writer Luis Feldstein Soto contributed to this report.

Dade manager Pereira resigns
County leader quits with swipe at news media

By Celia W. Dugger
Herald Staff Writer

A composed and somber Sergio Pereira announced his resignation Wednesday night, signalling the end of his tempestuous two years as Dade County manager. He said he will stay on until Feb. 29 to ensure a smooth transition.

His decision to leave came as The Miami Herald prepared to publish a story that said he did not report his sale of two houses in Hialeah on his 1985 income tax return.

Pereira's support from his bosses on the Metro Commission had eroded in the last two weeks after revelations in The Herald that he did not disclose his role in an unrelated West Dade land transaction that brought him $127,878 with no investment on his part.

After a day of speculation that he would quit, Pereira went live before television cameras at 11 p.m. to announce his resignation.

"It is clear that the unrelentless and unethical actions of some members of the media have contributed to a serious and unhealthy situation for our community and county government," said Pereira, 43.

"I am proud of my record as county manager and I believe I have accomplished a great deal," he said.

The Dade state attorney's office is investigating Pereira's part in the West Dade deal, as well as his use of county helicopters. And his role in the controversial Suit Case has not yet been resolved. A grand jury indicted him in October for buying allegedly stolen suits from a Miami duplex, but the charges were dropped on a technicality.

Wednesday evening, two dozen of Pereira's friends and co-workers from Metro-Dade huddled with him in the Coconut Grove offices of his attorney Hank Adorno.

First to arrive was a tight-knit group of secretaries who have worked for the manager since he first took office in January 1986. The women, who looked stricken, crowded into the elevator. One of them, Cirie Campos, sobbed.

Deputy County Manager Dewey Knight, whom Pereira recommended to commissioners as interim manager, as well as several of Pereira's closest assistants, joined him later.

The commissioners were at the Sheraton Bal Harbour for a dinner in honor of Commissioner Sherman Winn. They watched a stage show that featured men in skintight bikinis and a live alligator, but they were thinking about the Pereira controversy.

"I think he's been a good manager," said Metro Mayor Steve Clark. "No one has ever knocked his ability to manage. Other things may have happened of a personal nature. I have no knowledge of that."

Commissioner Clara Oesterle, who had asked Pereira to step aside while the investigations involving him were completed, said she was unhappy

that Pereira had not provided the commission with the full real estate records disclosure it requested.

"I was very disappointed to see the things he turned in to us were not complete. In fact, it was an abortion," she said.

Commissioner Barbara Carey said she was sad his career with Metro had to end this way.

"It's a disappointment for any ethnic group to have someone rise to that level, and then have to go out this way," she said. "His continuing to be there was polarizing the community along ethnic lines."

Pereira, the first Cuban-born county manager, has depicted the critical news coverage of his tenure as ethnically motivated. Spanish-language radio stations had continually defended him.

Herald reporters first questioned Pereira and Adorno about the Hialeah land deal Tuesday, and submitted questions in writing Wednesday morning. Adorno sent a response to the newspaper at noon Wednesday and sent copies to the commission.

By late afternoon, rumors swept through the Metro administration building that Pereira would resign. Throughout the evening and night, television and radio stations interrupted their programming to announce the inevitability of Pereira's resignation. Each cut-in was brief and followed by regular programming — except on Spanish-language WQBA-AM.

WQBA, which has vigorously defended the county manager in recent weeks, aired a special call-in program for listeners to express their outrage. Calls were taken by news director Tomas Regalado, who said Miami was "very upset" by Pereira's departure.

The Metro Commission is expected to meet soon to designate an interim manager. Several commissioners said they hope Deputy County

Manager Knight will step in as he has in the past when other managers departed.

Metro Commissioner Jorge Valdes, who has been one of Pereira's staunchest defenders, said he wants the manager's successor to be recruited from within Dade County.

"I'm not going to vote for any county manager that would come from outside," he said.

But Oesterle said she would probably favor a nationwide search, though she would want to find out first the wishes of the other commissioners.

"We have some very good assistant county managers. If one of them can do the work and do it well, we should look at them," she said.

The commissioners' questions about Pereira's finances will probably go unanswered. They will not be provided with more records they requested from Pereira, said Metro spokesman Bill Johnson.

Said Johnson: "Those were records he said he would turn over to keep a job he no longer wants."

Herald staff writers Christine Evans, Lourdes Fernandez, Dave Von Drehle and Luis Feldstein Soto also contributed to this report.

Privately he had a heart
Public rarely saw humanist side of Pereira

By Justin Gillis
Herald Staff Writer

The man and his coterie of loyal aides always said he was misunderstood.

Publicly, Sergio Pereira was a back-slapping, cigar-chomping, glad-handing boss who seemed to run Dade County government as if it were his kingdom, ordering expensive furniture, hopping around in county helicopters, dressing in heavy jewelry and expensive Italian suits.

El caudillo, one of his critics called him. The big man.

Privately, he was a humanist. If his flaws always seemed bigger than life, so did his heart.

"I am not going to appoint someone because he is or is not a green, gay Filipino," Pereira once said, explaining his refusal to promote Hispanics as rapidly as some critics wanted. "I'm hung up on talent. I'm not hung up on color or nationality. I am sorry, but I'll just die that way."

It was a side of him that county commissioners, reporters and his closest aides noticed often, one the public almost never saw. He came across publicly as arrogant. But he was really a friendly man with a ready laugh, a quick wit and a sense that the world was a little mad.

While he labored unnoticed over county budgets, fretted over public housing, struggled to reform a bloated transit legacy with the painful step of chopping 200 jobs, he managed to land in a series of bizarre controversies — unrelated to job performance — that ultimately cost him his career.

When he joined the county, he submitted a resume that can charitably be described as misleading. He was ultimately caught.

When he became county manager,

he ordered a custom marble desk and conference table that set taxpayers back $10,000. He took flying lessons in county helicopters at public expense. He bought fine suits of uncertain origin from a dubious retailer.

He was finally undone by the disclosure that he was wheeling and dealing in real estate while holding public office.

Pereira plowed away at his job, trying hard not to take the controversies seriously.

In many ways he was a perfect leader for a troubled town. He was the first Cuban-born manager of the city of Miami, the first Cuban-born manager of Dade County. He was a focus of pride for many Hispanics. He dealt easily with blacks and with the white male power structure of downtown Miami.

Miami Commissioner Miller Dawkins once said Pereira would be a perfect city manager because "he's Cuban, he acts black and he looks white."

He survived in the topsy-turvy world of Miami city politics, and he thrived as manager of Metropolitan Dade County. He gradually converted the 5–4 majority that chose him county manager in late 1985 into unanimous support.

Pereira thrived in part with the help of Charles Scurr, a loyal, precise, urbane executive assistant who counseled the manager often on how to avoid controversy and do the right thing. Despite such advice, Pereira's personal life—Scurr once called it a "mess"—ultimately caught up with him.

Pereira leaves a dual legacy, warm-hearted patriarch to those who

PEREIRA'S ACCOMPLISHMENTS

Last week, Sergio Pereira distributed to the media a list of what he considered his major accomplishments as Dade County manager, including:

REORGANIZING Little HUD, the county department that oversees public housing projects.

RESTRUCTURING the transportation department to provide more efficient service to the public.

SAVING more than $4 million with personnel cuts in 1986.

INTRODUCING countywide drug testing and counseling for employees.

COORDINATING Pope John Paul II's visit to Dade County last September.

ADDING more than 216 buses to the county fleet.

NEGOTIATING a 15-year contract for the operation of the Solid Waste Resources Recovery Plant.

RESTRUCTURING the county's long-term bond debt to take advantage of lower interest rates.

HELPING Dade County become the first local government in the United States to raise $1 million for the United Way.

PEREIRA'S PROBLEMS

FEBRUARY 1985 — While applying for the Miami city manager's job, Pereira's academic credentials are questioned by Korn/Ferry, a search firm hired to recommend candidates. Korn/Ferry's managing vice president, Norman Roberts, said Pereira told him he received an undergraduate degree from Montclair State College in New Jersey in 1967 and a master's degree from the University of Utah in 1969. The check revealed he didn't graduate from either school. The city hires him anyway.

JANUARY 1986 — County commissioners are surprised to learn that Pereira had spent $31,513 on new office furniture. He bought a $9,400 aqua-green marble desk and two tables, a $9,950 custom-built bleached oak credenza and an $8,900 custom-built, cream-colored leather sofa.

SEPTEMBER 1987 — The Dade County state attorney's office investigates Pereira for learning to fly Metro-Dade Police helicopters at public expense. During the first six months of the year, he logged 29.4 hours in the air. The investigation is still pending.

OCTOBER 1987 — The Dade County grand jury indicts Pereira for buying stolen designer suits from a cut-rate haberdasher who peddled clothing from a rented Miami duplex. He is charged with three third-degree felonies for buying seven stolen suits at the duplex, where suits worth up to $900 went for as little as $150 without tax. Pereira said he didn't know the suits were hot. The Metro Commission suspends him with pay, but reinstates him a month later when Dade Circuit Judge David Gersten dismisses the indictment on a technicality.

JANUARY 1988 — A Miami Herald story reveals that Pereira failed to report a $127,878 profit in a secret land deal in 1985. Pereira was one of a group of investors who acquired a contract to purchase a 4½-acre parcel in West Dade from a Miami lawyer who is now a federal fugitive convicted of laundering drug money through a land deal. Pereira claimed the profit on his income tax return, but did not include it on his financial disclosure form for the county. The Metro Commission later gives him a vote of confidence.

THE LETTER OF RESIGNATION

This is the text of the letter County Manager Pereira sent to Metro commissioners Wednesday night. At a press conference, he read virtually the same statement.

Dear Mayor and Commissioners:

It is with the deepest regret that I tender to you my resignation as your county manager effective Feb. 29, 1988.

I have dedicated the last 15 years of my life to serving the people of our great community. Public service has been more than a job for me, it has been my life. I have served to the best of my ability and with distinction and integrity. I am proud of my record as county manager, and with your support we have achieved a great many accomplishments.

I have consulted with the leaders of our Hispanic, black and Anglo communities as well as with my friends, colleagues, supporters and especially with my family. It is clear that the unrelentless and unethical actions of some members of the media have contributed to a serious and unhealthy situation for our community and county government. I have always had the best interests of our community at heart. I now sincerely believe that it is in the best interest of the community for me to step down as county manager.

I am recommending that Deputy County Manager Dewey Knight be designated as interim manager. If you concur, I will immediately begin the transition process with Mr. Knight and anticipate that very shortly we will be able to effectuate a smooth and complete transfer. I want to reassure our citizens that all county services will continue to be provided with the same level of excellence and commitment that has been our trademark. I personally plan to spend some time with my family, put this experience in perspective, and evaluate the opportunities before me.

I want to thank you, Mr. Mayor, and each member of the commission for your continuing support and counsel. I want to thank the many hard-working and dedicated professional men and women of Dade County who make our government work so well. I also want to thank my staff and my many friends, colleagues and supporters in the community, for without them, none of our achievements would have been possible. Finally, and above all, I want to thank my family.

Sincerely,
Sergio Pereira

knew him and insufferable dandy to those who didn't.

Under his silk shirts, Pereira sometimes wore a gold chain with two charms. Dangling side by side from his neck were a Playboy bunny and the Virgin of Guadalupe.

Pereira's tax return omitted house sales

**By Lisa Getter
and Justin Gillis**
Herald Staff Writers

Dade County Manager Sergio Pereira did not report on his 1985 income tax return the sale of two houses he built in a controversial Hialeah development.

Pereira resigned Wednesday night, a day after Miami Herald reporters first questioned him about the Hialeah land transaction. He refused to comment on the sale of the houses.

Earlier Wednesday, Pereira's attorney, Hank Adorno, said the sales were not reported to the Internal Revenue Service because Pereira's accountant determined there was no profit.

Adorno said Pereira and his former wife actually lost a small amount of money in the 1985 transactions, but he would not release records documenting any loss.

A detailed review of public records at the county courthouse and Hialeah City Hall indicates that the Pereiras sold the homes for $46,300 more than the listed price of the land and the construction costs estimated on the building permits. There is nothing in the public records to show what, if any, other costs Pereira might have had.

James Richardson, public affairs specialist for the IRS, said a taxpayer who developed property and sold it would be obligated to report the transaction even if there was no profit.

"The individuals would still need to show that on their return," Richardson said.

"If there is a problem, it's a problem the Internal Revenue Service can raise with us, not The *Miami Herald*," Adorno said. "It's none of your business. It's a private matter."

Pereira's 1985 tax return would normally be private, but he disclosed the entire return recently to quell a controversy over an unrelated 1985 land transaction, involving land in unincorporated Dade County near Sweetwater.

In that transaction, Pereira earned $127,878 — more than his public salary that year — with no investment of money on his part. Pereira did not list that transaction, as required by law, on a state financial disclosure form filled out 10 weeks after he reported the profits on his tax return.

Pereira said the fact that he reported that land transaction on his tax return proved that he simply forgot it when filling out the public disclosure form.

Pereira reported his ownership of the Hialeah property, located in a subdivision called Mango Hill, on a 1984 state disclosure form. Deeds show that he and his wife, who held the property in their own names, sold the two houses the next year.

"He did what he was supposed to do, report it on his state ethics form," Adorno said.

Portions withheld

When Pereira first released his 1985 tax return last week, he withheld some portions, and it was not clear whether he had reported the Mango Hill property sale to the IRS.

Under continued pressure from county commissioners, Pereira this week released the withheld portions of his 1985 return and his entire return from 1986.

The Mango Hill transaction does not appear on either return.

"If for some reason the accountant was wrong, he'll report it and show whatever loss he had," Adorno said. "If the accountant is wrong, it's not Sergio's fault." The accountant, Felix Caceres, said he could not discuss Pereira's tax return without permission.

Mango Hill has been under investigation by the U.S. attorney's office since 1985, when it was the subject of a report in The Miami Herald entitled *Hialeah: Zoned for Profit.*

That report quoted two developers of Mango Hill who complained that public officials in Hialeah had pressured the developers into selling lots to them at low prices. At the time, those same officials were reviewing plans for the development at City Hall.

The developers said the public officials sold some lots for quick profits, gave some to their friends and developed others.

No charges

Philip Spiegelman, an official of Mango Hill's developer, Del-Form Inc., said at the time, "Everyone got greedy." No charges have been filed as a result of the Mango Hill investigation.

Adorno, Pereira's attorney, said Wednesday in a letter to The Herald that neither Pereira nor his wife "had anything to do with the zoning of the Mango Hill lots, nor did they request or receive any assistance from any public official with respect to the purchase, development and sale of these two lots."

Developer Spiegelman said he did not remember Pereira's purchase of the lots.

Spiegelman, who has been questioned extensively by the FBI on Mango Hill transactions, now heads his own Broward development firm. He declined extensive comment.

"Whatever is in the public record, God bless you," Spiegelman said.

Courthouse records indicate that Pereira and his former wife, Esther Perez Pereira, bought lots 3 and 4 of Block 6 of Mango Hill on May 31, 1984, from Del-Form for $40,000.

In June 1984 contractors working for Pereira took out various construction permits on the two lots. The contractors estimated on building permits that they would construct identical three-bedroom, two-bath houses on the property for $26,000 apiece.

Contractors are required to give a written estimate of the cost of construction when they take out building permits. The law requires that the estimate be fairly accurate, since the fee to take out the permit is based on the estimated construction cost.

An architect and another developer who worked in that part of Mango Hill said the estimate of $26,000 per house in construction costs sounded about right. "It's not an expensive market, but it's a good market," said architect Oscar J. Gonzalez. "Whatever you build there gets sold."

On July 23, 1984, the Pereiras took out a loan of $81,200 from Consolidated Bank in Hialeah, pledging the land as collateral. The loan was apparently intended, at least in part, to pay for construction of the houses.

It is not clear who built Pereira's houses.

Adorno, Pereira's attorney, said he believed Vicente Leal, who owned numerous parcels in Mango Hill and was a member of the city's planning and zoning board at the time, built the houses for Pereira.

Leal's name appears on architectural plans for the two houses.

Leal is a leading figure in Hialeah land transactions. He has never publicly discussed his role in Mango Hill. His attorney, Frank Holden, did not return telephone calls.

The general contractor listed on plans filed at Hialeah City Hall for the Pereira houses was G&M Construction. The owner listed in state records for that firm, Mario E. Garcia, also did not return telephone calls.

City Hall records show that construction proceeded on the two houses — at 1148 and 1158 W. 40th Pl. — through the latter part of 1984. Construction was finally completed and the houses certified for occupancy on Dec. 17, 1984.

Pereira did not sell the houses until well into the next year.

The first house, at 1148 W. 40th Pl., was sold on Aug. 16, 1985, to Francisco T. Gonzalez and his wife, Estrella, for $68,400.

Estrella Gonzalez described Pereira as "the best person in the world."

"He behaved very well with us," she said. "He didn't trick us or anything."

The second house, at 1158 W. 40th Pl., was sold on Sept. 18, 1985, to Oscar Martinez and his wife Guilermina for $69,900. They refused to comment.

The sale prices of the houses, as reported in public records, were in line with others in the neighborhood.

The public records indicate that Pereira and his wife paid $40,000 to buy the land. The estimates filed by the contractors put the cost to build the houses at about $52,000. That put the Pereira's estimated costs reported in public records at $92,000. They sold the properties for $138,300. The difference is $46,300.

Adorno said the total costs exceeded the sale prices, but he refused to make public the documents that would prove a loss.

"Did you ever hear of cost overruns, architectural fees, professional fees, change orders?" Adorno said. "Write whatever you guys want, but you guys are buying a lawsuit. There's no way you guys are going to be right."

Herald staff writer Tina Montalvo contributed to this report.

EXAMPLE 2

Mayor's brother gets small-town paving contracts

The following package of stories (see Fig. A.2), beginning with the piece FIRM HEADED BY MAYOR'S KIN QUADRUPLES WORK IN ENDICOTT, originally printed in the *Binghamton* (N.Y.) *Sun-Bulletin* on May 3, 1982, and reprinted here with permission, shows that by no stretch of the imagination does a reporter have to work in a major city to uncover apparent corruption and conflicts of interest. Although the sums involved here are small by big-city standards, they loom relatively large when compared with Endicott taxes and the local level of governmental expenditures. In any case, as is often said in other circumstances, it's the principle that counts.

This story highlights a classic method used by contractors and officials to avoid soliciting formal bids for a job. From a corrupt point of view, after all, formal bidding for a construction contract is bad because it means the qualified firm that bids the lowest price for the job wins the contract and because the taxpayers pay as little as possible to get the job done. When, however, an official's goal is to give the job to a favored firm rather than give the taxpayers the best possible deal, the official wants to avoid formal bidding. In this case, officials apparently avoided formal bidding by splitting the job into two smaller jobs, both of them costing less than the amount that would require soliciting formal bids.

The story itself is a model of thoroughness. For instance, the reporter, Paul Shukovsky, under the subhead "2-year leap of 350%" (page 205), compares in great detail and from several perspectives the amount of work Battaglini Corporation did for Endicott with the amount of work other local contractors did for the village. By doing so, Shukovsky successfully counters the inevitable accusation that the newspaper is singling out Battaglini Corporation unfairly.

Just above that subhead, Shukovsky details his attempts to reach

Battaglini for comment, including mailing Battaglini a certified letter asking him to call. Readers often suspect that reporters don't try diligently enough to reach the subjects of investigative stories for comment; this paragraph goes a long way toward countering that accusation.

Shukovsky also makes a substantial effort to give Mayor Corino her

Library's autonomy displeases Crabb

By DAVID SCHWARTZ

How would you like to spend $700,000, but not have any control over what you get in return?

That's exactly what the city faces each year when the Binghamton Public Library's budget allocation is passed, and while Mayor Juanita Crabb is none too happy about the situation, there doesn't seem to be much of anything she can do to change it.

In an interview yesterday, Crabb expressed her dissatisfaction with the library's financial relationship with the city. In the 1981 budget alone, the city shelled out $717,000, or roughly 75 percent of the library's total operating expenses. That simple fact, Crabb said, should entitle the city

to have a say in how those expenses are administered.

"Yet the (Library Board of Trustees) is completely autonomous," she stated. "We have no control over how the money is used."

On a related front, Crabb was critical of the board's recent decision to purchase some property adjacent to the main branch on Exchange Street, at a time when the financially plagued library is considering whether or not to shut down two of its other branches completely.

The trustees — while eager to receive input from the city concerning the library's affairs — defended both their right to autonomy and their decision to purchase property for future expansion.

A library board's right to autonomy has

been upheld in the state courts, said Trustee Muriel Major. And even so, she argued, each member of the board is appointed by the city legislature, the city must approve or reject the library's budget request and the mayor in fact does sit on the board, though only as an *ex officio* member without a vote.

"We've always complained that we don't get enough help or interest from the city," Major said, adding that since Crabb took office in January the interest has sharpened and has been welcomed by the board. The fact remains, however, that " . . . we are not a city department," Major said.

Veteran Trustee Lawrence Doyle defended the board's decision to spend $62,000 on the property next door to the main library. He stressed the fact that all the money used for the deal came out of an endowment fund — bequests to the library — and not a penny was extracted from the city-funded operating budget. The main library is bordered on all sides by streets and buildings, Major said. There is absolutely no room to move,

and when the burned-out property adjacent to the decaying library annex went up for sale, if they failed to buy it, any possibility for future expansion would have been completely ruled out.

"If we had not taken advantage of this opportunity, 10 years from now we would be held very much accountable. You have to think in terms of the future," she said.

Trustee James Brewster said that with the overcrowding problems the library is already facing, future expansion might indeed become a necessity. He said the trustees, in buying the property, are simply "following through" on the lead already set by the city itself when $1 million in community development funds were allocated to restore the library as a historical landmark just four years ago.

With so much already invested in the building, and considering that it is a "four-county central branch library," Brewster insists that the purchase of property for future development " . . . is a very sound decision."

Pledging allegiance

Residents of Binghamton's North Shore Apartments, 45 Exchange St., take part in a flag dedication yesterday at the apartment complex. The flag, which once flew over the Capitol in Washington, D.C., was presented to the residents by Rep. Matthew F. McHugh, D-Ithaca.

CHUCK HAUPT PHOTO

Local

The Sun-Bulletin
May 3, 1982
Page 3A

Body found along tracks

By JERRY SULLIVAN

The dead body of an 18-year-old Endicott man was found on the Conrail tracks near Lawndale Avenue in Endwell yesterday morning, some eight hours after he was apparently struck by an eastbound train.

Roger Ovens, of 755 Dickson St. in western Endicott, was pronounced dead at the scene by Broome County Coroner Dr. Melvin Jones at about 11:30 a.m. Jones said Ovens died "instantaneously" of a fractured skull and laceration of the brain.

Ovens' body was discovered by Broome County Sheriff's Deputy Paul S. Kucera soon after he responded to a 9:52 a.m. report of a man down on the tracks near the Rollarena-Endwell. Kucera found a severed

left leg with a shoe attached lying on the eastbound track. He then saw Ovens' body lying on the south side of the track.

Ovens is survived by his parents, William R. and Elizabeth Ovens, of 755 Dickson St., Endicott; his grandmothers, Bessie Warner of Owego and Jennie Ovens of Binghamton; two brothers, Donald and Gerald; a sister, Cheryl; and numerous relatives.

"This boy has been around these tracks for 18 years," William Ovens said last night. "It had to be a freak. He had to wait for the west (-bound train) and run right smack into the east."

Broome County Sheriff Anthony C. Ruffo, who responded to the scene, said the accident is under investigation.

Firm headed by mayor's kin quadruples work in Endicott

By PAUL SHUKOVSKY

Endicott Mayor Marion L. Corino's brother, paving contractor Robert D. Battaglini, is the president of a company that has more than quadrupled its dollar amount of work done for the village since Corino took office in January 1980.

In 1979, the year before Corino was elected mayor, Bob Battaglini Corp.'s gross revenue from the village was $19,971. Last year, it was $90,012. None of Battaglini Corp.'s work for the village since Corino took office was obtained through competitive bidding, according to statements and records examined by The Sun-Bulletin.

In one instance last spring, the Battaglini Corp. was awarded a stone-and-oil paving job through procedures that allowed the village to legally circumvent formal bidding — but ended up costing the taxpayers $1,002 more than the originally quoted price of the job.

The job, on Governeurs Lane and Prince Edward Court, was given to the Battaglini Corp. through a procedure one village official called "shopping by telephone."

Battaglini Corp. officials had given the village engineer a telephone quote for the entire job at a rate that would have resulted in a bill of $8,060.85 — well over the $5,000 limit above which state law mandates all

contracts must be awarded through formal bid.

The work was subsequently split up — with Battaglini Corp. doing only a portion of the job and ultimately receiving $2,448 for the job. The rest of the paving project was handled by Central Asphalt Inc., which received $6,615 from the village at a state bid rate. Municipalities are legally allowed to purchase materials at a state bid rate without going through formal bidding.

If the Battaglini Corp. had been paid for the entire job as had been discussed originally, the village might have been in violation of state law. But because the job was split — and billed to the village separately than it would have, based on Battaglini Corp.'s telephone quote.

The village might have saved $823 by giving the job to the contractor who gave the next higher quote, rather than to the Battaglini Corp.

When village public works officials were asked why the job was split so that the Battaglini Corp. did not provide the stone and oil, they said they could not recall the circumstances. Officials of the only suppliers in Broome County for the type of oil used on the job said the Battaglini Corp. would not have been allowed to purchase oil from their companies on credit.

In at least two other instances, Battaglini Corp. did work for the village that apparently exceeded the $5,000 bidding limit, but the jobs were split up for billing purposes into several payments, each under the $5,000 limit. None of the jobs was obtained through competitive bidding, according to village records.

Village records obtained through the state Freedom of Information Act reveal that Battaglini Corp. was given at least 26 jobs in 1981 and four jobs in 1980 that cost more than $1,000, but less than the $5,000 formal bid limit.

The Sun-Bulletin found no evidence that Corino profited from her brother's work for the village. State law would have been violated only if evidence of such profit could be shown.

The village received three separate bills, each under the $5,000 bid limit, for construction of the North Side Park parking lot last summer, which cost Endicott's taxpayers a total of $9,013.45. The job was given to Battaglini Corp. without competitive bidding.

Village Superintendent of Public Works Eugene A. Kudgus said village officials originally planned not to pave the lot. It was later decided pavement was needed because the clay soil became too muddy when wet, Kudgus said.

Marion L. Corino

Kudgus, when asked if the job was split up to avoid competitive bidding, said: "Absolutely not."

In another case last summer, the Battaglini Corp. was hired to raise dozens of manholes and water valve castings. The job cost Endicott $14,550, but payment to the Battaglini Corp. was made in three separate installments, each under the $5,000 bidding limit.

"The reason I broke them down was be-

See ENDICOTT, Page 4A

A.2. The *Binghamton* (N.Y.) *Sun-Bulletin* May 3, 1982, story about the mayor of Endicott.

LOCAL

ENDICOTT—

Continued from Page 3A

cause I saw it as different jobs in different parts of the village," Kudgus said. He said other contractors besides Battaglini Corp. also raised manholes and water valve castings.

Battaglini Corp. last summer was awarded a contract for emergency sewer work on Pine Street and Murphy Avenue. The contract, which exceeded the $5,000 bidding limit, was given to Battaglini Corp. under the emergency exemption allowing a bypass of bidding requirements.

Statements indicating that those sewers had been a long-standing problem raise questions whether the work qualified as an emergency.

Corino, who repeatedly denied any impropriety, said she would look into the Governeurs Lane-Prince Edward Court situation.

Repeated attempts to reach Battaglini were unsuccessful. A telephone message left at his home went unanswered as did a certified letter asking him to get in touch with a reporter which was subsequently returned unclaimed. A phone number for Bob Battaglini Corp. in Endicott has been disconnected.

2-year leap of 350%

Village records show Battaglini Corp.'s gross revenue from the Village of Endicott jumped about 350 percent from 1979 — the year before Corino became mayor — to 1981.

To put the increase into perspective, Battaglini Corp.'s percentage of all construction dollars spent by the village jumped from 5.98 percent of the total in 1979 to 12.33 percent in 1981 — an increase of 106 percent.

Battaglini Corp.'s share of the total construction work in 1980 was 5.58 percent. Endicott spent $333,677 in 1979 for construction labor and $730,016 in 1981, based on figures supplied in March by the Village Treasurer's Office. Adjustments were made in the figures to correct for money paid out for materials rather than labor at the suggestion of Kudgus.

The only other contractors who showed a percentage increase greater than the Battaglini Corp. were those that did less work for the village. For example, Parlor City Contracting Company Inc.'s share of village business increased 365 percent from $5,110 in 1979 to $23,804 in 1980. Gary Dyer Excavating and Tank Service Inc., whose total billing was less than half that of Battaglini Corp., showed a 298 percent increase from 1979 to 1981.

Of the 20 contractors who worked for Endicott in 1981, only two were paid more money than Battaglini Corp. — Neil I. Guiles Excavating & Paving Inc. of Vestal and Dellapenna Brothers Inc. of Johnson City. Dellapenna did not show a percentage increase as great as did Battaglini Corp. Dellapenna's volume increased 82.82 percent from 1979 to 1981. With the exception of one small job in 1979, Guiles did not work for the village before 1981, according to village records.

Guiles, who was paid $93,094 in 1981, received all his work through competitive bidding. Dellapenna was paid $162,692 in 1981, also through bidding. Kudgus said. Of the 14 contractors who worked for the village in 1979, the year before Corino took office, Battaglini Corp. ranked sixth in money received.

Village Engineer John Ferguson denied there had been pressure to hire Battaglini Corp., though he added, "It is always easier to deal with someone who has no connections."

Ferguson said he was unaware that Battaglini Corp.'s work for the village had increased. He said that before he hires someone, he must get approval from Kudgus, who then gets approval from Corino. The village board is informed later.

Corino agreed, saying: "This is the normal chain of command. But they don't take every request for a purchase to me. They decide on the contractors."

"I don't know why he said that," Corino said when asked about Ferguson's statement on the Battaglini Corp. having connections.

Kudgus explained that, until very recently, "we shop by telephone," when jobs are below the $5,000 limit. Ferguson picks the names of a few contractors appropriate for the type of work involved, calls them, and the job is awarded to the contractor that gives the lowest quote, Kudgus said.

"We usually pick people we know are qualified, can do the work and have a good record of experience," Kudgus said. "He (Battaglini) has been around a long time. You can't exclude somebody just because of the last name.

"We work according to the letter of the law. He (Battaglini) has by no means the lion's share of the work."

When asked why Battaglini Corp. got so much work through Endicott's "shop-by-telephone" system, Kudgus said: "I don't know. You might say he has been underutilized. I know as for the finished product, he has done as good work as anybody in the area. He was available when others were not. Other than that, I don't know what to tell you."

Endicott's "shop-by-telephone" procedures appear to be less stringent when compared with those in Binghamton, Johnson City and the Town of Union. Binghamton and Union officials said that although they may initially make telephone calls to contractors on jobs below the $5,000 bid limit — the purpose of the calls is to request written quotes. Johnson City's Public Works chief said all work in that village is through formal bidding.

Kudgus also denied that he had been pressured to hire Battaglini Corp. "It looks weird, I'll agree. But should we not call him (Battaglini) because of what his last name is?" Kudgus said.

Kudgus said Village Attorney Joseph Nestor approved hiring Battaglini Corp.

Nestor said that, as far as he knew, giving Battaglini Corp. work is not a conflict of interest because Corino does not have a financial interest in the company.

Corino said that, although she keeps track of which jobs are being done in the village, she does not necessarily know which contractor is doing the work.

"I know that it (street construction) is going on. But if I knew every time they called a contractor and every time they raised a catch basin, I don't think I could operate efficiently," said the part-time mayor.

"I doubt you will find any part-time mayor with the amount of business done in the Village of Endicott with 12 large departments, who could keep track daily," she said.

The oil-and-stone paving of Governeurs Lane and Prince Edward Court was one of the jobs that the Village of Endicott gave to the Bob Battaglini Corp.

Village treated work on sewers as an emergency

Last June, a heavy thunderstorm overtaxed Endicott sewers and caused raw sewage to back up into basements on Pine Street and Murphy Avenue.

Mayor Corino became aware of the situation when Dominic Salamida, of 1005 Pine St., visited her to complain. An internal village memorandum shows that Village Superintendent of Public Works Eugene A. Kudgus instructed Village Engineer John Ferguson to treat the situation as an emergency. "John — go ahead w/ Emergency Repairs before next storm," the memo says.

Corino acknowledges instructing Kudgus to correct the situation immediately.

The Pine Street problem was handled by giving the $5,081 job to Bob Battaglini Corp.

State law, recognizing that emergencies can occur that require immediate action, allows for the suspension of formal bidding in such cases.

The sewer problem apparently had existed for years, however, and it wasn't a mystery to either the village board or Corino.

Salamida said he had complained to the board several times about it and Corino said it was her understanding that the sewage situation had been a problem in the Pine Street area for years. She said she had not known about it when she had been a board member, however.

Court rulings on the subject make the point that emergencies allowing bid suspension must be "unforeseen."

Kudgus said it was estimated that the sewer job would cost less than $5,000 but an unexpected problem brought the final bill above that figure. Kudgus could provide no documentation to support his point.

If the work had cost less than $5,000, it would not have been required to go to bid and therefore no emergency would have had to be declared.

— PAUL SHUKOVSKY

Corino promised street repairs

When Endicott Mayor Marion Corino ran for office in 1979, she made a campaign pledge to improve street maintenance. "I knew this (street improvement) is one of the things I saw that had to be done," Corino said in a recent interview. Some of the streets, such as Garfield and Madison, were "almost impossible to travel on," she said.

Corino said not much street work was done in 1980 — her first year in office — because it took time to plan the extensive efforts ahead.

There are about 43 miles of streets in the village. In 1980, about one mile (2 percent) was resurfaced or reconditioned. That figured jumped to 9 miles (21 percent) in 1981 and about 8 miles (18 percent) is planned for this year, according to figures obtained from the public works department.

Few people are as familiar with a municipality's roads as the police officers that patrol them. Endicott's policemen say the streets have improved.

"There is no question the streets have gotten better," said Endicott Police Lt. W.D. Ford Jr. "There is no comparison to the mess they were in before (Corino became mayor)."

Did village taxpayers get the best deal?

Last spring, the Village of Endicott saw to it that Governeurs Lane and Prince Edward Court got paved.

But records show that village taxpayers might not have received the best deal they could have for their money.

An internal work sheet, obtained from Village Superintendent of Public Works Eugene A. Kudgus, shows that last spring, a job that Village Engineer John Ferguson calculated would cost more than $5,000 was initially given entirely to Battaglini Corp. without going out to bid.

Ferguson telephoned four contractors to obtain prices for an oil and stone paving job on Governeurs Lane and Prince Edward Court. His work sheet shows he expected the job would cost a total of $8,060.85, based on the lowest quote he obtained, which was from Battaglini Corp.

The job actually cost village taxpayers $1,002 more than the price Battaglini gave Ferguson over the telephone, according to an internal Department of Public Works document, which was obtained by *The Sun-Bulletin*, and village payment vouchers.

Ferguson's work sheet shows that Battaglini said the company would do the work for $1.35 per square yard. Central Asphalt Inc. quoted $1.38 and Neil I. Guiles Excavating and Paving Inc. quoted $1.40 for the job, the work sheet shows.

But after the bills came in and the checks were sent out, the village had paid $1.51 per square yard for the work — 16 cents per square yard more than was quoted to the village by Battaglini Corp.

If the village had given the job to either Central or Guiles instead of Battaglini Corp. — and the contractor completed the job at the quoted price — the village might have saved hundreds of dollars.

Records reveal that the escalated cost to the village was a result of splitting the job — two contractors doing a job originally quoted to one. Battaglini Corp. originally had proposed to do the entire job at a cheaper price than was ultimately paid out.

Battaglini Corp., although it gave an informal bid for the entire job including material, in fact billed the village for only 41 cents per square yard for its part of the job. The Battaglini Corp. bill came to $2,448.

Stone and oil, which was included in Battaglini Corp.'s original telephone quote, instead came from Central Asphalt, which billed the village $6,615 for the materials.

Battaglini Corp., which did not have a stone spreader or oil tank truck of its own, rented equipment from Central Asphalt, which also supplied the materials, said Delivan Gates of Central Asphalt in a tele-

See DEAL, Page 6A

DEAL—

Continued from Page 4A

phone interview. Gates said Battaglini Corp. provided supervision.

Gates said Battaglini Corp. would not have been allowed to purchase the stone and oil on credit from Central Asphalt at that time.

When the bills from Battaglini Corp. and Central Asphalt are added up and then divided by the total square yards of Governeurs Lane and Prince Edward Court, the actual cost of the job comes to $1.51 per square yard. The village paid $9,063 for a job that the records show Battaglini said would cost $8,060.55.

Ferguson said he didn't remember why the jobs were split up and said that, as he remembered it, the arrangement with Battaglini Corp. for the street work was verbal.

Subsequently, Kudgus said that he and Ferguson had recalled that the leftover oil from the Governeurs Lane-Prince Edward job was spread on another village street — work later billed as part of the Prince Edward job.

Kudgus could not document that explanation, stating that there were so many oil delivery slips from last year's contruction season that most were discarded.

The oil was purchased by the village at state contract price, which allowed the village to bypass formal bidding.

— PAUL SHUKOVSKY

A.2. *(continued)*

due as well. He quotes her denials and explanations, points out that there's no evidence she violated any state law, and highlights one of the factors in her favor in the sidebar entitled, CORINO PROMISED STREET REPAIRS. The other two sidebars, however, each dealing with a specific job, show how official preferences apparently worked against the interests of the taxpayers and may have violated state regulations and court rulings.

Shukovsky also relates the apparent corruption to the reader's own experience as much as possible by indicating exactly how much tax money apparently was lost in several instances. Because the average Endicott taxpayer is probably well aware of the amount of property tax he or she pays the village every year, such specificity does a lot to help bring the story home.

Unlike many other investigative reporters, Shukovsky also takes the trouble to compare Endicott's bid-solicitation procedures with those of neighboring cities, towns, and villages, thus putting those procedures in context and showing more fully their true nature.

Firm headed by mayor's kin quadruples work in Endicott

By Paul Shukovsky

Endicott Mayor Marion L. Corino's brother, paving contractor Robert D. Battaglini, is the president of a company that has more than quadrupled its dollar amount of work done for the village since Corino took office in January 1980.

In 1979, the year before Corino was elected mayor, Bob Battaglini Corp.'s gross revenue from the village was $19,971. Last year it was $90,012. None of the Battaglini Corp.'s work for the village since Corino took office was obtained through competitive bidding, according to statements by vil-

lage officials and records examined by The Sun-Bulletin.

In one instance last spring, the Battaglini Corp. was awarded a stone-and-oil paving job through procedures that allowed the village to legally circumvent formal bidding—but ended up costing the taxpayers $1,002 more than the originally quoted price of the job.

The job, on Governeurs Lane and Prince Edward Court, was given to the Battaglini Corp. through a procedure one village official called "shopping by telephone."

Battaglini Corp. officials had given the village engineer a telephone

The stories in example 2 are reprinted with permission of the *Binghamton Press Sun Bulletin*.

quote for the entire job at a rate that would have resulted in a bill of $8,060.85 — well over the $5,000 limit above which state law mandates all contracts must be awarded through formal bid.

The work was subsequently split up — with Battaglini Corp. doing only a portion of the job and ultimately receiving $2,448 for the job. The rest of the paving project was handled by Central Asphalt Inc., which received $6,615 from the village at a state bid rate. Municipalities are legally allowed to purchase materials at a state bid rate without going through formal bidding.

If the Battaglini Corp. had been paid for the entire job as had been discussed originally, the village might have been in violation of state law. But because the job was split — and billed to the village separately — Endicott ended up paying $1,002 more than it would have, based on Battaglini Corp.'s telephone quote.

The village might have saved $823 by giving the job to the contractor who gave the next higher quote, rather than to the Battaglini Corp.

When village public works officials were asked why the job was split so that the Battaglini Corp. did not provide the stone and oil, they said they could not recall the circumstances. Officials of the only suppliers in Broome County for the type of oil used on the job said the Battaglini Corp. would not have been allowed to purchase oil from their companies on credit.

In at least two other instances, Battaglini Corp. did work for the village that apparently exceeded the $5,000 bidding limit, but the jobs were split up for billing purposes into several payments, each under the $5,000 limit. None of the jobs was obtained through competitive bidding, according to village records.

Village records obtained through the state Freedom of Information Act reveal that Battaglini Corp. was given at least 26 jobs in 1981 and four jobs in 1980 that cost more than $1,000, but less than the $5,000 formal bid limit.

The Sun-Bulletin found no evidence that Corino profited from her brother's work for the village. State law would have been violated only if evidence of such profit could be shown.

The village received three separate bills, each under the $5,000 bid limit, for construction of the North Side Park parking lot last summer, which cost Endicott's taxpayers a total of $9,013.45. The job was given to Battaglini Corp. without competitive bidding.

Village Superintendent of Public Works Eugene A. Kudgus said village officials originally planned not to pave the lot. It was later decided pavement was needed because the clay soil became too muddy when wet, Kudgus said.

Kudgus, when asked if the job was split to avoid competitive bidding, said: "Absolutely not."

In another case last summer, the Battaglini Corp. was hired to raise dozens of manholes and water valve castings. The job cost Endicott $14,550, but payment to the Battaglini Corp. was made in three separate installments, each under the $5,000 bidding limit.

"The reason I broke them down was because I saw it as different jobs in different parts of the village," Kudgus said. He said other contractors besides Battaglini Corp. also raised manholes and water valve castings.

Battaglini Corp. last summer was awarded a contract for emergency sewer work on Pine Street and Murphy Avenue. The contract, which exceeded the $5,000 bidding limit, was given to Battaglini Corp. under the emergency exemption allowing a bypass of bidding requirements.

Statements indicating that those sewers had been a long-standing problem raise questions whether the work qualified as an emergency.

Corino, who repeatedly denied any impropriety, said she would look into the Governeurs Lane-Prince Edward Court situation.

Repeated attempts to reach Battaglini were unsuccessful. A telephone message left at his home went unanswered as did a certified letter asking him to get in touch with a reporter which was subsequently returned unclaimed. A phone number for Bob Battaglini Corp. in Endicott has recently been disconnected.

2-year leap of 350%

Village records show Battaglini Corp.'s gross revenue from the Village of Endicott jumped about 350 percent from 1979—the year before Corino became mayor—to 1981.

To put the increase into perspective, Battaglini Corp.'s percentage of all construction dollars spent by the village jumped from 5.98 percent of the total in 1979 to 12.33 percent in 1981—an increase of 106 percent.

Battaglini Corp.'s share of the total construction work in 1980 was 5.58 percent. Endicott spent $337,667 in 1979 for construction labor and $730,016 in 1981, based on figures supplied in March by the Village Treasurer's Office. Adjustments were made in the figures to correct for money paid out for materials rather than labor at the suggestion of Kudgus.

The only other contractors who showed a percentage increase greater than the Battaglini Corp. were those that did less work for the village. For example, Parlor City Contracting Company Inc.'s share of village business increased 365 percent from $5,110 in 1979 to $23,804 in 1980. Gary Dyer Excavating and Tank Service Inc., whose total billing was less than half that of Battaglini Corp., showed a 298 percent increase from 1979 to 1981.

Of the 20 contractors who worked for Endicott in 1981, only two were paid more money than Battaglini Corp.—Neil I. Guiles Excavating & Paving Inc. of Vestal and Dellapenna Brothers Inc. of Johnson City. Dellapenna did not show a percentage increase as great as did Battaglini Corp. Dellapenna's volume increased 82.82 percent from 1979 to 1981. With the exception of one small job in 1979, Guiles did not work for the village before 1981, according to village records.

Guiles, who was paid $93,094 in 1981, received all his work through competitive bidding. Dellapenna was paid $162,692 in 1981, also through bidding, Kudgus said. Of the 14 contractors who worked for the village in 1979, the year before Corino took office, Battaglini Corp. ranked sixth in money received.

Village Engineer John Ferguson denied there had been pressure to hire Battaglini Corp., though he added, "It is always easier to deal with someone who has no connections."

Ferguson said he was unaware that Battaglini Corp.'s work for the village had increased. He said that before he hires someone, he must get approval from Kudgus, who then gets approval from Corino. The village board is informed later.

Corino agreed, saying: "This is the normal chain of command. But they don't take every request for a purchase to me. They decide on the contractors."

"I don't know why he said that," Corino said when asked about Ferguson's statement on the Battaglini Corp. having connections.

Kudgus explained that, until very recently, "we shop by telephone," when jobs are below the $5,000. Ferguson picks the names of a few contractors appropriate for the type of work involved, calls them, and the job is awarded to the contractor that gives the lowest quote, Kudgus said.

"We usually pick people we know are qualified, can do the work and have a good record of experience," Kudgus said. "He (Battaglini) has been around a long time. You can't exclude somebody just because of the last name.

"We work according to the letter of the law. He (Battaglini) has by no means the lion's share of the work."

When asked why Battaglini Corp. got so much work through Endicott's "shop-by-telephone" system, Kudgus said: "I don't know. You might say he has been underutilized. I know as for the finished product, he has done as good work as anybody in the area. He was available when others were not. Other than that, I don't know what to tell you."

Endicott's "shop-by-telephone" procedures appear to be less stringent when compared with those in Binghamton, Johnson City and the Town of Union. Binghamton and Union officials said that although they may initially make telephone calls to contractors on jobs below the $5,000

CORINO PROMISED STREET REPAIRS

When Endicott Mayor Marion Corino ran for office in 1979, she made a campaign pledge to improve street maintenance. "I know this (street improvement) is one of the things I saw that had to be done," Corino said in a recent interview. Some of the streets, such as Garfield and Madison, were "almost impossible to travel on," she said.

Corino said not much street work was done in 1980—her first year in office—because it took time to plan the extensive efforts ahead.

There are about 43 miles of streets in the village. In 1980, about one mile (2 percent) was resurfaced or reconditioned. That figure jumped to 9 miles (21 percent) in 1981 and about 8 miles (18 percent) is planned for this year, according to figures obtained from the public works department.

Few people are as familiar with a municipality's roads as the police officers that patrol them. Endicott's policemen say the streets have improved.

"There is no question the streets have gotten better," said Endicott Police Lt. W.D. Ford, Jr. "There is no comparison to the mess they were in before (Corino became mayor)."

bid limit — the purpose of the calls is to request written quotes. Johnson City's Public Works chief said all work in that village is through formal bidding.

Kudgus also denied that he had been pressured to hire Battaglini Corp. "It looks weird, I'll agree. But should we not call him (Battaglini) because of what his last name is?" Kudgus said.

Kudgus said Village Attorney Jo-

VILLAGE TREATED WORK ON SEWERS AS AN EMERGENCY

Last June, a heavy thunderstorm overtaxed Endicott sewers and caused raw sewage to back up into basements on Pine Street and Murphy Avenue.

Mayor Corino became aware of the situation when Dominic Salamida, of 1005 Pine St., visited her to complain. An internal village memorandum shows that Village Superintendent of Public Works Eugene A. Kudgus instructed Village Engineer John Ferguson to treat the situation as an emergency. "John — go ahead with Emergency Repairs before next storm," the memo says.

Corino acknowledges instructing Kudgus to correct the situation immediately.

The Pine Street problem was handled by giving the $5,081 job to Bob Battaglini Corp.

State law, recognizing that emergencies can occur that require immediate action, allows for the suspension of formal bidding in such cases.

The sewer problem apparently had existed for years, however, and it wasn't a mystery to either the village board or Corino.

Salamida said he had complained to the board several times about it and Corino said it was her understanding that the sewage situation had been a problem in the Pine Street area for years. She said she had not known about it when she had been a board member, however.

Court rulings on the subject make the point that emergencies allowing bid suspension must be "unforeseen."

Kudgus said it was estimated that the sewer job would cost less than $5,000 but an unexpected problem brought the final bill above that figure. Kudgus would provide no documentation to support his point.

If the work had cost less than $5,000, it would not have been required to go to bid and therefore no emergency would have had to be declared.

seph Nestor approved hiring Battaglini Corp.

Nestor said that, as far as he knew, giving Battaglini Corp. work is not a conflict of interest because Corino does not have a financial interest in the company.

Corino said that, although she keeps track of which jobs are being done in the village, she does not necessarily know which contractor is doing the work.

"I know that it (street construction) is going on. But if I knew every time they called a contractor and every time they raised a catch basin, I don't think I could operate efficiently," said the part-time mayor.

"I doubt you will find any part-time mayor with the amount of business done in the Village of Endicott with 12 large departments, who could keep track daily," she said.

Did village taxpayers get the best deal?

Last spring, the Village of Endicott saw to it that Governeurs Lane and Prince Edward Court got paved.

But records show that village taxpayers might not have received the best deal they could have for their money.

An internal work sheet, obtained from Village Superintendent of Public Works Eugene A. Kudgus, shows that last spring, a job that Village Engineer John Ferguson calculated would cost more than $5,000 was initially given entirely to Battaglini Corp. without going out to bid.

Ferguson telephoned four contractors to obtain prices for an oil and stone paving job on Governeurs Lane and Prince Edward Court. His work sheet shows he expected the job would cost a total of $8,060.85, based on the lowest quote he obtained, which was from Battaglini Corp.

The job actually cost village taxpayers $1,002 more than the price Battaglini gave Ferguson over the telephone, according to an internal Department of Public Works document, which was obtained by The Sun-Bulletin, and village payment vouchers.

Ferguson's work sheet shows that

Battaglini said the company would do the work for $1.35 per square yard. Central Asphalt Inc. quoted $1.38 and Neil I. Guiles Excavating and Paving Inc. quoted $1.40 for the job, the work sheet shows.

But after the bills came in and the checks were sent out, the village had paid $1.51 per square yard for the work — 16 cents per square yard more than was quoted to the village by Battaglini Corp.

If the village had given the job to either Central or Guiles instead of Battaglini Corp. — and the contractor completed the job at the quoted price — the village might have saved hundreds of dollars.

Records reveal that the escalated cost to the village was a result of splitting the job — two contractors doing a job originally quoted to one. Battaglini Corp. originally had proposed to do the entire job at a cheaper price than was ultimately paid out.

Battaglini Corp., although it gave an informal bid for the entire job including material, in fact billed the village for only 41 cents per square yard for its part of the job. The Battaglini Corp. bill came to $2,448.

Stone and oil, which was included

in Battaglini Corp.'s original telephone quote, instead came from Central Asphalt, which billed the village $6,615 for the materials.

Battaglini Corp., which did not have a stone spreader or oil tank truck of its own, rented equipment from Central Asphalt, which also supplied the materials, said Delivan Gates of Central Asphalt in a telephone interview. Gates said Battaglini Corp. provided supervision.

Gates said Battaglini Corp. would not have been allowed to purchase the stone and oil on credit from Central Asphalt at that time.

When the bills from Battaglini Corp. and Central Asphalt are added up and then divided by the total square yards of Governeurs Lane and Prince Edward Court, the actual cost of the job comes to $1.51 per square yard. The village paid $9,063 for a job that the records show Battaglini said would cost $8,060.55.

Ferguson said he didn't remember why the jobs were split up and said that as he remembered it, the arrangement with Battaglini Corp. for the street work was verbal.

Subsequently, Kudgus said that he and Ferguson had recalled that the leftover oil from the Governeurs Lane-Prince Edward job was spread on another village street—work later billed as part of the Prince Edward job.

Kudgus could not document that explanation, stating that there were so many oil delivery slips from last year's construction season that most were discarded.

The oil was purchased by the village at state contract price, which allowed the village to bypass formal bidding.

—Paul Shukovsky

EXAMPLE 3

Small-school students fall behind

Thc package of stories, charts, and sidebars grouped under the headline SMALL-SCHOOL STUDENTS FALL BEHIND, FACE BARRIERS TO COLLEGE (see Fig. A.3), originally published in the *Minneapolis Star and Tribune,* on April 20, 1986, and reprinted here with permission, is an excellent illustration of a story that could not have been written without the aid of computers nor without the aid of a state law guaranteeing access to public data, the Minnesota Data Practices Act. (Even with the act, the *Star and Tribune* had to persuade the state attorney general to rule that the data were public before state education agencies would allow the newspaper access to them.)

Only a computer could have analyzed data from 451 high schools, based on scores from 118,336 Preliminary Scholastic Aptitude Tests (PSATs) taken over five years. A reporter who attempted to analyze such a mass of data with a pencil and paper would soon be playing Napoleon Bonaparte in a padded cell.

Work on this story began when reporter David Anderson, the coauthor of this book, realized he had four or five friends, all graduates of small to tiny Minnesota schools, who had successful high-tech careers. He decided to find out why, expecting to find that small, rural schools prepared students better in math and science. He initially assumed that city schools teach drug dealing and hubcap stealing while suburban and small-town schools emphasize Reeboks and business management. But when he began collecting data and talking to testing experts, he found otherwise. (Investigative Reporters and Editors published a synopsis of this story and Anderson's comments on it in *Top Investigations from 1985 & 1986: The IRE Book 3.*)

This story touches on many sensitive matters including but not lim-

A.3. The *Minneapolis Star and Tribune* April 20, 1986, story about student achievement in Minnesota's small schools.

Tests

Continued from page 1A

Curriculum, expert teachers are keys at Pipestone

By Pat Doyle
and Dave Andersen
Staff Writers

Staff Photos by Bruce Bisping

Freshman Michelle Hollingsworth worked a problem in Ray Blecker's algebra class. There was no talking, no distraction, no horseplay.

Ray Blecker: "Now I'm going to call on some of you quiet people who haven't gotten involved today."

What the experts say/

Kenneth Keller
President, University of Minnesota

Harold Howe II
Professor of education, Harvard University Graduate School; member, College Board Commission on Precollege Guidance and Counseling

Walt Haney
Professor of education, Center for Study of Testing, Evaluation and Educational Policy, Boston College

---

A.3. *(continued)*

Family atmosphere holds Verdi students

Comparing Pipestone and Verdi (1981 to 1985 averages)

Big schools have top PSAT scores

Curriculum improves PSAT scores

Big schools lead in ACT scores

About the reporters

A.3. *(continued)*

ited to the pride many parents and students take in the schools they send their children to or attend themselves, whatever the test scores of the students the school produces. The stories bend over backward, therefore, to show the advantages of attending a small school while carefully explaining why lower PSAT scores could hurt a student's college and career prospects.

The paper laid out its statistical apparatus and the data in six charts included in the story package. Anderson advises anyone who contemplates doing a similar story to check every formula and every number in the data carefully, "as schools faring poorly will go over the report with a spectrophotometer." He also advises obtaining the services of a statistician of impeccable credentials to help analyze the data and using at least a 286 computer with 640K RAM and a very fast disk drive. He also suggests that reporters writing similar stories probably will need to write or hire someone to write a program to identify data anomalies, such as a school in which the student body drops from 400 to 100 in one year, then goes back up to 390, indicating that the data provided for that year are probably wrong.

Anderson also recommends talking to the students and their parents and not just relying on raw data. He and his fellow reporters obviously did this, and the story reflects their work. Stories based on data alone are often quite tedious and possibly inaccurate; this story is neither. The two major sidebars bring life to the statistics and make them more vivid, more understandable, and quite believable.

Stories written early in the present investigative era, which began with the unraveling of the Watergate conspiracy in 1974, often didn't bother to propose solutions to the situations they uncovered. This story, written twelve years after Deep Throat began wagging his or her tongue, provides numerous proposed solutions. Some are in the main story itself; others are the major subject of the sidebar titled WHAT THE EXPERTS SAY (page 222).

Early investigative reporters were also unlikely to include in their stories detailed criticism of the methods they themselves had used. This story, to its great credit, does: See Walt Haney's comments under WHAT THE EXPERTS SAY. But early investigative reporters were also unlikely to use computers to analyze data and to make the underlying mathematical and substantive decisions involved in such analyses, which are the decisions Haney criticizes. Those sorts of decisions were crucial to this story, which attempts to compare apples and oranges (big schools and small ones) on an equitable basis.

Anderson told the IRE that in response to the story, a number of school officials called to ask that the newspaper repeat the analysis in four years because they intended to make major curriculum and hiring changes. Others called to say they were glad to see their schools get credit for something other than sports victories. A number called to denounce the investigation as flawed, a case of big-city-paper rural baiting; some said the study was unfair because many rural schools judge their agriculture and shop courses to be of primary importance and college preparation as secondary.

A number of schools either quietly or publicly laid plans to control the number and types of students taking the test in future years in hopes of improving the scores in their schools, rather than improving their curricula or spending the extra money to hire teachers with degrees in science, math, or foreign languages. Anderson said the *Star and Tribune* planned several follow-up stories, including one piece aimed at catching administrators who took this route to make themselves look good without making the schools any better.

Small-school students fall behind, face barriers to college
College prep tests/How Minnesota schools score

By Dave Anderson
Staff Writer

Students in small Minnesota high schools score significantly lower on the math and science portions of college entrance exams than those who attend larger schools, even though their fourth-grade math and science abilities were nearly identical.

These math skills are increasingly important for students seeking careers in a technological age. The reasons for the difference in scores are complex, but one important factor is that larger schools generally have broader college preparatory curricula.

The Star and Tribune analyzed data from 451 Minnesota public high

schools, based on scores from 118,336 Preliminary Scholastic Aptitude Tests (PSAT) taken over five years. The school-by-school results, never before made public, show:

• On the average, the bigger the school, the better its students scored on the PSAT, the college entrance test most commonly taken by Minnesota high school juniors. The median size of a junior class in the top 10 percent of schools on the PSAT is 218; in the bottom 10 percent it's 31.

• Average math scores fall off dramatically in small schools, the approximately one-third of Minnesota public high schools that had 35 or fewer students in the junior class.

In tiny schools, those averaging

The story in example 3 is reprinted with permission of the *Star Tribune*.

10 juniors, students generally fall in the bottom quarter of Minnesota public high schools in the math scores.

• While school size is a factor, the location of the school is not. Students who took the tests at larger outstate schools—in Pipestone, Rochester, Detroit Lakes and Fergus Falls, for instance—scored virtually the same as students at top-ranked schools in the Twin Cities area such as Edina, Alexander Ramsey, St. Anthony and Bloomington Jefferson.

Students in some large city schools did poorly. St. Paul, Humboldt and Minneapolis Henry, Edison and North all average in the bottom 10 percent of schools on math scores. (North has made dramatic improvements recently.)

• Some average-size schools are producing excellent results, but they are exceptions. The state's top 20 public schools include Zumbrota and Kenyon, which are near the state median of 58 in junior class size but have more than average curriculum offerings.

The analysis also showed that private schools with strong curricula, such as St. Paul Academy and Summit School, Breck and Blake, are among the best high schools in Minnesota in preparing students for college.

About 6 percent of Minnesota's high school students attend small public schools and about 7 percent attend private or parochial schools.

• More than two-thirds of Minnesota youngsters go to college and, compared with students nationwide, they are well-prepared. Even at the smallest Minnesota schools, most students score well enough to get into college.

The research found that junior class size by itself is a small part of the equation. But it is important because a small difference in scores can affect a student's rank on the PSAT by as

much as 15 percentile points nationally. This can affect some teenagers' opportunities to get into the colleges and the careers of their choice.

But school officials haven't known how their students compared with youngsters at other schools because the school-by-school college preparatory results have been treated secretively.

The average scores for the school years 1980–81 through 1984–85 were obtained recently by the Star and Tribune under the Minnesota Data Practices Act. They were analyzed by the newspaper's research department and by Ted Anderson, a University of Minnesota professor of sociology.

About half the differences in scores among schools, a substantial amount for such a study, can be explained by a combination of four characteristics of schools or school districts: the percentage of students who took the test, the percentage of college graduates in the district, the percentage of minority enrollment, and the size of the junior class.

The newspaper adjusted the scores when comparing schools to take into account the biggest variable, the different percentages of students taking the test at each school.

The analysis found that the town where students live and the size of the schools they attend, as well as how smart they are and how hard they work, determine how they will do on college entrance examinations.

Experts say school size is also important because:

• It is one indication of the breadth of curriculum and teacher training in math and science.

• It creates a barrier for small-school youngsters, who start educationally even—or even a bit ahead of—their big-school counterparts. Small-school students face barriers in getting into technical programs at schools like the University of Minnesota, and the university's effort to raise its standards can be expected to raise those barriers even higher.

• It can be changed by local school boards and legislators through consolidation, increased spending, pairing, sharing or linking classes electronically.

Experts say the reasons that small schools don't do as well as large ones are fairly obvious:

First, small schools often have too few students to justify offering higher-level college preparation courses such as advanced algebra, trigonometry, analytic geometry, calculus and physics. And research indicates that the more of these courses a student takes, the better the students will do on college entrance exams.

Second, some small schools, especially those farther from population centers, cannot or will not spend the money to hire and keep teachers with specialized training.

In more than half the state's small schools, math was taught last year by teachers who didn't major or minor in mathematics and thus were not certified to teach it fulltime. Of the 132 teachers in this category, 105 were teaching in the smallest one-third of the state's schools.

Pipestone, a larger school that provides exceptional math and science instruction, has hired experienced teachers, said Principal George Wagner, but "a lot of school boards want the administrators to hire people right out of college because that way they are getting a cheaper teacher."

Third, college-bound students at small high schools don't always get the stimulation from other bright students that is common in larger schools. In a school with 30 juniors, for instance, 16 may be planning on college and perhaps seven of those will be studying subjects requiring advanced math or science.

"There is no question but that our students learn a great deal from their peers," said Dave Larson, head of the math department at Edina High School. "Often a peer is able to put it another way and explain some points a colleague missed the first time in class or in the book. It also reinforces a certain pride and prestige, particularly among the students in the enriched classes."

He also said that, like many larger schools, Edina teaches algebra in eighth grade, so many students are studying trigonometry and other advanced subjects by the time they are juniors.

Small schools do have advantages.

They almost always have lower student-teacher ratios, allowing teachers to spend more time with individual students.

"You can get studies to show both that small schools are good and small schools are bad," said Keigh Hubel, professor of education at Southwest State University in Marshall. "Small schools may be behind in course offerings and test scores but they are also behind in vandalism, drug use, alienation, expulsions and dismissals. They also have higher graduation rates than large schools."

Leroy Domagala, superintendent of schools in Balaton, said, "We have 40 percent of our kids going to college and 95 percent of them graduate. We're offering quality education, and we oppose mandated curriculums. If it's in the interest of the community, we'll offer the course. We shouldn't be forced to do it because someone in Minneapolis said we should."

The students in small schools seem to be just as intelligent and just as able to learn as those in large schools.

A state Department of Education

study of scores from the relatively new Minnesota Educational Achievement Program (MEAP) test—which is given to 4th, 7th, 8th and 11th graders—found that 4th graders in the small districts do slightly better in math than those in larger districts.

"What this tells you is that kids across Minnesota start pretty much equal in math ability," said William McMillan, director of that testing program and a former math teacher.

"In lower grades they are all pretty much taught the same. But by the time they get to be juniors in high school the curriculum differences begin to take their toll."

The influence of curriculum also is reflected in scores for the American College Testing (ACT) exam.

In that test, which is administered in the senior year, 35 percent of the math section is based on a student's understanding of intermediate algebra, numeration concepts and advanced topics. And a quarter of the natural sciences test is allotted to questions about physics, a subject not offered in many small Minnesota schools.

The highest average ACT scores were in schools with the largest enrollments (and typically strong curricula and well-trained teachers), with the most dramatic drop-off between schools with 100 students in a graduating class to schools with 25.

In Illinois, a study of ACT scores by the state superintendent of public instruction found even greater differences based on school size. After that study was completed, Illinois officials recommended consolidating all high schools with fewer than 72 students in a graduating class.

A few words about pre-college tests: There are two leading testing organizations. The College Board in New York and its subcontractor, the Educational Testing Service in Princeton, N.J., administer the PSAT to high school juniors and the Scholastic Aptitude Test (SAT) in the senior year. The PSAT, despite the name "Preliminary" is particularly important in Minnesota because the scores are used by most of the state's colleges as part of their formulas to determine who is admitted. American College Testing, Iowa City, Iowa, administers its ACT to high school seniors.

Consolidation is one alternative in Minnesota, although not always the best.

Since school size is an indication of curriculum, another approach to improving the test scores of students is to improve the math and science curriculum for students at small schools.

This year, for the first time, many high school students can take college-level courses at nearby state universities at school district expense.

But many small schools are too far from a state university for commuting, and most universities are in towns with large high schools that already offer advanced courses.

Consolidating schools—or sharing courses and specialized teachers—has potential because more than 100 rural schools in Minnesota are fewer than 15 miles from neighboring schools. Many are within seven miles.

In other cases, consolidation would be difficult because of longer distances. And educational experts say consolidation in itself would be unlikely to improve students' scores much without improved curriculum or better-trained teachers.

Consolidation traditionally has been opposed in many towns because the local high school is very important to the community.

A school supplies jobs for local people and buys products from local merchants. It gives citizens more control over their children's education. It keeps children in town, and small size means that almost everyone who wants to can make the football team or play in the school band. And it keeps alive community traditions.

Some rural parents already have demonstrated that they want a larger school for their children.

Over the years, several thousand have transferred their children to bigger schools. They have paid thousands of dollars in tuition, and many have lobbied for school closings, pairing and other programs to improve education. But they are a minority.

Gov. Rudy Perpich took up their cause when he proposed allowing parents to send their juniors and seniors to any public high school they wish. But the idea was rejected by the 1985 Legislature because of strong opposition from school officials.

Another new idea is the proposal by University of Minnesota President Kenneth Keller to improve academic quality by tightening admissions standards.

That may hit harder at students from small schools, since PSAT scores are an important component of the formulas many colleges at the university use to determine who gets admitted.

A student who is slightly above average in class rank and PSAT scores will be admitted to the College of Liberal Arts. Any high school student living in the Upper Midwest qualifies for admission to the General College.

But some colleges at the university, particularly the Institute of Technology, have admissions standards that make entrance difficult. Even the valedictorian in a large school would need a PSAT math score well above the national average.

IT's admission formula also requires four years of math, including trigonometry or higher level courses, plus two semesters of chemistry and two semesters of physics.

Only a few small schools contacted for this article offer physics and chemistry, and they offered only one semester of each.

Staff writers Pat Doyle, Diane Mundt and Pat Pheifer contributed to this article.

About the Reporters

These articles were prepared by staff writers Dave Anderson and Pat Doyle.

Anderson, 44, joined the Star and Tribune in May 1977 as a general assignment reporter, and served two years as a supervisor of public affairs reporting at the Minneapolis Star.

He is a graduate of Roosevelt University in Chicago, has written a textbook on advanced reporting techniques and has been covering state news in Minnesota since 1984.

Doyle, 33, joined the Star and Tribune in September 1984 as a reporter for the State Desk and has been covering education issues since February. He is a 1975 graduate of Marquette University, Milwaukee.

Curriculum, expert teachers are keys at Pipestone

By Pat Doyle and Dave Anderson
Staff Writers
Pipestone, Minn.

Ray Bleeker writes an equation on an overhead projector and peers through eyeglasses at his freshman algebra class at Pipestone High School. "Don't get scared," he cautions. "You'll be able to understand this. This is all new to you, so it has to sink in. Before we go any further, I want you to ask some questions. If we get it wrong, then we have some more talking to do."

Bleeker, 58, works in a 1918 classroom with a battered blackboard, polished wooden floors and an Apple computer. The desk-tops are custom designed with temperature conversion tables and geometric figures. Posters and banners bear messages such as "Welcome to mathematics, the door to your future," and "If you are going to college, you'll need math now."

The messages apparently have sunk in.

Over the past five years, Pipestone students have scored higher on the Preliminary Scholastic Aptitude Tests (PSAT) college entrance exams than any other students of any of the other 450 public high schools in Minnesota. Even when the scores are adjusted to account for the percentage of students who take the test, Pipestone's students are tops in the state in math scores.

The school's average math score on the latest PSAT, taken in October, was 63—high enough to put a student in the top 6 percent nationally among college-bound juniors. Pipestone's score was as high as the score at prestigious Choate School in Connecticut

and better than scores at a number of highly regarded public schools in Scarsdale, N.Y.; Winnetka, Ill.; Los Alamos, N.M., and Palo Alto, Calif.

Advanced curriculum, expert teachers and a generous budget partly explain the spectacular performance at Pipestone, school officials say.

The Pipestone School District spends 9.8 percent more per pupil on regular instruction and 6.3 percent more per pupil on total operating expenses than other districts of smaller size.

Some of the money is used to provide college preparatory courses exceeding state requirements. The courses include three years of French, two years of German and five years of math, including advanced algebra, trigonometry and calculus. Also included are psychology and economics.

In an attempt to improve curriculum, Pipestone recently sent a teacher to Japan to study math teaching methods there.

Pipestone's enrollment—387 students in grades 9 through 12—is large enough to justify hiring special instructors and offering top courses, said Principal George Wagner.

He said a school with fewer than 25 students per grade probably couldn't justify hiring a physics or chemistry teacher. "If you had one-half the kids interested in the courses, you'd be looking at 12, and I don't think you could afford it," he said.

But Pipestone's edge over many rural schools in spending, size and teacher expertise doesn't explain why its students do better than those in large public schools or even in the state's better private schools, such as Blake.

For instance, although Pipestone's average teacher salary of $23,000 exceeds pay scales in smaller rural schools in its area, it trails the average salary of $29,640 in Twin Cities area public schools.

The test scores "are pretty much the function of the staff," Wagner said. "Most have a master's degree plus. I'd like to take a lot more credit as a principal, but I have to be honest.

"We are constantly revising our programs to see how we can improve them . . . We've gone to trimesters then back to semesters. We try new things and what works we keep."

Students and administrators give much of the credit to teachers such as Bleeker who inspire students to excel.

"He gets a lot of respect," said senior Steve Stratton, who took Bleeker's algebra three years ago and plans to become a doctor. "He doesn't really sit up there and command it. He just gets it.

"The first day I had him in 9th grade, everybody was kind of scared of him. Nobody screwed around. After two days I wasn't scared, but I still respected him."

Said Brad Westfield, a senior who will go to California State Polytechnic University in Pomona to study engineering: "If a student is trying, he'll be there to help. He makes himself available in the morning before school and after school."

Bleeker punctuates each step of a lesson with admonishments, questions and encouragement.

In a recent class, he interrupted an algebra lesson to tell students: "This is your time to jump up and down if you don't understand. Because it will haunt you for the next several weeks if you don't understand."

Students chewed on pencils and pens in concentration. But Bleeker wasn't satisfied that all of them grasped the lesson.

"Now I'm going to call on some of you quiet people who haven't gotten involved today," he said.

Bill Larson, who teaches advanced algebra, trigonometry and calculus, also receives high grades from his students.

With sleeves rolled up, Larson worked on a blackboard while his students figured advanced algebra problems on calculators. There is no talking, no distraction and no horseplay. When he left the room for a couple of minutes, the students seemed not to notice. They continued to scribble, erase and huddle over quadratic equations.

Larson enforces discipline quietly. "If I see they're daydreaming, rather than just holler, I'll just stop the discussion and the silence will bring everyone to," he said. "The students think, 'Who's not paying attention?' They look around to see who it is."

Pipestone also produced some of the highest individual scores in the state.

Senior Boyd Bucher spent last summer at Harvard studying astronomy and calculus. The experience, offered to top high school students, "was kind of challenging, but it wasn't too hard," said Bucher, who will attend the Massachusetts Institute of Technology next year to study physics. Bucher said he regards Pipestone science teacher Bill Lane as "one of the smartest people I know."

Junior Scott Hess, a farmer's son, achieved a perfect math score on his PSATs and hopes one day to design computer programs.

(Unlike teachers in many small schools, Lane, Bleeker and Larson have degrees in the subjects they teach. They have advanced degrees as well.)

Most of the parents are farmers or blue-collar workers, Wagner said.

Only 8.5 percent of the adults in

the community have college degrees, compared with 43.1 percent in Edina.

Not surprisingly, every year Pipestone lures students from smaller school districts.

This year four families who pay taxes in other districts are paying $911 apiece in tuition to send their children to Pipestone, and another family had one of their sons adopted by an older brother to attend the school, Wagner said.

Verdi, which has considerably lower test scores, has been the biggest contributor over the years.

Pipestone guidance counselor Richard Kvamme attributes some of the success of the school's students to peer pressure.

"We have a program now where every year we have kids come back from college to talk to the students. They say they're glad they took the extra math classes."

What the experts say:

Kenneth Keller
President, University of Minnesota:

I think it will be good if the state and university do something to help these small schools that don't offer advanced courses. The [tougher admissions standards] considered by the university should encourage schools to make changes.

If the state didn't just put money into districts, but found ways to use money to help these schools stimulate the kind of changes that ought to be there, schools might offer advanced courses.

I would like to see more districts working together to provide more opportunities.

Teachers could travel between schools to teach and schools could do a better job using computers to aid instruction.

Certainly offering pre-college math courses seems to be a wise thing. I think we owe it to children. A lack of science courses will mean that some students will take extra time to catch up in college. I wouldn't insist on calculus. They (small schools) just don't have the numbers (of students) or the money.

I don't think it's realistic to talk about closing schools at this point. I think there is a great deal of local pride. It's more than politics. Small local schools maybe have other values for students, enabling them to be close to home, to see friends. It's not a question of whether the education is equal in large and small schools, but whether there are tradeoffs.

Some small schools do well. I feel there are too many exceptions to say small class size led to low math scores.

Harold Howe II
Professor of education, Harvard University Graduate School; member, College Boards Commission on Pre-college Guidance and Counseling:

There are three possibilities for a solution to this problem:

• Moving further in the direction of consolidation.

• Putting much more money into these districts to allow them to attract the teachers they can't now and maintain very small classes in subjects such as calculus.

• Various innovations such as TV, traveling teachers and computer hookups with other school systems.

I would hesitate to suggest the entire state go for just one of these. In certain places consolidation may make sense. In other places you would have them riding three hours on a bus, for all I know. Therefore more money or some kind of inventive approach to isolated education systems would make more sense.

Nobody has a good answer to how you build something to replace the loyalty, community feeling and sense of pride that exists around a small school.

The state could help communities that are going to give up their schools. Perhaps some recreational programs could be continued, with state money, even though the school has consolidated.

But I don't see any way to set aside the fact that when physics, math, language and literature are not available . . . that alternate benefits provided by small schools cannot make up for that.

I think it is a fundamental deprivation of college-bound kids not to have the opportunity for those experiences.

Walt Haney

Professor of education, Center for Study of Testing, Evaluation and Educational Policy, Boston College:

The difference between scoring in the 44th and 60th percentile is not go-

ing to make that much difference today. Given the demographic trends expected for the next five to eight years, it will be easy to get into college. But it may make some minor difference in some cases.

You should take the time to find out what schools offer which classes in math. You also should have used a better measure for socio-economic status such as jobs.

But mainly you are attempting to determine what is happening to individual students based on group averages, and that is very dangerous. You should look at socio-economic status of individual households.

A couple of other minor things bothered me. The verbal [test] does measure verbal reasoning. But reasoning is a very tenuous thing. Research has shown the verbal reasoning ability is not nearly as influenced by instruction as math, but it is affected.

The College Board is saying [otherwise] because they don't like anyone using their data. Our studies show it's a lot easier to coach for math than verbal, but that there is some achievement in the verbal.

Studies have also found that taking the course is much more important than qualifications of the teacher.

Your story raises some important policy issues, mainly the need to increase the teaching of science and math in small schools. But I would personally say further scrutiny is warranted and would certainly not change policy based on this.

Family atmosphere holds Verdi students

By Dave Anderson
Staff Writer
Verdi, Minn.

This year's nine-member senior class at the Verdi Public School is triple the size of last year's.

And, barring transfers or tragedies, it will be triple the size of next year's graduating class in this tiny farming town near the South Dakota border.

Courses taken by fewer than a dozen students are the norm; it's not uncommon to see two or three students in a classroom.

The six freshmen, five sophomores, three juniors and nine seniors—a total enrollment of 23—are believed to make Verdi the state's smallest high school.

It is not that Verdi students would have to travel dozens of miles to a larger school. There are three other high schools within a 20-minute drive, including Pipestone, the state's top-scoring public school. In fact, in recent years half the families in the Verdi district have sent their children elsewhere.

But Verdi's students say they like their little school.

Eighty-four of them, from kindergarten through 12th grade, share a 60-year-old building with 13 classrooms, two libraries, a cafeteria, a small gym, two computers and a teacher's lounge frequented by students.

Relationships among students and teachers are relaxed and a student with a problem does not need to wade through a labyrinth of rules and bureaucracy to get a solution.

But most of all there is great pride in doing so well for being so small.

Yet there are drawbacks to having fewer students than some high schools have English teachers.

Size and consolidation are such emotion-charged issues in Verdi that many of the students agreed to discuss the drawbacks of attending such a small school only if their names were not used.

But those problems, students said, relate more to sports and social activities than academics.

Last year a senior complained that no one went to school dances because "there was no one to come."

"You don't see much dating within the school . . .," said one girl. "We're all more like friends. By the time you get to dating age you have such strong friendships with everyone you wouldn't think of dating them. They're all more like family."

Boys' basketball and football is now paired with Lake Benton, 8 miles to the east, and girls can be Lake Benton cheerleaders.

"In sports almost everyone has to go out to have enough for a team," said senior Tracy Rosenboom. "That puts too much pressure on some students and you wind up with people on a team who don't really want to be on the team."

Rosenboom, who plays volleyball for Verdi and is a basketball cheerleader for Lake Benton, likes the family atmosphere of a small school. In a physics class of two, for instance, "You just sit down and have a conversation and discuss things," she said. "It's not so formal and you're not afraid to ask stupid questions."

Rosenboom and classmate Lisa Aberson are planning to attend

Mankato State University — Rosenboom for elementary education, Aberson for art education.

Like many students in small high schools, they have taken some courses elsewhere. Aberson drove to Tyler High School each morning for an art class that is not offered at Verdi. Rosenboom drove to a vocational school for trigonometry.

A Minneapolis Star and Tribune study found that students from small schools average lower in college entrance exams.

But, despite its size, Verdi's students over five years have averaged better than those in 30 percent of the state's schools on the Preliminary Scholastic Aptitude Tests (PSAT). Still, its average is about 8 points below the statewide average and 27 points behind nearby Pipestone.

Verdi's size also requires faculty members to put in more preparation time.

Al Steinhoff, for example, teaches American history to 7th and 10th graders, geography to 8th graders, civics to sophomores, driver education to juniors and social studies to seniors — in addition to being acting principal.

Another problem is money. Because some costs remain relatively fixed, it is considerably more expensive to educate children in small schools.

Verdi had one professional staff member for about every 6.6 students in 1984, compared with the statewide average 1 to 16.

But teaching costs came to $1,326 per child, while the statewide figure was $1,152. Some other costs were double the statewide average, and total operating expenses came to about $3,340 per student, $750 higher than the statewide average of $2,590.

At Verdi the teachers subsidize the district by agreeing to a pay scale based on 85 percent of the average in surrounding school districts. Were it not for the lower salaries and part-time superintendent, expenses would be even higher. Steinhoff said a lot of the teachers stay there because of other ties to the community. "There are two kinds of people in the world," he said. "Some will go anyplace for a certain job. Others will take any job in a certain place.

"Perhaps students from schools like ours don't do as well on the tests because we put more emphasis on morals, values and patriotism than memorizing. We are more concerned with what kind of people we turn out.

"This is an awful nice school," he added. "We don't draw combat pay here."

EXAMPLE 4

Journalists accept "honorariums" from government

The following story, MOON-
LIGHTING FOR THE GOVERNMENT, by George Garneau, was originally
published in *Editor & Publisher* magazine on February 18, 1989, and is
reproduced here with permission.

It's an excellent example of a story about ethics in journalism. It's
an example of the use of the Freedom of Information Act to uncover
apparent wrongdoing. It's an example of how reporters can be led down
the road toward corruption and co-optation. And it's an example of how
reporters, like many other people, apply strict ethical standards to others
but protect themselves with rationalizations when someone suggests they
apply the same standards to themselves. As Garneau writes, "Journalists, many of whom thrive on exposing conflicts of interest and personal
affairs of public officials, take a broader view when it comes to their
own."

Moonlighting for the government

*Dozens of journalists who cover the government are paid
by the government to appear on government-produced
radio and TV programs*

By George Garneau

Journalists who cover the U.S.
government for prominent national
news organizations regularly moonlight for agencies of the same U.S.
government.

Dozens of mainstream Fourth Estate practitioners lend their names,
faces and reputations — for pay — to ra-

dio and television programs and publications of the U.S. government, according to records obtained by *E&P* under the Freedom of Information Act.

The United States Information Agency and Voice of America pay outside journalists from several hundred dollars to thousands of dollars a year in "honorariums" for appearing on programs broadcast around the world. Reporters can earn $100 for a 10-minute talk show to $475 for moderating one-hour discussion and interview shows.

Staffers for *Time, Newsweek, U.S. News and World Report, Christian Science Monitor,* the *Baltimore Sun* and the *New Republic* have participated along with syndicated columnists and free-lance journalists.

The practice is part of a long-simmering ethical controversy sharply dividing Washington journalists. It recently fueled discord among journalists elected to control congressional press passes. When a committee banned VOA employment of Capitol magazine and newsletter reporters and required fuller disclosure about outside income, its majority was ousted by vote of reporters.

Journalists, many of whom thrive on exposing conflicts of interest and personal affairs of public officials, take a broader view when it comes to their own.

"I have felt the wrath of reporters who drape themselves in the First Amendment and then claim it is nobody's business but their own if they earn money from the people about whom they write," said Rick Maze, Times Journal Co., reporter who was voted off the periodical committee. T-J Co. owns six D.C.-area papers.

In an article appearing on the *New York Times* op-ed page, Maze said, "It's virtually breathtaking to see the arrogance that surfaces among some journalists when the tables turn and questions arise about their possible conflicts of interest."

Views about journalists participating in USIA are polarized. Participants see no conflict of interest. Critics see an outright conflict at worst and an appearance of conflict at best.

"Absurd," said New Republic magazine editor Michael Kinsley of rules barring congressional correspondents from receiving pay to appear on government programs.

Conflicts are "not a trivial problem," he said, adding, "I cannot see how working for our own government is more corrupting than accepting honoraria from corporations, lobbying groups and so on, all of which are untouched by the rules.

"Of the many ways journalists can compromise themselves, occasional – or even regular – stints with the VOA seem relatively harmless."

Lars-Erik Nelson, Washington, D.C., bureau chief of the New York *Daily News,* disagrees.

"We're not here to work for the government, we're here to cover the government," Nelson said.

VOA "is engaged in government propaganda to which journalists should not lend their credibility," he said, adding it recalls an era when reporters wrote speeches for politicians and then reported on the speeches.

"I don't do it any more," said Henry Trewhitt, the U.S. News & World Report diplomatic correspondent who earned more than $30,000 over two years for numerous USIA appearances, records show. He said he saw no conflict, but quit after his employer banned the practice in January.

"There is certainly a question and I recognize it as a valid question," Trewhitt said. "This has been something I have done for many years and VOA never tried to influence anything I said. As long as I was my own man in the process, it wasn't something I was concerned about."

What if he had to cover USIA?

"I would have a problem with that, I think. The question simply never came up."

"We felt the time had come to avoid the appearance of conflict," said Kathy Bushkin, U.S. News & World Report director of editorial administration.

A memo told staff: "While we have never thought that our reporters were compromised by USIA programs, we do not believe it is appropriate to accept fees for these government-sponsored broadcasts."

Charles Corddry, a Baltimore Sun defense correspondent whose records show he earned $1,100 over two years—$100 for each appearance on a 10-minute discussion show, America Today—said his employer did not object.

"I did not feel there was any conflict in what I did," he said, declining to explain.

USIA plans to spend $951 million in 1990, more than double its 1981 budget. With a stated objective of increasing international understanding of American society and U.S. foreign policy, it operates in 127 nations, often with ties to U.S. embassies.

VOA, whose radio programs beam around the world, including communist nations, gets the bulk of funding, though USIA's satellite TV network, Worldnet, has grown to reach 80 nations.

USIA, whose director is appointed by the president, is prohibited by law from distributing information domestically. Through its certification authority over international distribution of independent films, USIA has "a virtual license to engage in censorship," a federal appeals court said last year.

VOA airs Press Conference U.S.A., its version of Meet the Press, and Issues in the News, its version of the McLaughlin Group.

Payments to participants "assure the credibility and continuity" of programs, according to VOA spokesperson Beth Kinsley, who said appearances were "not a promotion of the government," but conformed to VOA's mandate to present diverse views and opinions.

"It would be difficult to air if we had to rely on them appearing for free," she said. "We don't think there is any problem with payment. Some take it, some don't."

Worldnet pays "honorariums" to journalists who appear on roundtable discussions and who moderate "dialogues" in which foreign journalists interview officials in Washington by teleconference.

They are paid "for their expertise," according to William Eames, USIA deputy director.

In 1986, the Daily Correspondents Gallery banned members from receiving VOA paychecks. Michael Shanahan, then gallery chairman and currently McClatchy newspapers political correspondent, said, "I just thought it was flat wrong. I didn't think there was any gray area at all. We pretend to be the keepers of the gate in writing about politics. If we're going to set up an accrediting agency that tells the world, 'These reporters are free of real or apparent conflicts of interest,' you can't purport to write about the government and get paid by the government."

Shanahan "never believed anybody was on the take or tainted or toned down stories because of money received from VOA, but anybody can look at that and say, 'I wonder if he's getting paid.' It's a direct and apparent conflict of interest."

"When the issue came up two years ago, we laid the law down," said

Chuck Lewis, outgoing Associated Press Washington bureau chief. "The AP staff is not allowed to appear on VOA programs. It makes no difference if it's free or if they are compensated."

"It's an appearance problem," said Lewis, explaining that viewers and listeners don't know if journalists are paid or not.

Last November, the Periodical Press Gallery, aware of members earning substantial sums despite rules banning government employment, spelled it out: no paid USIA or VOA appearances.

Shirley Hobbs Scheibla, a *Barron's* Washington editor, said journalists "shouldn't be appearing on VOA because it is an acknowledged propaganda arm and we aren't supposed to have propagandists accredited to the gallery."

Journalists who appear on the programs, however, say they are free to express their views and often criticize the government.

Times Journal Co. vice president and editorial director James Doyle, in a letter to the Periodical Press Gallery, said his appearances on VOA shows were "as unfettered" as commercial journalism and talk shows.

Journalists should contribute to VOA and USIA and should be paid, he said, and "should not impede the efforts of those agencies to present good American journalism to the world."

To deny their press accreditation would "distort" press gallery rules and "stifle, in no small way, the free expression that American journalists enjoy."

Pat Clawson, who recently won election to the periodical gallery's executive committee, said he would not work for the government, but journalists have a right to, and their news organizations, not a committee established by Congress, should decide.

"I think we have very serious ethical problems in journalism, but this is not one of them," said syndicated columnist Georgie Anne Geyer, a frequent USIA guest on programs and overseas trips.

Geyer, who nets $5,000 for speeches, said USIA pay is so low as to be insulting, but she participates almost as "charity" because "I see nothing wrong with serving the principles of my country."

"I am one of the most ethical journalists in this country," Geyer added, calling USIA "just another wing of journalism."

She finds no conflict in working for USIA and denied her views were swayed by the income paid her. She draws the line at writing speeches for government officials, and pointed out that well-paid reporters at big papers can afford the luxury of no outside income.

Journalists who appear on government-produced programs dismiss suggestions they would be compromised by a few hundred dollars.

"I spend most of my time attacking the State Department," said syndicated columnist M. Stanton Evans, who often appears for VOA. He called the objections by some journalists a "totally phony issue."

"Nonsense. A kind of puritanical foolishness," said David Aikman of Time magazine after moderating a VOA show. He said criticisms were especially ironic coming from reporters who receive free office space in the Capitol Building.

The code of ethics of the nation's biggest journalism association, Society of Professional Journalists, says only that journalists should protect their personal and professional lives "from conflict of interest, real or apparent," and moonlighting should be avoided "if it compromises the integrity of journalists and their employers."

EXAMPLE 5

Judges golf when they should be in court

The television investigative story "Hennepin County District Court Judges" was aired October 17–20, 1983, and is reproduced in transcript form, with permission (video cues added). It was produced by John Lindsay, written and reported by Al Austin, photographed and edited by Peter Molenda, and investigated and researched by Mary Feidt and Don Shelby.

The story is an excellent example of TV's strengths as an investigative medium. It's one thing to read about judges playing golf when they should be working. It's another thing to watch them play golf when the on-screen clock shows that they're playing during working hours on a workday. It's one thing to read about how the judges squirm when confronted. It's another to watch them do so on camera.

This program made a special point, as all good investigative reports should do, of answering the questions the viewer is always asking in one form or another: What's this got to do with me? Why should I care? The program's answers: Because you're paying these people, because they've asked for more of your money to pay other judges to help them out, and because if you need to go to court, you'll probably have to wait an extra two years for your case to come up because these people spend their time on the golf course rather than on the bench.

The program also made a point of naming and commending, at least implicitly, the hardworking judges who vacationed on vacation time rather than on work time. Commending those judges was the proper thing to do, but it also made the goldbricking judges look worse. And it allowed the reporters to sidestep the possible charge that they were hyping their story by trying to tar all the judges with the same sensationalist brush.

The report also did a good job of dramatizing the backlog of cases these judges presumably should have been taking care of — by showing a reporter sitting at a desk piled with files — files containing unresolved court cases.

Following the standard TV format, the program clearly separated its commentary on the situation from its reporting of it but, again following standard TV practice, used the commentary as the kicker on the broadcast, thus adding punch to the opinion. Under standard newspaper practice, the editorial comment on such an investigation would end up on the editorial page, where few would read it.

HENNEPIN COUNTY
DISTRICT COURT JUDGES

PART I

PAT ON CAMERA	INTRO: (PAT MILES) The WCCO-TV I-Team spent the summer watching the Hennepin County Court judges at work. As it turned out, though, much of the observing was not done in the court- room. Al Austin is here with part one of the in- vestigation.
PAT/AL AUSTIN TWO SHOT	
AL AUSTIN ON CAM	AL AUSTIN: For more than a year, we heard attorneys in Hennepin County saying privately that while the District Court was complaining of overwork and asking the Legislature for more judges to relieve the burden, some District judges seemed not to have enough to do. Especially in the summer . . . This summer we investigated.
AUSTIN REPORT (ON TAPE) STARTS HERE	VIDEO
WIDE SHOT— GOVERNMENT CENTER FOLLOWED BY SHOTS OF JUDGES ARRIVING AT CENTER	AUSTIN: What we did was serve as a kind of time clock for some of the judges. Marking their arrivals and departures on the job at the Henne- pin County Government Center. There are 24 District judges in Hennepin County. They hear

---

The story in example 5 is reprinted with permission of WCCO Television, Minneapolis.

STILL PHOTOS OF
JUDGES

everything from small lawsuits to murder cases. They're paid 55-thousand dollars a year and they get 6 weeks paid vacation a year. The Legislature added 4 judges to the Hennepin County bench last year to help handle the 6 thousand new criminal and civil cases filed each year and the backlog of old cases.

SHOTS OF FILING
CABINETS; ASSISTANT
THUMBING THROUGH
FILES

SETUP SHOT (AUSTIN
AND ATTORNEY SAM
MCCLOUD)

That backlog is heavy. A lawsuit filed now in Hennepin County likely would not come to trial for 3 years. That's nearly twice the delay found acceptable in a recent national study done for court administrators. Attorneys agree that the delay is a serious problem that can cause unfair settlements.

SOUND-ON-TAPE (SOT):
MCCLOUD

SAM MCCLOUD (attorney): That problem could be solved if we were willing to spend more money on judges. In other words, hire additional judges.

AUSTIN STANDUP
OUTSIDE
GOVERNMENT
CENTER

AUSTIN: That opinion has wide support. Spokesmen for the district court say 4 to 6 more judges are needed and the Minnesota Trial Lawyers Association has asked the Legislature for more judges for Hennepin County and more pay for judges.

The question is are the current judges doing all they can to relieve the backlog?

SHOTS OF JUDGES
WALKING INSIDE
CENTER. (INDIVIDUAL
NAMES
SUPERIMPOSED)

AUSTIN: A district judge's summer routine calls for him to spend 2 weeks handling criminal matters. The rest of the time he is largely free to work on a block of about 70 or 80 backlogged civil cases, at his own pace. Keeping his own time card, so to speak. It's called Summer Block and it's a system the judges, themselves, voted in.

FULL-SCREEN
GRAPHIC WHICH
INCLUDES VIDEO OF
JUDGE KANTOROWICZ

Here is our time card for one . . . Judge Richard Kantorowicz. Judge Kantorowicz arose from the Northside DFL machine, became a Minneapolis Alderman, then a municipal judge. He was appointed to the district bench in 1973.

AUGUST 1ST   3 37
SUPERIMPOSED ON
GRAPHIC
AUSTIN STANDUP ON
GOLF COURSE

Monday, August 1st. Judge Kantorowicz arrived at the Government Center at 8:35 A.M. He stayed 3 hours and 37 minutes.

This is Theodore Wirth Golf Course, just a few blocks from Judge Kantorowicz's home. The

Judge left the Courthouse at 10 minutes after Noon, went to lunch, then drove home, changed his clothes and arrived here at the golf course at 1:35. It's now 2:25 and there he is just leaving the third green.

WIDE SHOT OF JUDGE
KANTOROWICZ
PLAYING GOLF

AUSTIN: The Judge played golf until almost 4:00 and then went home. He would be back on the golf course the next day, Tuesday, at 12:45 and after golf, again go home for the day. At most, Tuesday was a 4 hour day at court.

ANOTHER GRAPHIC
INCLUDING VIDEO OF
THE JUDGE AND DATE
SUPERIMPOSED

ANOTHER GRAPHIC
W/DATE
SUPERIMPOSED

Wednesday. Judge Kantorowicz is not seen at the Government Center all day. His clerk says he is at a meeting and, quote "May not be in today." The court's daily calendar makes no mention of Kantorowicz having business outside the Government Center.

TIGHT SHOT COURT
CALENDAR. NAME
HIGHLIGHTED

ANOTHER GRAPHIC
W/DATE
SUPERIMPOSED

Thursday. Again, he was not seen to enter the Government Center at all. The clerk said he would be in and out.

AUSTIN STANDUP IN
FRONT OF JUDGE'S
HOME

At 1:00, a car let Judge Kantorowicz out here, at his home. He took a set of golf clubs out of the car and went inside. Then at 2:30 he left the house and went, not to the Government Center, but to this printshop.

SHOT OF PRINTSHOP
AND CAMPAIGN
PAMPHLETS

AUSTIN: The shop was printing primary campaign literature for Alderman Al Daugherty. The production supervisor of the printshop said Judge Kantorowicz was instructing him on how to print this Daugherty brochure. Kantorowicz was in the shop for 30 minutes and then went home.

STILL PHOTO OF
KANTOROWICZ
OUTSIDE PRINTSHOP

ANOTHER GRAPHIC
WITH THE JUDGE AND
DATE SUPERIMPOSED

Friday, August 5th into the Government Center for 3 hours and 15 minutes. He left for the day at 11:20. In midafternoon he returned to the same printing company to work on Alderman Daugherty's campaign literature. He stayed there 35 minutes and then went home.

SHOT OF PRINTSHOP

WALKING SHOT OF
JUDGE AND ANOTHER
MAN

FULL SCREEN
GRAPHIC W/DATES
AND HOURS THE
JUDGE WORKED
DURING FIRST FIVE
DAYS OF AUGUST

And so, for the first week in August, the time card for Judge Kantorowicz shows 10 hours 52 minutes at court.

SHOTS OF THE
JUDGE – WALKING
AND ON THE GOLF
COURSE

We watched for Judge Kantorowicz's arrivals and departures for 16 days. Only twice in those 16 days did he put in more than a half day at the Government Center. Often it was much less. And 5 days, our observation showed he did not go to the Government Center at all. Frequently he could be found at the golf course during court hours.

MORE GOLF

Thursday, August 18th. Just finishing a round of golf at 3:30. Monday August 22nd. Starting a round at 12:43 pm. After he finishes the golf, he will go home. Tuesday, August 23rd. Half past three and he's on the 17th hole.

MORE WALKING
SHOTS. GOLF COURSE

For those 16 workdays, three weeks and one day, our time card shows Judge Kantorowicz putting in an average of just 13 hours a week. Some of those days we don't know where he went and he won't say, but each time we kept track of him, we found no sign that he was engaged in judicial business. He carried no briefcase away from the Government Center and neither the court calendar nor the daily assignment sheets or other court records indicated that any of this time was counted against his 6 weeks vacation. Or gave any other reason for the Judge to be absent. Rather those records showed him to be working.

STILL SHOTS OF
LETTERS

We sent Judge Kantorowicz 2 letters asking for an interview or for information that might explain his absences or explain the rest of his summer work schedule. And we repeatedly phoned his office. He never responded.

AUSTIN CONFRONTS
JUDGE ON THE
SIDEWALK

AUSTIN: "Why won't you answer questions about your work?"

KANTOROWICZ: "Because the point of the story is that we have a spokesman for ourselves. You guys are in a ratings war. Your I-Team is strictly a ratings war. I'm not involved in that . . . "

AUSTIN: "Judge Fitzgerald, even if he would talk to us, he could not explain your comings and goings, could he? Don't you want us to have the truth? Don't you think it's proper that . . . "

KANTOROWICZ: "I think that this is really, really, really lousy journalism."

AUSTIN: "Why, Sir?"

KANTOROWICZ: "Accosting me on the street and then after you start the conversation, you tell me I'm being recorded."

AUSTIN: "I can't reach you by phone or by letter, so how else am I supposed to reach you?"

SHOTS OF JUDGE
WALKING

AUSTIN: We don't know how Judge Kantorowicz spent the rest of his summer. We know that despite all the leisure time we observed, he managed to dispose of all but 4 of the block of 64 cases assigned to him for the summer. Evidently the judge fulfilled the requirements of the summer block system he had helped institute.

SHOT OF DISTRICT
JUDGE

Chief District Judge Patrick Fitzgerald said, it is acceptable for a judge to take off when his work's done for the day. The job is not a 9 to 5 job, Fitzgerald said.

GOLF COURSE SHOTS

But the question remained. How much more could Judge Kantorowicz have done to reduce the three year backlog of cases in Hennepin County?

END OF TAPE REPORT

AUSTIN ON CAM

CLOSE: (AUSTIN) Judge Kantorowicz is by no means typical of the other Hennepin County District Court judges. Some of them seem to work all the time and others were only slightly less industrious. But neither was Judge Kantorowicz an isolated case. Several of his brethren spent precious little time at the Government Center. We'll tell you about them tomorrow night.

PART II

PAT ON CAM

INTRO: (PAT MILES) If you file a lawsuit in Hennepin County today, expect it to take almost 3 years to come to trial. WCCO Television's I-

	Team discovered the casual work schedules of
PAT/AL AUSTIN TWO SHOT	some district court judges may play a part in that delay. Al Austin is here with us with part 2 of the I-Team's investigation. Al . . .
AUSTIN ON CAM	AUSTIN: Last night we focused on the activities of Hennepin County District Court Judge Richard Kantorowicz. During the 16 days we watched
GOLF COURSE SHOTS	him this summer, he appeared to be working an average of just 13 hours a week, spending much of the rest of the time on the golf course. We
BACK ON CAM	found other district judges on golf courses as well, and in bars, at lake cabins and on tennis courts during the work day.
AUSTIN REPORT (ON TAPE) STARTS HERE	VIDEO
STILL PHOTO OF RILEY	AUSTIN: This is Judge Neil Riley. Widely respected for his activities in support of nonprofit organizations, Judge Riley is perhaps the best known of all Hennepin County Court judges. He
SHOT OF JUDGE WALKING	has a reputation of dispensing speedy justice, settling cases before they come to trial. Sometimes he holds hearings at unusual times, Saturday mornings, for instance. But we did not see him work much during regular court hours. We kept track of Judge Riley for 15 days.
GRAPHIC	On Monday, August 15th, Judge Riley arrived at work at 8:30. He left at 5 minutes til noon. Drove home to Wayzata and did not return
JUDGE AT POOLSIDE	to court that day. He did not go into work at all on Tuesday or on Wednesday. Instead, he spent Wednesday at home sitting on his dock reading and playing tennis at a neighbor's house. Yet, both days he was scheduled to be at work.
	The following day, Thursday, Riley put in an hour and 25 minutes at the Government Center. And then he left for the day, telling two acquaintances that he was going to play tennis with his son-in-law.
JUDGE PLAYING TENNIS, ETC.	Friday, again Judge Riley was scheduled to work. Again, he stayed home. He took the sun on his dock, he played volleyball and he played tennis twice, in the morning and again in the afternoon.
GRAPHIC	During the whole week, Judge Riley spent less than 5 hours at the County Government Cen-

SHOTS OF TENNIS

ter and court records show that none of the days he stayed home was counted against his vacation time. The records showed he had already taken 6 weeks vacation this year, though he had more time accumulated. In the 15 days we watched, Judge Riley's average day at the office was 2 hours and 25 minutes—including 6 days when he did not come in at all.

Judge Riley declined to explain his absences to us.

AUSTIN STANDUP AT DESK

Judge Riley and the other judges were working under a new system this summer called summer block. Rather than the customary method of assigning cases one at a time to whichever judge became available, the judges had voted to divide up more than a thousand old civil cases. Mostly, uncomplicated cases that could be settled without a jury trial. And to work on them through the summer. Judge Riley was given 95 cases, Judge Kantorowicz 64 and so forth. Each judge would then dispose of his own cases however he wished.

SHOTS OF JUDGE WALKING

SHOTS OF PROVO IN HIS OFFICE

True to his reputation for speed, Judge Riley disposed of 90 cases. That was more than any other judge. And court administrator Jack Provo, who declined an on-camera interview, says it was a very productive season for the entire court . . . more productive than last summer. And, says Provo, if the system allowed some short workdays, so be it.

STILL OF PROVO

PROVO (AUDIO): If a judge is done with his businesses, there is no more court business that you can bring in front of that judge, that judge is free to do what he or she wants.

WALKING SHOT OF IVERSON

AUSTIN: By the end of August, Judge Irving Iverson had finished all but 2 of his 79 cases assigned to him for the summer. And so, he was gone the entire week before Labor Day. His clerk told callers he was on vacation.

STILL PHOTO OF JUDGE

Here he is outside his lake cabin outside Alexandria, Minnesota. Early afternoon Friday, September 2nd.

STILL OF PROVO

PROVO: Well, it amounts to a very short week on the job, I would submit that the judge probably has time off coming through vacation.

COURT RECORD

AUSTIN: But, court records listed Judge Iverson as working . . . made no mention of his using vacation time that week. Those records showed that he had taken almost 7 weeks vacation between February and June.

STILL OF LETTER

Judge Iverson did not answer our written requests that he explain his absences and contacted in person, he declined an interview.

AUSTIN CONFRONTS JUDGE IN THE STREET

AUSTIN: Would you tell me why, why you won't talk about your work?

SHOTS OF JUDGE

IVERSON: Well, I . . . I just don't approve of the methods being used.

AUSTIN: Judge Chester Durda was also absent several full days. But, more often Judge Durda worked mornings and took afternoons off. At least he did during the 14 days we kept a time clock on him.

GRAPHIC AND STILL PHOTOS OF JUDGE

On July 28, a Thursday, Judge Durda arrived for work at 9 past 9. At 12:37, he left, drove to this restaurant in Northeast Minneapolis, and stayed there until 3:00. Then drove to Tai Ping Restaurant in Golden Valley. He was still there when the workday ended at 4:30. The following three days he kept to a similar routine. On Wednesday, August 3rd, Judge Durda arrived at work at 9:05, left at 2 minutes past noon. That's his car, the maroon Buick. He drove to the Bierman Athletic Building at the University of Minnesota—he's an active Gophers booster—and was inside that building for almost an hour. Then, he drove to the Lincoln Del, where he sat at the bar drinking with a group of men for 2 hours and 15 minutes. Then he went home for the day.

SHOTS OF JUDGE IN VARIOUS PLACES

In the 14 days we watched, only once did Judge Durda spend more than a half day at the Government Center. Not once did we see him engaged in any judicial business elsewhere. 5 of the 14 days our observations and calls to his clerk indicated he did not show up at all. Court records made no mention of vacation or any other reason for him to be off. He was scheduled to be at work. Like the other judges, Durda would provide no explanation.

SHOT OF COURT RECORDS

AUSTIN CONFRONTS THE JUDGE OUTSIDE CENTER	DURDA: I'm tied up with a hundred cases this morning, I've got a full afternoon.
	AUSTIN: Could we do it this evening then? Could we talk this evening?
	DURDA: The Chief Judge speaks for the entire bench.
	AUSTIN: But he can't speak for your personal activities and that's what's in question. You know on some days when you were absent . . .
	DURDA: I don't think you ought to even be recording this. That isn't fair. That's attack journalism.
	AUSTIN: Could we arrange . . .
	DURDA: I've had enough . . . that's it.
STILL PHOTOS OF JUDGES	AUSTIN: Durda, Iverson, Kantorowicz, Riley . . . all filled their summer quota of cases, or nearly so.
STILL OF PROVO END OF TAPE REPORT	PROVO (AUDIO): I will simply say this, this is a very productive bench. It's a very hardworking bench and that's the bottom line.
AUSTIN ON CAM	CLOSE: (AUSTIN) Many attorneys agree with Administrator Provo and tomorrow night, we'll meet some judges who look to us to be especially hardworking. We'll also examine the connection between judges with nothing to do and trials with no judges to hear them and the 3 year backlog of civil cases that sits there waiting.

PART III

DAVE ON CAM DAVE AND AL AUSTIN TWO SHOT	INTRO: (DAVE MOORE) As you are undoubtedly aware, this week the WCCO I-Team is examining the work habits of some Hennepin County District Court judges. Al Austin is here with part 3 of the investigation.
AUSTIN ON CAM	AUSTIN: Dave, under a system the Hennepin County District Court judges devised themselves

this summer, so long as each judge pulled his 2 weeks of criminal court duty and disposed of a stack of old civil cases, he could do with his time what he wished. In previous reports we've showed how 4 judges found great amounts of leisure time in that system—taking whole days off, working 15 hours a week or less. There were other judges who managed lesser amounts of time off.

AUSTIN REPORT (ON TAPE) STARTS HERE	VIDEO
SHOTS OF JUDGE WALKING	AUSTIN: Judge A. Paul Lommen has been a district judge in Hennepin County for 12 years and before that he was a municipal judge. This summer he was assigned 74 old lawsuits to resolve between mid-June and early September. Evidently, this workload was not excessive. During the 12 days we clocked Judge Lommen's arrivals and departures on the job, his average day was just 3 hours and 21 minutes. Three of those days, he didn't show up at the County Government Center at all. Even though court records showed him to be at work. And other days, one after another, Judge Lommen left work about lunchtime and went home to stay. Never taking a briefcase home with him.
GRAPHIC	
SHOT OF CENTER	
MORE SHOTS OF JUDGE WALKING	
GRAPHIC	Wednesday, August 31st. He arrived at work at 9:31 and left at 12:29. Made some brief stops downtown, then caught a bus and went home. He was still there as the court day ended. Next day, Thursday, he left the Government Center a few minutes past noon, walked around town for an hour, returned to the Government Center for just 30 minutes, then caught a bus home. A member of his staff told callers he had gone to a seminar.
STILL OF JUDGE WITH STATEMENT SUPERIMPOSED	We asked Judge Lommen for an explanation of his work routine. Yesterday he sent a reply. It reads, in part: "On a number of occasions, there were time gaps when no case was immediately available for trial. When I had finished whatever work was scheduled for the day, it was my practice to leave the Government Center for the day. The productivity of the court did not suffer because of this practice. In fact, the productivity of the court was higher than ever this summer." Quote Judge Lommen.

SHOT OF JUDGE WALKING	Short as they were, Judge Lommen's workdays were longer than 4 other judges' we reported on earlier. At least on those days we observed them. And yet, many attorneys say the Hennepin County bench is hardworking . . . overworked.
STILLS OF OTHER JUDGES	And some judges did seem to be.
STILL OF THE JUDGES	We asked attorneys — who are the hardworking judges? Practically all mentioned Robert Bowen and Doris Huspeni. Our observations agree. Those two judges were regularly at work all day except when they took official vacations.
	Judges Delila Pierce, Crane Winton, Jonathon Lebedoff, Lindsay Arthur, William Posten, Eugene Minenko and Charles Porter worked long hours too.
SHOTS OF JUDGES WALKING	There were several judges we didn't watch, either because they were on vacations or special assignments in other buildings. Some judges alternate between full workdays and half days. Like Chief District Judge Patrick Fitzgerald.
SHOT OF JUDGE'S CAR DRIVING OFF FOLLOWED BY GRAPHIC	We kept a time clock on him 12 days. Six of them he worked all day; the other 6 were half days at the office. We don't know what he did all those afternoons he was gone. We only kept track of where he went once. Friday, August 26. Judge Fitzgerald left work at 11:33 and went right to the
SHOT OF JUDGE ON GOLF COURSE	Minneapolis Golf Club, where he spent the afternoon.
	Judge Fitzgerald granted us an off-camera interview as spokesman for the entire bench but, he repeatedly refused to explain his absences or to say if he considered it proper for judges to miss whole days of work. He kept repeating the same answer for both questions . . .
STILL PHOTO OF JUDGE	FITZGERALD: If you are contending that there is any kind of misconduct on the part of any members of the District Court bench, I refer you to the Minnesota Board on Judicial Responsibility.
AUSTIN STANDUP AT DESK	AUSTIN: Who's hurt by idle judges? Well, on August 18th, the Thursday when Judge Fitzgerald worked a half day, and Judges Kantorowicz and Riley worked just 2 hours each, and Judges Durda and Iverson were gone all day . . . 4 criminal trials were postponed because — according to court records — no judges were available.
(VIDEO OF COURT RECORDS SHOWING TRIALS POSTPONED USED HERE)	

The next day, Friday, 2 more trials were postponed—no judges available. On that day 18 of the 24 district judges were gone all afternoon. The following Wednesday, with 1 judge missing and several others off early, another criminal trial was postponed—no judges available.

ATTORNEY DAVID GHERITY SOUND-ON-TAPE (SOT)

AUSTIN (to David Gherity, attorney): Your client showed up, and his friends and family showed up . . .

GHERITY: Yes, he certainly did . . . and his mother was there and his friends were there also . . .

AUSTIN: And no trial . . .

GHERITY: And no trial.

SHOT OF BURRINGTON AT A TABLE

SHOT OF DESTROYED HOUSE

AUSTIN: But it's people like Joyce Burrington who have the long wait for judges. Her house exploded in the spring of 1979. She sued the utility company, hoping for money to rebuild.

JOYCE BURRINGTON SOT

AUSTIN: How long did it take you to get the money?

BURRINGTON: Three months shy of four years.

AUSTIN: Almost four years . . .

BURRINGTON: Almost four years. This is my first encounter with the court system. I had no idea anything would take four years like this . . . not when it seemed to be basically a cut and dried case as far as I was concerned.

END OF TAPE REPORT

AUSTIN ON CAM

CLOSE: (AUSTIN) Not all that 4 year wait was the fault of the court backlog. Joyce Burrington's case wasn't filed until several months after the explosion and attorneys weren't ready for the trial for nearly 2 years after that. But court officials themselves agree the delay is about double what it should be. Is there a connection between judges who don't show up for work and trials that have no judges to hear them? Could judges who are working only 2 or 3 hours a day do something about the court backlog by putting in full workdays? Spokesmen for the court say it's not that simple and Court Administrator Jack Provo, who works for the judges, says if they run out of work to do, that's his fault. But is it? The final report in this series tonight at 10.

PART IV

PAT ON CAM

PAT AND AUSTIN TWO SHOT

INTRO: (PAT MILES) For the past three nights the WCCO I-Team has revealed some questionable work habits among certain Hennepin County Court judges. Tonight, Al Austin is here with the final report and commentary. Al . . .

AUSTIN ON CAM

AUSTIN: We kept informal time cards on some of the Hennepin County District Court judges for about five weeks without their knowledge. We found about half the judges working long full days.

AUSTIN REPORT (ON TAPE) STARTS HERE

VIDEO

SHOTS OF JUDGES WALKING, GOLFING, PLAYING TENNIS . . .

AUSTIN: But, we also found Judge Richard Kantorowicz putting in just thirteen hours a week while we watched him. Found him missing from the Government Center days at a time, spending time on the golf course rather than in Court, designing campaign literature for an alderman during the workday.

We found Judge Neil Riley keeping similar short hours, spending his time at home or on the tennis court.

Found Judge Irving Iverson taking a full week off without counting it as a vacation — though a judge gets six weeks vacation a year.

We found Judge Chester Durda only once in fourteen days putting more than a half day at work. Sometimes taking full days off without claiming vacation time. Spending large chunks of the workday in restaurants and bars.

And we found Chief Judge Patrick Fitzgerald taking about half his afternoons off. Playing golf the afternoon we kept track of him. He said there's nothing wrong with judges doing

SHOTS OF
GOVERNMENT
CENTER EXTERIOR

that if they get their work done. Work they assigned themselves.

And while these and other judges were enjoying leisure time, their clerks and stenographers were left at loose ends. Their courtrooms were left empty. A three year backlog of civil cases waited and grew. And scheduled trials were being postponed for want of judges to hear them.

Spokesmen for the court say it's not a nine-to-five job. Judges sometimes work nights or weekends or at home and need time to reflect. And there are scheduling complications. . . .

COMMENTARY:

SHOTS OF JUDGES
WALKING

"COMMENTARY"
SUPERIMPOSED OVER
VIDEO

But is it possible that judges, intelligent professionals, faced with a huge backlog of cases and asking for more judges to help out with the work . . . that these judges can't find more than ten or fifteen hours of work to do a week? If they can't why not take an official vacation? Some judges did. Judges Bowen, Shiefelbein, Sedgwick, Pierce, Huspani, Arthur, Leslie, all got some of their six weeks vacation time out of the way this summer and still managed to do most of their summer work.

But some, no matter how they may characterize it, worked the system for extra vacation time. The system they worked out for themselves. Intentionally or not, they installed an incentive plan for themselves. The faster they got rid of

AUSTIN STANDUP
OUTSIDE
GOVERNMENT
CENTER

their stacks of cases, the more time off.

You probably noticed that not many judges had anything to say in these reports. Even though the reports were about judges. Some of these public officials made it clear they didn't feel they owed us an explanation. They resented what we were doing—watching them, asking questions. And they withdrew into the sanctity of their courts where our camera could not go.

AUSTIN STANDUP
OUTSIDE
GOVERNMENT
CENTER

You didn't hear much from attorneys either. Even on the most routine questions of fact, attorneys who were frank with us to begin with, grew silent and refused interviews when they learned we were checking up on the judges. "They're my friends, I have to face them in court," said one. "I'm afraid what might happen," said another.

"COMMENTARY"
SUPERIMPOSED OVER
VIDEO OF
GOVERNMENT
CENTER

And a third said, "You're flirting with power here. My clients could get hurt."

One other thing you didn't see . . . the inside of a courtroom. In their resentment of our project, the judges refused us permission to take pictures even of empty unused courtrooms. Wait a minute, we thought. Those aren't their courtrooms. Those courts belong to us all.

EXAMPLE 6

Federal officials
spend themselves silly

The following transcript of a radio investigation, which aired on WEEI NEWSRADIO 590 in Boston, April 2–4, 1986, and is printed here with permission, was reported by Gene Hartigan. It's an excellent example of the use of the Freedom of Information Act by a radio investigator to uncover substantial waste of taxpayer money by federal officials operating in the radio's listening area.

Hartigan had to analyze the 1,300 pages of documents his FOIA request sprung loose, and he also interviewed a great many past and present employees and directors of the erring agency, the Federal Emergency Management Agency (FEMA). If you're considering a similar investigation, Hartigan urges you to study the material you receive as a result of an FOIA request to make sure it's what you requested. He also urges learning a great deal about how the agency you're investigating works so that your questions are on target when you finally get to ask them.

Nowhere in this story did Hartigan accept at face value any explanation for apparent unnecessary spending put forward by an apparent perpetrator. Instead, he checked each explanation with another, apparently honest official in the agency, or he checked the facts himself to see what could have been done at less expense to the taxpayers. He emerged with a picture of part of an agency engaged in grossly unnecessary spending, the filing of fraudulent expense claims, and unnecessary junketing at taxpayer expense.

Hartigan's work indicates how helpful it is to do investigative reporting regularly: The tip that began this story came from past and present employees of the agency who had heard one of Hartigan's previous series.

Segment 1, FEMA Story, Wednesday, April 2, 1986, 7:30 a.m./8:30 a.m.

In Washington they are telling us there is a budget crisis. And while the president and Congress are finding ways to cut spending, one federal agency in New England ran up over $200,000 in bills to oversee disaster relief efforts for hurricane Gloria.

The Federal Emergency Management Agency, FEMA, is responsible for administering the relief efforts in the aftermath of hurricane Gloria. The storm did less damage than expected, but still caused Massachusetts, Rhode Island and Connecticut to be declared eligible for federal disaster assistance.

Last October the New England regional office of FEMA in Boston opened three disaster field offices, the first in Norwich, Connecticut, a second in Rhode Island and the third in Worcester, Massachusetts. These three offices would coordinate disaster assistance efforts with local officials.

This series of reports will focus on two central questions. First, are there sufficient budget controls in FEMA to prevent financial abuses in this time of massive federal budget deficits and is there evidence that local FEMA officials have wasted taxpayers' money in the conduct of agency programs?

The person occupying the office of chief of the disaster assistance program division has broad budgetary authority, including wide discretionary spending latitude. Has FEMA taken sufficient care to guarantee the occupant of that office has a track record of sound budget decision making? The available evidence raises serious questions on this point.

Information gathered by WEEI's investigative unit raises serious questions about the operation of the FEMA disaster effort. A review of records by WEEI indicates a pattern of excessive spending for supplies, equipment and personal expenses, all under the direction of FEMA chief of disaster assistance programs, Albert Gammal, who also served as federal coordinating officer for hurricane Gloria.

Gammal, originally a political appointee from the late 60s, has since attained civil service status. Gammal's early political strength was demonstrated in 1962 when he helped deliver the Worcester Republican delegation to former senator Edward Brooke, who at the time was running for attorney general against Elliot Richardson.

In 1969 he was appointed regional administrator for the General Services Administration, GSA. But in 1976, the Boston office of GSA under the direction of Albert Gammal became the focus of both a GSA internal audit and a *Globe* spotlight series that revealed the GSA office under Gammal's direction stood charged with awarding millions of dollars in government contracts to favored firms.

The GSA audit cited a pattern of abuses and violations of federal laws that benefited select contractors. WEEI has been unable to document that any legal

---

The story in example 6 is reprinted with permission of WEEI NEWSRADIO 590, Boston.

or administrative action was taken against Gammal as a result of the GSA audits.

In my next report, a disaster field office opens in Connecticut and the personal expense money starts to flow.

For the WEEI investigative unit, I'm Gene Hartigan.

Segment 2, FEMA Story, Wednesday, April 2, 1986, 4:30 p.m./5:30 p.m.

A review of records supplied by the regional office of the Federal Emergency Management Agency, FEMA, has revealed excessive spending for supplies, expenses and salaries topping $200,000. All under the direction of disaster coordinator Albert Gammal and FEMA regional director Henry Vickers.

Last September hurricane Gloria threatened the New England states with 130 mile per hour winds only to subside before hitting the coast. Enough damage did occur to require federal assistance. The distribution of that money is the responsibility of FEMA.

When FEMA personnel moved into Connecticut to open a disaster operations field office October 14, little did taxpayers know it would cost them over $75,000 for their two month stay. Those costs would result from personal meals, lodging, and some 20 rental cars including the use of Lincoln Continental sedans for three FEMA personnel flown in from California and Virginia.

The field office was under the direction of regional FEMA disaster assistance director Albert Gammal. It was to assist local officials with hurricane damage assessment and sign off on funding requests by cities and towns in Connecticut.

A review of records obtained by WEEI under the Freedom of Information Act show the following. From October 14, 1985, through December 3, 1985, persons under the direction of FEMA assigned to the Connecticut field office ran up bills for hotels, food, mileage, parking and tolls totaling $38,000. Other expense vouchers for rental cars, office overhead and miscellaneous total an additional $33,000.

FEMA personnel assigned in this region on temporary duty assignment receive $75 per day per diem and qualified for reimbursement for mileage, tolls and miscellaneous expenses.

Also, GSA government-recommended policy, which sets standards for FEMA, suggests no receipts be required unless the item or service costs over $25 each.

While FEMA disaster federal coordinating officer Gammal defends these expenses, random interviews with cities and towns in Connecticut raise questions why such large expenditures were necessary.

Interviews by WEEI's investigative unit with the disaster project officers of New Haven, Jewett City, Griswold and Montville, Connecticut show they had little if any personal contact with FEMA personnel during the assistance operation.

In all four cases each indicated their contact was handled by the Army

Corps of Engineers assigned to assess damage, and the resulting paperwork was mailed to the FEMA office or given to corps personnel. To date WEEI has surveyed _____ cities and towns to determine the extent to which the cost of field offices improved the delivery of services.

For example, New Haven's coordinator on hurricane Gloria, Michael Betz, told WEEI he never had a face to face meeting with anyone from FEMA in connection with Gloria. What is most unusual with the towns of Griswold, Jewett City and Montville is all are within 20 miles of the FEMA field office in Norwich, Connecticut, but none obtained personal assistance from FEMA with their claims.

Additional questions have been raised in WEEI's review of documents which show that personnel assigned to the Connecticut operation secured 20 rental cars and in less than 60 days ran up a bill for $6,400. Included in the listing of cars were three Lincoln sedans.

In one case the original car received was returned and a Lincoln was picked up to replace it. FEMA management told WEEI that car size is not a valid question as they, FEMA, negotiate for a set rate that covers all cars. Yet by their own admission and a review of rental agreements obtained by WEEI, differing rates on hourly, daily and weekly rates from two vendors were used. Disaster officer Gammal, who supervised the Connecticut operation, told WEEI he had no knowledge of the car rentals in Connecticut.

In my next report, while the damage is declared on the coast of Massachusetts, Al Gammal sets up a field office 46 miles inland in Worcester.

For the WEEI investigative unit, I'm Gene Hartigan.

Segment 3, FEMA Story, Thursday, April 3, 1986, 7:30 a.m./8:30 a.m.

ANCHOR INTRO: Last October President Reagan declared six eastern Massachusetts counties eligible for disaster relief as a result of hurricane Gloria. Additionally seven cities and towns from Worcester west were also declared eligible. On October 28 the Federal Emergency Management Agency, FEMA, under the direction of Albert Gammal moved the disaster assistance operation from its Boston office to a field office 46 miles away in Worcester. In part three of his investigative series, Gene Hartigan outlines how the move to Worcester set up the opportunity for regular staff and reservists to receive expense monies they would have otherwise not been eligible for.

HARTIGAN: The Worcester field office was put in place to assess storm damage and interact with cities and towns who would file for federal monies. But a random call to the communities that ring Worcester itself show that on only one occasion did any official called by WEEI visit the Worcester field office.

Records obtained by WEEI's investigative unit under the Freedom of Information Act show that reimbursements to regular staff of the Boston FEMA office for the 2½ month period October to January totaled $13,000 for hotels, food, parking, tolls and mileage expenses.

In contrast, WEEI has learned that the operation of FEMA disaster efforts at the 1981 Lynn fire, which included personal assistance, finding emergency housing, and public assistance, operated out of a disaster field office in Lynn. There were no hotels used for staff and very few expenses were filed for. This is quite the opposite from records obtained by WEEI which show staff employees out of the Boston office who would not normally receive per diem were being compensated because they were temporarily assigned to the Worcester office, just 46 miles from their regular Boston duties.

Most notable were expenses of $4,100 paid to one employee, a temporary hire clerk, who was traveling only 28 miles from Wayland to Worcester and according to her own expense voucher was leaving work nightly at no later than 6 P.M., yet stayed overnight in Worcester and Norwich, Connecticut, hotels 37 nights at government expense.

Also there were expenses paid to another regular staffer for $3,801. FEMA records show this secretary in the Boston FEMA regional office, who lives in Milton just a short ride from the office in Boston. Then there is the case of another FEMA employee who was assigned a rental car that she took home to the town of Hull at Christmas but did not return to Worcester until January 1st, keeping the car all week at government expense. When questioned, FEMA's Al Gammal told WEEI she had planned to come to work at the Boston office and work post Christmas, but had taken sick.

In another car related claim, one reservist filed for both mileage and reimbursement for gasoline charges at the same time, which appears to be double billing. In the case of two other FEMA special hires, their expense vouchers show them leaving Worcester on November 5 and 6 to visit the same cities and towns, at the same times, in two separate cars. A FEMA spokesman said scheduling of duties caused a conflict and required them to travel in separate vehicles.

When questioned about expense filing, Al Gammal told WEEI expense vouchers are "checked thoroughly at two levels. Every one is gone over with a fine tooth comb."

In my next report, furnishing the Worcester office, an expensive three month proposition.

For the WEEI investigative unit, I'm Gene Hartigan.

Segment 4, FEMA Story, Thursday, April 3, 1986, 4:30 p.m./5:30 p.m.

ANCHOR INTRO: On October 28 the Federal Emergency Management Administration, FEMA, opened a disaster field office in Worcester to deal with the effects of hurricane Gloria and oversee providing federal disaster funds to qualifying towns. But what some sources familiar with the operation of FEMA say could have been coordinated out of Boston would end up costing the taxpayers over $200,000 in expenses and special salaries for the three month operation. In part four of his special series, investigative reporter Gene Hartigan outlines some of the costs that contributed to the high costs of administrating hurricane Gloria's aftermath.

HARTIGAN: The Worcester field office was put in place to assess storm damage and interact with cities and towns who would file for federal disaster assistance. But random calls to communities in the state have yet to turn up evidence to substantiate FEMA claims of need of a field office.

Records obtained by WEEI's investigative unit under the Freedom of Information Act show some of the more expensive items include the installation of temporary phone and computer service lines at a cost of $2,065, and just three months later another $1,043 to have them disconnected. In addition the cost of office supplies, tables, chairs, and miscellaneous costs totaled $25,300. Records for phone service requested by WEEI have yet to be made available for review.

Records also show FEMA publicly advertised the presence of its field offices at a cost of $10,300 in 29 major newspapers. The records obtained by WEEI show that two major newspapers, the *Middlesex News* and the *Boston Globe* issued collection notices to FEMA, and the *Middlesex News* placed their bill with a collection agency.

What is curious in all this is FEMA operates a special emergency center in Maynard, just 22 miles from the temporary office set up in Worcester and just 24 miles from the Boston regional office. When asked why this site was not utilized both federal coordinating officer Al Gammal and FEMA regional director Henry Vickers indicated certain classified government equipment located at the site prohibited its use for such activities.

Yet when questioned, FEMA representatives admitted to WEEI that meetings had been held at the Maynard facility, most notable a meeting of area fire chiefs who met to discuss arson prevention. And a personal tour of the emergency site by WEEI confirms two floors of offices, already equipped with phone service, computer equipment operating 24 hours a day. The classified equipment is isolated in a controlled access area.

In my next report, training the specially hired reservists at resort hotels on the Cape and at Goat Island in Newport, Rhode Island, the costs continue to rise.

For the WEEI investigative unit, I'm Gene Hartigan.

Segment 5, FEMA Story, Friday, April 4, 1986, 7:30 a.m./8:30 a.m.

ANCHOR INTRO: A review of records obtained by WEEI shows that the Federal Emergency Management Agency, FEMA, spent over $200,000 in expenses, overhead and special salaries to administer the disaster assistance program associated with last fall's hurricane Gloria. In part five of his series, investigative reporter Gene Hartigan outlines additional expenses resulting from government paid training sessions at luxury resorts.

HARTIGAN: From over 1,300 pages of information obtained under the Freedom of Information Act, WEEI has learned that training sessions held in February and November 1985 cost the taxpayers an additional $31,600 in expenses for hotels, food, mileage and tolls, not including salaries. These are expenses that would have been dramatically reduced if the meetings had been held in Boston. The meetings were held to train special hire reservists who work on disaster relief.

On February 25, last year, FEMA began a five day, four night training session at the Goat Island Sheraton resort in Newport, Rhode Island for 91 staff and special hire reservists. The cost of the session was $21,171. What is significant is WEEI has confirmed that at least 56 of those attending live in the greater Boston area.

Similarly on November 4 last year, a week after the Worcester office opened, FEMA held a second five day four night training session at the New Seabury resort in Mashpee on Cape Cod. Yet 30 staff and special hire reservists attended costing the government $10,485. Again, WEEI has confirmed at least 19 attending lived in Greater Boston. The holding of this session is curious as FEMA officials have said in previous conversations their time was taken up with organizing the field office in Worcester.

Although in both cases attendees were charged a discounted government rate for rooms, the effect of holding the conferences in Newport and New Seabury was to sharply increase the cost of mileage and lodging.

When questioned about the meeting site choice, federal coordinating officer Gammal said it was necessary to get the undivided attention of those attending adding, "There is a lot more accomplished and you can work late into the night." Yet a review of their published schedule for both training sessions shows no meeting was scheduled past 6 P.M. Gammal also indicated setting up such a session around Boston would "cost $2,000 to $3,000 minimum."

Yet a check of some Boston hotels by WEEI turned up the following. Just a short ride from the downtown FEMA headquarters was a hotel eager to host such a conference. The hotel proprietor said he could not only accommodate the number of attendees but was willing to provide the conference facilities free to get the business.

It should be noted that all persons attending the conference are often advanced several hundred dollars cash by FEMA and turn in vouchers after the event, and do not have to turn in receipts for any items under $25.

In my next report, a look at some serious questions about FEMA's regional office and some comparisons with other regions on the East Coast.

For the WEEI investigative unit, I'm Gene Hartigan.

Segment 6, FEMA story, Friday, April 4, 1986, 4:30 p.m./5:30 p.m.

ANCHOR INTRO: A review of records obtained by WEEI shows that the Federal Emergency Management Agency, FEMA, spent over $200,000 in expenses, overhead and special salaries to administer the disaster assistance program in southern New England in the wake of hurricane Gloria. But the question still remains to what end was the money spent. In the last of his six part series, investigative reporter Gene Hartigan reviews some of these costs and outlines comparisons with other regional offices along the eastern United States.

HARTIGAN: WEEI's investigative unit reviewed 1,300 pages of documents obtained under the Freedom of Information Act and questioned FEMA regional officials along with past and present employees of the agency. Some interviews suggest FEMA's response to hurricane Gloria could have been managed from the Boston regional headquarters, eliminating the need for field offices that would have resulted in substantial savings to the taxpayers.

A disturbing fact pointed to by several sources interviewed by WEEI was FEMA staff employees collectively spent over 800 nights in hotels at a cost of over $30,000 in connection with hurricane Gloria field office operations. Yet WEEI has called communities around Massachusetts and Connecticut and found little evidence that FEMA personnel had much direct contact with local officials. In fact most indicate their on-site work was conducted by the Army Corps of Engineers, whose budget and expenses are separate from costs tallied in this report.

A WEEI survey of FEMA regional offices along the East Coast found that all the other regions interviewed stated they would seek state owned facilities when federal sites were not available. In Connecticut, Al Gammal contracted with a private company for space that for 60 days cost the government $8,000 on office rent alone. Gammal said this was the only space available people would rent for 60 days.

The three regions also agreed that policies were followed on auto rentals that recommended midsize or compact size cars or special use vehicles such as vans or wheel drive vehicles, but most important stressed the concept of pooling when possible.

Most telling was a comment by region three disaster coordinator Bob Adamick of Philadelphia, who when asked about using Lincolns as rentals said, "No way, not at all. It sure wouldn't look good, unless the president or vice president were coming by to inspect."

Both regional director Henry Vickers and federal coordinating officer Al Gammal praised the dedication of the special hire reservists. But what should be noted is that these reservists are paid, plus receive expenses. WEEI has obtained a listing of annualized pay for FEMA reservists. Of 85 names provided, just shy of 50 percent have pay levels of $25,000 or more, with the lowest annualized pay being $15,800. It should be noted reservists are additionally compensated for overtime.

Questions raised by people interviewed include, why was a disaster field office established just 46 miles from the FEMA headquarters in Boston and a Connecticut office established just 64 miles south of Worcester when the whole state of Connecticut was declared a disaster? And why was an office set up inland when space was available in Boston which was closer to the site of the majority of the disaster declaration?

Additionally, records show computer transmission costs from the Connecticut field office cost the government $3,500 over Southern New England Telephone lines, work that could have been accomplished in the regional office on government lines at greatly reduced costs, sources indicate.

It should be noted the president's disaster declaration was a public assistance disaster, which means funds were available for cities, towns and designated nonprofit agencies. No disaster funds were being distributed to individuals. As it is known in government circles this was an "administrative disaster, a paperwork disaster."

By his own admission, regional FEMA administrator Henry Vickers told WEEI that had the storm hit Boston he would have administered the efforts "from right here" (in Boston). Which contradicts earlier FEMA claims of no available space.

Finally, after years of handling disasters and a great deal of experience in the field, several sources interviewed by WEEI are questioning why FEMA had not yet developed a disaster plan that could be implemented using local facilities and costing the taxpayer a lot less money.

For the WEEI investigative unit, I'm Gene Hartigan.

EXAMPLE 7

Reporters moonlight as speech writers for politicians

T he problem of ethics in journalism is, as we have said, one subject newspapers rarely touch. The following article by Bob Wyrick and Pete Bowles, published by *Newsday* on October 26, 1972, and reprinted here with permission, is quite unusual, so unusual that we're reprinting it in spite of its age. It supports a contention often disputed by editors: that a publication or station can and should publish or broadcast articles about the doings of competing news outlets and their employees even if those employees have not been arrested, elected, or otherwise made into public figures. It is also an example of the sort of investigation that reaches print only when a reporter decides to look critically and in detail at the implications of facts known to many. Finally, the story demonstrates the use of a computer by investigative reporters, in this case to match the names of newspaper employees with names on the state payroll.

In one respect, however, the story is not unusual. It is written with little drama and is crammed full of details, many of which are dropped on the reader early in the story. The article, therefore, illustrates the pitfalls of assuming that an audience will be as interested in a particular investigation as the reporter who researched and wrote it.

The story abounds with the rationalizations encountered daily by investigative reporters. But in this case, it is reporters who are the subjects of the investigation and who are trying to justify moonlighting for the same politicians they cover during the day. The story was originally Wyrick's idea, both reporters said in interviews. Wyrick came to *Newsday* after working on a small Florida newspaper. Assigned to the pressroom in the state supreme court building in Mineola, New York, Wyrick noticed that, in his words, other *Newsday* reporters "would write press releases at night for the politicians they covered during the day and sometimes printed their own releases." This dual-employment practice "was common knowledge, but no one gave a shit," Wyrick said. "It seemed like just no one cared."

Although Wyrick was initially shocked at this practice, it took him two years at *Newsday* to get around to proposing a story on the subject. He sent a memo, including documentation of a couple of cases, to his editors and asked permission to do the story. He knew, he said, that the story "had potential to involve *Newsday* people as well as others" and that "the editors at *Newsday* were friends with the editors at other papers." He also knew that management might "think it very touchy to have staff morale screwed up by a guy poking around." But to Wyrick's surprise, he was given the go-ahead on the story shortly after he sent in his memo.

Wyrick said he and Bowles gathered the names of some staffers on the other papers from newspaper union membership lists. They already knew—from firsthand observation or reliable tips—that many of their fellow reporters engaged in dual political employment.

Wyrick said that he and Bowles then "talked to a lot of these guys on the take and asked them who else was on the take." Wyrick said, "We would lay a piece of paper [a press release] in front of them and ask, 'Did you write this?' If they said yes, we then said, 'Are you so generous you did it for free?' They were ratting on each other. I don't have any respect for any of them. They shouldn't have been newspapermen in the first place."

The Wyrick-Bowles technique uncovered many dually employed journalists, but it also missed a couple, Wyrick said. One of them was a man who at that time was a *Newsday* political writer in Suffolk County. "I asked him if he knew of any reporters on the take," Wyrick said, "and his answer was no. I didn't ask him about himself. He was highly respected." But later, according to Wyrick, two other *Newsday* reporters revealed that this same man had been paid $7,000 to $8,000 annually by a local political boss. The payments came to light during a lawsuit when some old Republican party records were examined, Wyrick said.

Wyrick said the ethics story was written three or four times. "There was a lot of writing by committee," Wyrick said. "But I don't think it had anything to do with fear. There was a lot of writing by committee at *Newsday*." During the rewriting, however, what Wyrick saw as an important fact was inadvertently left out: Stan Hinden, a former *Newsday* political editor who was paid for writing stories for the civil service union newspaper, had written permission from his boss to do so.

According to Bowles, the original idea behind the *Newsday* exposé was to write a story about all the reporters in both New York state and the New York City area who were paid kickbacks and fees by various businesses, as well as about those reporters who worked for politicians. For instance, Bowles said, one airline offered free trips to Australia to reporters who boosted tourism by placing photographs of Australian bathing beauties in the paper. Also, Bowles said, the American Cigar Institute offered compensation to reporters and editors who successfully placed photographs of cigar smokers in their newspapers. Finally, Bowles said, the two decided to focus their attention on reporters in their own bailiwick—Long Island—who were working for politicians they were supposed to be covering objectively.

Bowles said that he and Wyrick requested and received from the state government the records of anyone who had been employed by the joint legislative committees in Albany, because, according to Bowles, "we were told that many of these were no-show jobs" and that many were held by reporters. This list was one of those run through the computer, as the story explains. Bowles said the two *Newsday* reporters also obtained, from sympathizers, lists of employees of other newspapers and, directly from *Newsday*'s management, lists of its own past and present employees.

Both reporters said that most of their information was obtained directly from fellow reporters who had known about the dual-employment practice for years and from the politicians involved. Not all their fellow reporters were cooperative. "There was lots of mistrust in our office. Some people thought it was a dirty deal for us to be going after other reporters," Bowles said. "When the story came out, lots of people were relieved that we only went after people who had been working for politicians" and not people holding nonpolitical governmental jobs. Some people whose jobs were in such gray areas were eliminated from the story, Bowles said.

Bowles insisted that the story as originally written was "much harder than it finally came out." He said, "The editors worried about running it and wanted it rewritten a number of times. They may have been getting pressure from other papers who didn't think it was fair for our newspaper to attack their reporters. . . . Finally, they made us put a feature lead on it."

Bowles detailed one example of friendship's altering the content of the story. According to Bowles, *New York Daily News* editor Mike O'Neill was a friend of the *Newsday* editor in charge of the story, David Laventhol. "O'Neill refused to be interviewed by us," Bowles said. "But because of his friendship with Laventhol, he was able to give Laventhol a printed statement [on dual employment], which was included in the story. It wasn't right. Other people wouldn't sit down for an interview, and we reported in the story that they refused to discuss the matter with us." Those people weren't allowed to submit prepared statements. Bowles said, however, that Laventhol resisted other apparent pressures, such as telephone calls from the *Long Island Press,* many of whose dually employed reporters were mentioned in the story.

Several years later, *Newsday* published three follow-up stories, also reprinted here. The first of these articles on former Nassau County Family Court judge Martin Ginsberg was written by Brian Donovan (February 8, 1975), the second by Dan Hertzberg (March 1, 1975), and the third by Bradford W. O'Hearn (March 13, 1975).

(*Newsday* articles reprinted and distributed by Iowa State University Press.)

Newsmen holding paid political jobs, a survey reveals

[*Newsday* reporter Bob Wyrick spent three months looking into the relationship of the press and politicians on Long Island. Reporter Pete Bowles worked with Wyrick and finished the investigation when Wyrick took a leave in late September for a year's study at Harvard University as a Neiman Fellow.]

Readers regularly find stories in their daily newspapers about the pronouncements and activities of government officials and politicians. What they may not realize, however, is that some of those articles are written or edited by journalists who receive second salaries from the people they write about.

A *Newsday* investigation has identified a tradition of newsmen accepting paid political jobs. The survey was confined to Long Island and to the major daily newspapers here: the *New York Daily News,* the *Long Island Press,* the *New York Times* and *Newsday.*

The *Newsday* survey found that:

Two newsmen currently are receiving second salaries as governmental public relations aides, and 16 others have held second jobs in government or politics in the last 10 years. Seven of the 18 have since left their newspapers for full-time public relations work, six with Republican administrations or political organizations.

At least seven of the 18 involved actually wrote or edited stories for their newspapers about the subjects from whom they were receiving a second salary. Four of the 18 received $10,000 or more a year in extra money from their political jobs.

About half of the 18 newsmen were getting two salaries without the permission of their newspapers, including at least one who disguised his involvement behind his wife's name.

Long Island political candidates employed working newspapermen during campaigns on at least 30 occasions during the past decade. The candidates included such powerful political figures as Nassau County Republican Chairman Joseph Margiotta; Assembly Majority Leader John E. Kingston (R–Westbury); Glen Cove Mayor-Supervisor Andrew J. Di-Paola, a Democrat who has received both the GOP and Democratic nominations for the State Supreme Court; Huntington Town Supervisor Jerome Ambro, also a Democrat; former Nassau County Executive Eugene Nickerson, a Democrat; Rep. Norman Lent (R–East Rockaway); and former Assembly Speaker Joseph Carlino (R–Long Beach).

As many as 11 newsmen were on double payrolls at one time during the 1967 election campaign, the peak period for such moonlighting in recent years. The practice appears to be declining. Political leaders of both major parties said that no newsmen had been hired for this year's campaign, mainly because of concern over the publication of the *Newsday* survey. Another reason given was that there was a substantial number of former newspapermen working in political or governmental jobs now. The two reporters in the *Newsday* survey still holding dual jobs are in governmental, not political, posts.

The *Newsday* survey was conducted against the backdrop of recent challenges to the credibility and objectivity of newspapers and other media. The 12-week survey included about 150 interviews and involved the use of an IBM 360 computer. In addition, hundreds of payroll records and documents listing political campaign expenditures were examined. The survey was limited to an attempt to identify cases involving reporters and editors being paid for doing political or governmental work, and thus did not deal with practices where ethical questions are less clear cut — such as a newsman

who does such work on the side but is not paid for it, or one involved personally in local civic issues, or one moonlighting for nonprofit organizations or educational institutions. For instance, Stan Hinden, former *Newsday* political editor, was paid for writing stories for the *Civil Service Leader,* a publication of the Civil Service Employees Association. He was succeeded in that part-time job by Bill Butler of the *Daily News.* Also, several *Newsday* reporters and editors, and a *Long Island Press* editor, have moonlighted (some still do) for Long Island colleges and charitable drives and institutions.

The two newsmen in the survey who currently are on government payrolls are: Harry C. Schlegel, an assistant city editor responsible for political assignments at the *New York Daily News* who also receives $900 a month as research director for the Joint Legislative Committee on Interstate Cooperation; and Sherman Phillips, a *Long Island Press* reporter who is registration supervisor at the Nassau County Board of Elections.

The six former journalists who now work for Republican administrations or political organizations are: Richard Miranda, who worked for a number of candidates while employed as a reporter at the *Press;* Tony Panzarella, who served as an aide to several Republicans, including Assembly Majority Leader Kingston, while writing for the *Press;* Gene Turner, who took a job with Margiotta while with the *Press;* Stan Pakula, who directed political campaigns while working at the *Press;* Robert McDonald, who was employed by a Nassau County agency while he was a reporter at the *Daily News;* and Robert Ryan, formerly of the *Press* and the *New York Herald Tribune,* who worked for Glen Cove Democrats and Huntington Republicans during his reporting career.

Frank Krauss, who is now a partner in a public relations firm, worked for former Assemblyman Martin Ginsberg (R–Plainview) while he was employed as a reporter at the *Daily News*. Krauss hid the fact by using his wife's name for the work for Ginsberg.

The remaining nine who showed up in the *Newsday* survey are:

Arnold Friedman, assistant managing editor of the *Press,* who was on the payroll of Rep. Seymour Halpern (R–Jamaica); former *Newsday* night photo editor Bill Sullivan, who was paid to try to get pictures of certain Republicans into the paper; Grover Ryder, Nassau County bureau chief for the *Daily News,* who until last year was on the Huntington town payroll; Dick Wettereau, night city editor for the *Press,* who worked for the North Hempstead GOP from 1959 through 1968; Henry McCann, a news editor at the *Press,* who worked for former Assemblyman Jerome Mc-Dougal, Jr.; Frank Mazza, a *Daily News* reporter who worked in a number of Democratic campaigns; Bernard Rabin, a *Daily News* reporter who once held a Long Beach city job; the late Ben White of the *News,* who was the key advisor to Nassau Democrats; and the late Dick Prussin of the *Press,* who served on a joint legislative committee for seven years.

Most of the newspapermen involved in the practice said the outside jobs did not interfere with their ability to give their readers a fair and objective story. "They sold their pen; they didn't sell their soul," said Bob McDonald, a former *News* reporter who is now press secretary to Nassau GOP Leader Joseph Margiotta and who also had outside accounts while working for the *News.* But another of the 18, former *News* reporter Frank Krauss, said he felt the abuse of the system of taking outside political work "was not what you wrote good about a guy—it was the bad things you knew about and never wrote."

Some politicians think differently. Alexander J. Brandshaft, chairman of the Huntington Republican Committee, put it this way: "If we bought a $5000 advertisement, it's not as good as one news story from a reporter. A paid political ad, no matter what you say, is still a paid political ad."

The concept of ethics in journalism has evolved slowly. The earliest American newspapers were frankly partisan and touted the politicians they favored in the news columns while either ignoring or vilifying their opponents. A more objective type of reporting emerged during the Civil War, and by the turn of the century it had become a firmly implanted practice in American journalism to separate editorial opinion from straight factual reporting of news.

Guy Ryan, president of Sigma Delta Chi, the national professional journalism society, said recently that he was surprised that any newspaper would allow its reporters and editors to work for politicians. "There's a danger in trying to serve two masters," he said. "A newsman not only has to play it straight but make it appear that we are playing it straight."

Long Island Press editor Dave Starr has declined to be interviewed about *Press* reporters who had political jobs. On March 16, Starr issued a policy statement to his Nassau staff that outside work was permitted as long as it "cannot be misinterpreted—to any degree—as influencing the news judgment or editorial policy of the paper." The memo also said, " . . . public relations work for an elected official or a political leader or a business firm could lead to charges of favored treatment."

Daily News Managing Editor

Mike O'Neill said: "The *News* has always opposed outside activities by the editorial employes which would compromise their obligations to objective reporting of the news.

"Like other newspapers, the *News* permits free-lance writing which is non-competitive. But as a matter of policy and by contract with the Newspaper Guild, *News* employes are specifically prohibited from using their connections with the paper 'to exploit in any way outside work or interest.'

"Staffers usually get advance guidance from their editors on what they can or cannot do. In the few instances where possible conflict of interest has arisen, the reporter has been asked to discontinue the outside activity, and, in every case, he has complied.

"The only example which *Newsday* cites of a *News* employe currently working for a government agency concerns Harry Schlegel of our city staff. Since 1966, Mr. Schlegel has carried out part-time research assignments for the Joint Legislative Committee on Interstate Co-operation. He took the job with the knowledge and approval of his superiors. The work is non-political: There is no conflict with his duties on the paper."

Newsday editor David Laventhol restated the paper's policy in a memorandum to the staff in December, 1969. The memo said: "An editorial staff member must not take part in anything that would compromise himself or *Newsday*. This is a broad area that would include official jobs, outside writing, loans, business transactions and political or civic activities. . . ."

The center of most newsmen's outside political activity is the press room in the State Supreme Court Building in Mineola, where the county maintains offices for key governmental reporters from *Newsday,* the *New York Daily News,* the *Long Island*

Press, and reporters for the *New York Times* (which also has a reporter in Suffolk), and assorted radio and television newsmen. (The *News* has seven full-time reporters assigned to Long Island, the *Press* about 24, and *Newsday* about 75.) "When a political job was available, the news spread like wildfire through the press room," a Republican source said.

The tradition of coziness between politicians and the reporters who work in the press room is a long one. In the early 1950's, then GOP leader and Nassau County Executive J. Russel Sprague handed out cash gifts of $50 to $100 to reporters and photographers at Christmas and election time. The practice was stopped in the mid-50's when a reporter for the now-defunct *New York Journal-American* began gathering information to write a news article about it.

Gene Turner, who on Oct. 6 succeeded Forrest Corson as executive assistant to the Nassau County Board of Supervisors at a salary of $30,000 and who previously headed the Hempstead Town public relations staff, said that he has referred reporters to Nassau County Republican Headquarters for political jobs. "I feel it's up to the reporter to make the moral judgment," Turner said. "And if he wants to work, the Republican Party is entitled to use him." This same view was reflected by officials of both parties, most of whom said they preferred to hire newsmen rather than public relations firms because newsmen did not charge as much, had a better knowledge of the area's problems and issues, and better contacts in the newspaper business.

Besides Turner, the party officials who steered reporters to political jobs included Nassau Democratic Party chairman Marvin Cristenfeld; former party chairman John F. English; County Executive Caso's press secretary, Robert Ryan; and Margiotta's press aide, Robert McDonald.

McDonald said, "Most of the guys we [the Republicans] hire, I grew up with in the press room. They come over and say, 'Is there anybody I can work for?' And then we put together a campaign . . . and we say, 'These are the guys [political candidates] we want you to work for.' You'd be surprised, in our circle, if you are not asked, if you don't get a candidate to work for, you feel like they are mad at you."

But many reporters have refused to become part of this circle. One of them is *Long Island Press* reporter Bob Weddle. English said that while he was Nassau Democratic leader he tried to get Weddle to go to work for the party on the side and was refused. Weddle, who lives in Bellmore, said that he did not accept the offer from English and other offers which were made over the years because it did not square with his personal code of ethics. Another reporter, Roy Silver, the long-time Nassau correspondent for the *New York Times,* said the Democrats once offered him a part-time job with the Nassau County Bridge Authority. Silver said he checked with his editors and was told not to accept the position because "sometime we might have to do a story about the authority."

About half of the 18 newsmen uncovered in the survey held their outside jobs with the knowledge and consent of an editor at their newspaper. The others took pains to keep their outside jobs secret. Frank Krauss took more pains than most.

During the three years that Krauss handled public relations assignments for then Assemblyman Martin Ginsberg (R–Plainview), while also working at the *News,* Krauss persuaded Ginsberg to put his wife's name on a state payroll to conceal the fact that Krauss was working for the assemblyman. Krauss, 32, said he received

$6,000 in state funds under his wife's name. "I felt it best that I keep it confidential," Krauss said in explaining why the name of his wife, Delphine J. Krauss, was listed on the payroll.

Mrs. Krauss' name appears under the job title "research counsel" on the payroll of the Joint Legislative Committee for Industrial Relations from Aug. 28, 1969, through March 31, 1970, at a salary of $2,500 and as an "assistant secretary" from Aug. 13, 1970, to March 31, 1971, for $3,500. Ginsberg, now a Nassau County Family Court judge, headed the health subcommittee of the joint committee during this period. Ginsberg, when asked why the job titles were listed in this manner, said: "They were just the positions that were available." Krauss said the money received under his wife's name was for public relations work he did for Ginsberg from late 1968 to 1971. "My wife didn't do anything," he said. Krauss wrote at least one story for the *News* about Ginsberg while holding the two jobs. Krauss left the *News* to become the press spokesman for North Hempstead Town in 1971.

Krauss, who is now a partner and vice president of Howard Public Relations Ltd. in Port Washington, said his duties for Ginsberg included writing news releases and brochures for his 1970 re-election campaign and writing publicity releases on Ginsberg's activities on the health subcommittee. "Some people might say it is an abuse [of taxpayer's money] to use a JLC payroll for a guy's personal advertising," Krauss said. "But how else can a guy get known?" Ginsberg said that under Krauss' direction his public image was modeled as a legislator who specialized in areas such as retarded children and the handicapped.

Ginsberg said that another *Daily News* reporter, Bernard Rabin, also worked for him under an arrangement similar to Krauss'. He made the statement after he was shown payroll records stating that Rabin's wife, Miriam Rabin, was paid $1,210 as an Assembly clerk for the first five months of 1971. Asked if Rabin had worked for him, Ginsberg replied: "The answer is yes . . . he handled my public relations—he put out campaign releases and wrote photo captions."

Ginsberg said that Rabin previously worked for him from 1966 through March, 1969, and was paid, under his wife's name, about $1,500 a year. Rabin, a *News* employe for 18 years who formerly worked out of Nassau County and now covers the Queens and Brooklyn courts, said his wife worked for Ginsberg and was paid "a lot less" than $1,500 a year. Told about Ginsberg's account that Rabin actually did the work, Rabin said: "That's one reason I wouldn't work for these guys—these politicians have big mouths."

Official minutes of the Long Beach Urban Renewal Agency show that Rabin was paid $1,500 a year as the agency's public information officer for three years—Jan. 9, 1967, to Jan. 1, 1970. Former Long Beach City Manager Foster Vogel, who also served on the urban renewal agency during this period, said he had recommended Rabin for the job of writing newsletters and press releases about the agency. Rabin, however, said that Vogel, the minutes and agency members were all mistaken. He said his wife had done the job. "I spoke to them [city officials] about the job but I couldn't do it," Rabin said. "I didn't have the time, and I didn't want anything where there might be an odor or anything."

The practice of reporters working for politicians has not gone entirely unnoticed. Last year, Huntington GOP leader Alexander Brandshaft formally complained to the *Daily News* that the Republicans were getting no exposure in the *News* because Huntington Democratic Town Supervisor Jerome Ambro had Grover Ryder, the *News'* Nassau bureau chief, on the town payroll for $6,000 a year.

Ryder said the management at the *News* felt that there was no justification for Brandshaft's complaint, but asked him to give up the town job nevertheless. "They said, 'We have to be as clean as a hound's tooth,'" Ryder said.

Ironically, Brandshaft has also had a reporter in his camp. In 1967, when Ryder was handling Ambro's campaign to unseat incumbent GOP Town Supervisor Quentin Sammis, the *News'* Long Island bureau chief, Bill Butler, was working for Sammis. (Both reporters said they worked without pay.) Brandshaft was the GOP co-leader in Huntington in 1967.

Sammis was defeated in that race and Ambro, the new town supervisor, gave Ryder a $6,000-a-year town public information job in January, 1968. Ryder said that he tried to keep his relationship with Ambro professional. "Ambro wouldn't try to get me to get anything in the paper because he knew I wouldn't do it," Ryder said. Ambro said he received no special treatment in the *Daily News* because of Ryder's town employment.

In 1969, Ryder replaced Butler as Long Island bureau chief for the *Daily News,* which put him in the position of helping to decide what was worth printing in the paper on a given day and assigning reporters to cover it. One *Daily News* reporter who asked not to be quoted by name said: "Ryder was in a direct conflict on the Ambro thing because he assigned reporters to cover Ambro's press conferences." Ryder said, "Most of the people in the press room didn't even know I worked for Ambro. I never called another reporter [from another paper] concerning Ambro." Reflecting on the whole situation of reporters' taking outside political work, Ryder said: "Some reporters do it with integrity; some do not. I think there is a very fine line there. It would perhaps be better that nobody did this."

A newsman who recently said he had had second thoughts about his outside political work was Richard Wettereau of Manhasset, night city editor at the *Press*. Wettereau said he had received $50 to $100 a week from the North Hempstead GOP for 10 years—1959 through 1968. During that same period, he was the North Shore beat reporter for the *Press* and wrote stories on North Hempstead, Glen Cove and Oyster Bay. "I gave it up because it just didn't fit right with me," he said. "There was nothing illegal or immoral about it, but I thought it was jeopardizing the position of unbiased news."

Some of the reporters who did accept jobs did not want to write stories about candidates who employed them, and frequently "traded off" with other reporters. Tony Panzarella, who worked 10 years as a *Long Island Press* reporter before taking a job early this year as an administrative assistant in the Nassau County Parks Department, said he relied heavily on other reporters to get stories placed for his candidates. "I'd give them a [press] release and ask them to do what they could," said Panzarella, who was on Assemblyman Kingston's legislative payroll for $100 a week and who said that he earned $10,000 a year extra from his outside work. Conversely, Panzarella was not likely to say no when another reporter asked him for a similar favor. He admitted that he frequently accommodated his reporter friends on other papers by writing stories in his paper based on press releases these reporters had prepared for their candidate.

Harry Schlegel is the assistant city editor for political and city hall assignments for the *Daily News*. Several reporters on the paper's Long Island staff pointed to Schlegel's political job as justification for their taking outside work. For a five-year period, he has been paid $54,316.34 in state funds. Since 1966, Schlegel, of 14 Kingsbury Rd., Garden City, has been on the state payroll as a research director for the Joint Legislative Committee on Interstate Cooperation, whose chairman is Sen. John Marchi (R–Staten Island). Marchi said he had asked Schlegel to take a leave of absence to help in Marchi's 1969 primary fight against Mayor Lindsay for the Republican mayoral nomination.

Schlegel said that former *Daily News* Editor Harry Nichols, now deceased, had given him permission to take the Marchi committee job originally but refused his request for a leave of absence to work for Marchi's campaign. "The boss [Nichols] said he wanted me around here to coordinate the campaign coverage," Schlegel said. As an editor, Schlegel helped decide what aspects of the campaign should be covered and directed a staff of reporters who wrote about the various issues.

In addition to this, Schlegel wrote eight news stories under his own byline about the Marchi-Lindsay mayoral campaign, including an interpretative article on June 19, 1969, on the computer analysis of the vote after Marchi beat Lindsay for the nomination. "I may have written [the Marchi-Lindsay stories], but it was on the assignment of my boss who knew I was working for Marchi," Schlegel said. "What could I tell him? That I wasn't going to write them? That would be insubordination."

Another editor in a position similar to Schlegel's was Arnold Friedman, of Floral Park, assistant managing editor of the *Long Island Press,* who was working for Rep. Seymour

Halpern (R–Jamaica). Congressional payroll records show that Friedman was paid $11,755.68 for 13 months' work for Halpern spread over 1967, '68, and '69, while Friedman was employed as night news editor responsible for the selection of news that went into the *Press*' Queens edition.

Friedman, asked if he had ever handled Halpern stories, said, "I don't recall anything specifically, but if I did I never let my professional integrity be compromised." Halpern, who is retiring this year, said that he paid Fried-man to "help in relation to speeches, committee testimony, newsletters [to constituents] and in-depth writing."

Articles about Halpern that appeared in the *Long Island Press* would normally be handled through the Queens-edition desk. Gene Turner, who was a combination copy editor–rewriteman on the Queens desk under Friedman before going to work for the Town of Hempstead, said, "He [Friedman] never asked me to give any favorable treatment to Halpern. I only handled them [Halpern assignments] routinely like any other story."

Turner said that his knowledge of the Friedman-Halpern business arrangement made him feel that it was nothing "out of the ordinary" to work an outside political public relations job. "In April, 1966, I moved from Queens to Uniondale," said Turner, who was earning about $10,000 a year. "I had two kids and a brand new house and I was worried about it. I called my friend Bob Ryan and said, 'Hey, I need some extra money,' because at the *Press* [salary] I could hardly carry my house." At that time, Turner had never heard of the man Ryan recommended. "Ryan said, 'There's this young legislator in Uniondale named Margiotta who needs some help,'" Turner recalled.

Turner was put on a state payroll and earned $500 for putting out newsletters for Margiotta and sending out a poll to his constituents. Turner said that he worked in Margiotta's 1966 campaign "as a gratis thing" without pay and took a full-time public relations job with the Town of Hempstead that same year.

Turner said he did not notify the *Press* management of his work for Margiotta. "I just chose not to," he said. "I felt they might say no for some obscure reason even though there was obviously no conflict." Turner said that none of Margiotta's stories came through the Queens-edition desk.

Panzarella said that he also kept all his outside public relations accounts secret except for $3,200 he earned last year for writing releases for *Catholic Charities*. Panzarella's record of outside public relations work dates back to the mid-1960's, when he earned $62 a week for handling press affairs for the Hicksville School District. More recently, Panzarella was on the legislative payroll of State Sen. Ralph Marino (R–Syosset) as a research assistant and said that he was paid $2,000 for four months' work in 1969 or 1970. From July, 1970, until last April, Panzarella was on Kingston's legislative payroll for $100 a week. In 1969, Panzarella was paid $300 by the Nassau County Republican Committee for writing press releases for a slate of Republican city council candidates in Long Beach.

Panzarella said there was no conflict in his dual jobs. "My office didn't even know that their [Kingston's and Marino's] press releases came from me," he said. "I never put a story in my typewriter concerning any of my accounts." However, the *Long Island Press* in October, 1970, carried a series of articles written by Panzarella that analyzed the campaigns of Nassau candidates, including Kingston and Marino.

Reporters were not the only source of help sought by political campaign workers. Former *Newsday* night photo editor William F. Sullivan was paid cash to help see to it that pictures of certain politicians received special treatment at *Newsday*. John Goertler, who was campaign photographer for Supreme Court Justice Sol Wachtler during his close but unsuccessful 1967 campaign to unseat Nickerson as county executive, said that he had paid Sullivan $200 cash to see to it that pictures of Wachtler and other Nassau GOP candidates were brought to the attention of the night city desk, where final decisions were made on which pictures would be published in *Newsday*. Wachtler said he was not aware of the Goertler-Sullivan arrangement.

Goertler said: "I gave my money to 'Sully' to make my job that much easier. It's tough to get a picture out of the darkroom to the night desk. If it never got past the photo editor [Sullivan], how could it get to the desk?" Sullivan, who lives in Merrick, said that when Wachtler's people brought in press releases with pictures attached, he would "take them out to the desk." He said he could not remember the exact amount of money he received. "It was $20 here, $50 there — there wasn't anything steady about the payments."

Newsday assistant publisher Stanley Asimov said that *Newsday* was unaware at the time of Sullivan's activities in the Wachtler campaign. However, Asimov said, in February 1968 the paper's management learned from several members of the photography staff that Sullivan had been paid by Oyster Bay Republican candidates to handle photography for the 1967 town campaign. Asimov said Sullivan was warned and given a second chance because he had 18 years of service with *Newsday*. But when Sullivan took administrative action the next day against some of the photographers who had spoken out about him, Asimov said, he was fired.

Sullivan said he could not recall how much he received in the Oyster Bay campaign, but Long Beach City Manager James Nagourney, a GOP publicity man at the time, said he put Sullivan on his payroll for two months before the election at a salary of $200 a week. Nagourney was managing the campaign for then Councilman Ralph J. Marino (now a state senator) against the late Michael Petito, then the Democratic Oyster Bay supervisor. "I made shots for whoever was running on the town ticket, not just Marino," Sullivan said. "I worked through Nagourney; for four or five jobs a week you'd get a weekly thing [payment]. It [the photography] was for the weeklies. Any of the stuff I did for them never got in *Newsday*."

Sherman Phillips of the *Press* is paid $10,997 as a registration supervisor at the Nassau County Board of Elections. He was hired to do public relations and promote mobile voter registration July 29, 1963, by English, who in addition to being Democratic leader was then a commissioner of elections. Phillips was the *Press'* night police reporter until last July, when he became a district reporter responsible for covering the North Shore from Great Neck to Roslyn. Phillips, who often wrote stories in the *Press* about the Board of Elections, said that he was never faced with the prospect of having to write a story about a Democratic politician who had gotten entangled in an embarrassing incident with the police. "If the thing came up, I'd do a story," he said. "There was never any conflict."

Richard L. Miranda, a reporter who left the *Press* Jan. 3, 1971, to become the $20,500-a-year press secretary for Hempstead Town Supervisor Alfonse D'Amato, said he averaged $2,000 a year from political jobs during his 12 years as a *Press* reporter. He said he worked for both Democrats and Republicans. "There was never a point in my newspaper career that I wasn't working for someone on the side," Miranda said. While with the *Press,* Miranda said, he primarily covered the police and district court in Nassau.

In 1963, while working for a group of insurgent Republicans in North Hempstead, Miranda said he spent more money on expenses than he was paid. Afterward, Miranda said, he worked for then State Sen. Norman Lent on two of Lent's legislative committees for an 18-month period in 1966 and 1967 and was paid $5,000 in state funds. In 1967, Miranda said, he also was paid $2,000 for working in the unsuccessful campaign of Democrat Patrick J. Purcell against GOP Supervisor Robert Meade in the Town of North Hempstead.

Later, Miranda worked six months as the press assistant to Assemblyman John Kingston (R–Westbury) and said he was paid $2,200. At the request of Robert Ryan (then head of Hempstead Town's public information department), Miranda went to work in 1969 as the public relations director for the Hempstead Town Local Development Corp. for a salary of $400 a month. He said he held the job with the corporation, which operates the Freeport Industrial Park, for almost two years.

After working in D'Amato's campaign for reelection as town tax receiver and after D'Amato had been designated to move up to supervisor because of the election of Presiding Supervisor Ralph Caso as county executive, Miranda was asked by D'Amato if he would like to be D'Amato's press assistant. "I was flabbergasted," Miranda recalled. "I never knew if I would fit into government—I had been on the other side so long."

A reporter for the *Daily News* who now specializes in transportation news, Frank Mazza, of Glen Head, was the only newsman of the 18 who declined to discuss his outside activities. Mazza worked for a number of Democratic campaigns over the years, including the Glen Cove City Council race of 1967, in which Mayor-Supervisor Andrew J. DiPaola was elected to office for the first time by the slim margin of 147 votes. The Glen Cove Democrats paid Mazza $2,020 for writing publicity releases and articles for a campaign newspaper. "We never used his position to get favorable news in the *News,*" former city Democratic Leader Vincent Suozzi said.

On Sept. 15, 1966, Mazza's byline appeared on a story in the *News* about a candidate he was working for, Edward B. Joachim, an Old Westbury attorney. The article identified Joachim as the Democratic candidate in the 17th Assembly District and detailed how Joachim had tipped off the district attorney's office to a Long Island call-girl ring.

Records show that Mazza was paid $5,000 in 1970 as a public relations consultant for the Nassau Coliseum Inc., a county agency, and that the Nassau County Democratic Committee gave him $500 in 1967 for publicity work. County Democratic Leader Marvin Cristenfeld said the party had used Mazza's services a number of times over the years. "I've called Frank from time to time and asked him if he was available to work [in a campaign] and then put him in touch with the candidate."

In the 1964 campaign that brought the downfall of Assembly Speaker Joseph Carlino (R–Long Beach), Hank McCann of the *Press* wrote the publicity releases for winner Jerome McDougal, Jr. McDougal, a former first vice president of the Nassau County Democratic Party, described McCann as "a good, two-fisted, four-fingered typewriter man" whom he paid $600 a month—a total of $2,400 to $3,000—for writing press releases during the campaign. McCann, now the *Press'* news editor and previously editor of the paper's Sunday magazine for 13 years, denied that he had made that much money. "My recollection is that I was paid $60 a week, which would be $250 a month," McCann said.

McCann said that he wrote television and entertainment columns for the Sunday magazine while working for McDougal and that he did the political work with the approval of his management.

Two of the earliest political activists among area reporters were the late Ben White of the *Daily News* and the late Richard Prussin of the *Press*. White, a reporter who scooped the world on the sex transformation of Christine Jorgensen, was on the Nassau Democratic Committee payroll in 1961, according to former Democratic Leader John English. "He [White] was as responsible as anyone else for Nickerson's winning the election [for county executive]," English said. "He was a key political advisor." English said White often referred to him reporters who were interested in taking on party assignments. After Nickerson's election, the county executive in 1962 recommended White for a $7,500-a-year public relations post at Meadowbrook Hospital, now the Nassau County Medical Center. White held the Meadowbrook job until his death in 1963. A former *Newsday* editor, he worked for the *News* on Long Island from 1946 until his death.

Prussin, a long-time *Press* reporter who died in 1968, was on the payroll of the Joint Legislative Committee on Mass Transportation, headed by the late State Sen. Edward Speno, from 1958 to 1965. Prussin was credited by Speno aides with playing a major role in the development of

Checking a GOP Claim

In the course of the *Newsday* survey, several Republican officials said that some *Newsday* reporters and editors had been paid secretly in recent years for political work by placing their wives' maiden names on Joint Legislative Committee payrolls in Albany.

Newsday asked for the names of those allegedly involved so that they could be included in the story, but the officials refused to name any. "You're going to get the [names of the] *Newsday* guys," said Bob Ryan, director of communications for Nassau County Executive Caso. "Because when you come out [with the story on the survey] the other papers are going to use them to embarrass you." Ryan, however, said that his statement did not mean he personally would furnish the information to other papers.

In an attempt to check out the Republican claims, *Newsday* used an IBM 360 computer to match the names and addresses of every current and former *Newsday* editorial employe against the names and addresses of all New York–area persons listed on all the State Joint Legislative Committee payrolls available back to 1965. The computer was programmed to identify matching addresses even when the names were different.

In checking the names of 700 newspaper employes against the 2,100 New York–area employes on the Joint Legislative Committee payrolls, no *Newsday* employes were found. But five reporters and editors from other newspapers were found.

Speno's national auto safety program.

Also among the early moonlighters were former newsmen Ryan, who is now County Executive Caso's public relations director, and McDonald, who is County GOP Leader Margiotta's press secretary.

Ryan recalled that his first outside political job was in the late 1950's while he was a reporter for the *Long Island Press*. He said that he and Stanley Pakula, currently the public information officer for the Town of Islip, shared a $500 fee for writing publicity releases for the Glen Cove Democrats. Pakula, who handled a number of political campaigns while working as a reporter at the *Press* from 1960 to 1963, recalled that the Glen Cove job was in 1961. In any event, after leaving the *Press* to work for the *New York Herald Tribune* in 1961, Ryan also did campaign work for a seven-man slate of Republican candidates running for office in Huntington Town. Ryan declined to say how much he was paid for the Huntington campaign.

McDonald, a long-time friend and associate of Ryan's, worked at the *News* 13 years before going to work for Margiotta in March, 1969. In 1965, shortly after Ryan had left the *Tribune* to work for Caso and while McDonald was still with the *News*, the two submitted a public relations proposal to the Nassau-Suffolk Regional Planning Board, but the package was rejected. McDonald was paid $6,000 in 1968 as the publicity agent for the Mitchell Field Development Corp., an agency set up by the county to plan the development of the former air base. The *News* published a story announcing that McDonald was going to work for Margiotta and mentioned the fact that he was the "public relations consultant" to the Mitchell Field agency.

Jury probing Ginsberg use of funds

A grand jury in Albany will begin an investigation next week into whether former Nassau Family Court Judge Martin Ginsberg illegally used public money to help pay for campaign publicity.

The jury will begin hearing testimony on Thursday, the same day that Ginsberg is scheduled to be sentenced on his recent perjury conviction in Nassau County. Ginsberg's attorney, John Sutter, called the new investigation the work of overzealous prosecutors and said he was confident that Ginsberg would not be indicted.

The Albany inquiry concerns Ginsberg's activities as a state assemblyman, a post he held before he received his judgeship in 1972. The witnesses subpoenaed include Bernard Rabin and Frank Krauss, whom Ginsberg has said wrote campaign releases for him while also working as reporters for the *New York Daily News*. Also ordered to appear are Rabin's and Krauss's wives, who were placed on state legislature payrolls and received payments totaling $7,210.

The grand jury will try to determine Ginsberg's role in arranging those payments and whether the wives actually did any work for the legislature, sources said. If the jurors decide that the money represented payments for Rabin's and Krauss's campaign work, the sources said, Ginsberg might be indicted on larceny charges.

Ginsberg's arrangement with Rabin, Krauss and their wives was disclosed by *Newsday* in an article published in October, 1972. In that article, Krauss was quoted as saying that his wife, Delphine, did not perform any state work in exchange for the $6,000 in state money she received during 1970 and 1971. Rabin's wife, Miriam, was paid $1,210 in 1971. The 1972 article said that Ginsberg had acknowledged arranging the state jobs for the two women.

Rabin, who still works for the *News,* could not be reached for comment yesterday. Krauss, who has left the paper to go into full-time public relations work, said that he would cooperate with the Albany probe. Sources said the Albany district attorney probably would grant Rabin, Krauss and their wives immunity in return for their testimony. Also subpoenaed yesterday was Pete Bowles, one of two *Newsday* reporters who wrote the 1972 article.

At the time of the article, no official action was taken against Ginsberg. But the issue was revived in December during Ginsberg's Nassau County trial on extortion, bribe-receiving and perjury charges. The prosecution introduced the articles as evidence in an attempt to rebut the testimony of Ginsberg's character witnesses. Shortly afterward, sources said, the Albany district attorney's office began making inquiries on the matter and decided to start an investigation.

Ginsberg was convicted on one perjury count and faces a maximum seven-year sentence. Albany County's chief assistant district attorney, Daniel Dwyer, said he expected the grand jury there to reach a decision next week on whether to indict Ginsberg.

New Ginsberg charge reported

Former Nassau County Court Judge Martin Ginsberg, convicted of perjury in December, has been indicted by a grand jury in Albany, sources close to the case said yesterday. The grand jury has heard testimony concerning allegations that Ginsberg illegally used public money to help pay for campaign publicity.

Ginsberg reportedly is ill in a hospital and could not be reached for comment. His lawyer, John Sutter, refused to comment.

Ginsberg was convicted in Nassau Dec. 27 of lying to a county grand jury about a $7,500 payment he received in 1970 from a tow-truck operator seeking county towing privileges. Ginsberg was given an unconditional discharge.

The Albany grand jury inquiry concerned Ginsberg's activities as a state assemblyman, a post he held before he received his judgeship in 1972. The investigation centered on Ginsberg's role in placing on state legislative payrolls the wives of two *New York Daily News* reporters, and on whether the wives actually did any work for the legislature. Ginsberg has said that the two reporters wrote campaign releases for him.

Daniel Dwyer, Albany County's chief assistant district attorney, said yesterday that the county grand jury had handed up four sealed indictments and had been discharged. Dwyer refused to say whether any of the four indictments involved the Ginsberg inquiry. However, other sources said the former judge had been named.

With Ginsberg now ill in the hospital, the unsealing of his indictment may be delayed. Normally, a sealed indictment in the county is opened when the individual named in it appears in

Albany for arraignment, Dwyer said.

The Albany grand jury heard testimony Feb. 13 from Bernard Rabin and Frank Krauss, who, Ginsberg has said, wrote campaign releases for him while also working as reporters for the *Daily News,* and from their wives, who were placed on state legislature payrolls and received payments totaling $7,210. Another witness was Pete Bowles, one of the two *Newsday* reporters who wrote an article in October, 1972, that revealed the arrangement between Ginsberg, Krauss, and Rabin.

It was learned during the grand jury inquiry that the grand jury was looking into possible charges of second- and third-degree grand larceny and official misconduct.

In the *Newsday* article, Krauss was quoted as saying that his wife, Delphine, did not perform any state work in exchange for the $6,000 in state money she received during 1970 and 1971. The article said that Ginsberg had acknowledged arranging for the state jobs for the two women. Krauss, who has left the *Daily News* to go into full-time public relations work, said yesterday that he and his wife were granted immunity in return for their testimony. Mrs. Rabin said that she and her husband, who still works for the *News,* also were granted immunity.

At the time of the *Newsday* article, no official action was taken against Ginsberg. But the issue was revived in December during Ginsberg's Nassau County trial on extortion, bribe-receiving and perjury charges. The article was introduced into evidence by the prosecution in an attempt to rebut the testimony of Ginsberg's character witnesses. Shortly afterward, sources said, the Albany district attorney's office began making inquiries on the matter and decided to begin an investigation.

Ginsberg denies larceny charges in Albany court

Former Assemblyman and Nassau Family Judge Martin Ginsberg pleaded innocent yesterday in Albany County Court to six charges of grand larceny and official misconduct for allegedly using state funds to pay for private campaign publicity.

Until this weekend, Ginsberg had been hospitalized for depression for about two weeks at South Oaks Hospital in Amityville. He was brought into the courtroom in a wheelchair, and one court observer said his face was ashen and his eyes vacant. "He looked like a cadaver, totally devoid of expression," the observer said.

As the court clerk read the first count in the indictments, Ginsberg replied in a low voice, "Not guilty, so help me God." His attorney, John J. Sutter, leaned over and spoke briefly to him, and to each of the remaining five counts Ginsberg replied only, "Not guilty." He also was accompanied by his wife, Joan, and a cousin, Irving Elfus.

The indictments charge that Ginsberg placed the wives of two *New York Daily News* reporters on state legislative payrolls while he was an assemblyman, but they actually did not work. Ginsberg has said that the two reporters wrote campaign releases for him. The allegations first were printed in *Newsday* in 1972. At the time Ginsberg acknowledged arranging the state jobs for the two women.

Ginsberg was convicted in December of lying to a Nassau grand jury about a $7,500 payment he received in 1970 from a tow-truck operator seeking county towing privileges. He was given an unconditional discharge in that case last month.

The three counts of official misconduct allege the same set of facts as the grand jury larceny indictments. Conviction on these counts could mean a maximum of one year in jail and a $1,000 fine or a fine twice any gain to Ginsberg.

Sutter said that Ginsberg, who refused to talk with reporters, was "shocked and numb" over the charges.

Ginsberg denies both the allegations and, if true, that they would constitute a violation of the law, Sutter said. Albany County Judge Arnold W. Proskin released Ginsberg without bail and gave Sutter 45 days to file motions. No trial date was set.

The indictments to which Ginsberg pleaded innocent yesterday grew out of an Albany County grand jury investigation that began after the allegations concerning the reporters were brought out in testimony in his trial last year.

Specifically, Ginsberg is charged with two counts of second-degree grand larceny in excess of $1,500, in which it is alleged that he placed Delphine Krauss, wife of former *Daily News* reporter Frank Krauss, on the state payroll, but that Ginsberg benefitted by "the work, labor and services rendered by Frank Krauss." The counts cover the 1969 and 1970 fiscal years. If convicted, he faces up to seven years in jail on each count.

He is also charged with one count of third-degree grand larceny exceeding $250, which alleges the same set of events involving Miriam Rabin and her husband, Bernard Rabin, who still works for the *News*. Conviction could bring a maximum of four years in jail. Neither the reporters nor their wives were charged in the indictments. Each was given immunity for their testimony.

INDEX

Aberson, Lisa, 224
Adamick, Bob, 253
Addison's disease, 35
Adorno, Hank, 189–99
Aikman, David, 229
Air Force Register, 56
Airline manifests, 42
Airport noise (story), 140–41
Alinsky, Saul, 56
All the President's Men, 9, 109–10
Ambro, Jerome, 259
American Cigar Institute, 257
American College Testing (ACT) Exam, 218
American Medical Association, dictionary, 60
Anderson, David, 210–25
Anderson, Jack, 7, 24, 29
Anderson, Ted, 216
Armas, Benigno, 189
Army Register, 56
Arrest records, 83
Asimov, Stanley, 266
Assessment, land, 73–75
Assignments, out-of-town, 113–14
Associated Press, 229
Audits, 43
Austin, Al, 230–45
Autopsy, on Jews, 115–16
Averages, in investigative stories, 141–43

Baltimore, city contracts (story), 26
Baltimore News American, 26
Baltimore Sun, 228.
Bank records, 43
Barlett, Donald, 82
Barron's, 229
Battaglini, Robert D., 203–9
Battaglini Corporation, 200, 209
Benes, Joel, 191
Bernstein, Carl, 9, 109–10

Bethesda Naval Hospital, 35
Better Government Association, 91
Betz, Michael, 249
Bid-splitting, 200–209
Binghamton (N.Y.) *Sun-Bulletin,* 200–209
Birth records, 43–44
Blake School, 220
Bleeker, Ray, 220–21
Blue Cross-Blue Shield, 47, 63–64
Boston Globe, 97, 251
Boston Herald, 98
Bowles, Pete, 255–58, 270–72
Boy Scouts of America, 15
Brandshaft, Alexander J., 260
Branzburg, Paul, 109
Brooke, Edward, 247
Bucher, Boyd, 221
Buckley, William, 24
Burrington, Joyce, 242
Busbee, George, 42
Bus driver (story), 133
Bush, George, 97
Bushkin, Kathy, 229
Business directories, 60
Business records, 44–46
Butler, Bill, 259
Bylined stories, 24

Caceres, Felix, 198
Caldwell-Pappas-Branzburg decision, 109
Camouflage questions, 126–27
Campaigns
  chain balloting, 93
  finance records of, 46–47
  fraud in, 87–98
  fund raising for, 95–96
Campos, Cirie, 192
Cancer (story), 34
Cardenas, Alberto, 190

273